LOVE and ADDICTION

LOVE *and* ADDICTION

STANTON PEELE
with Archie Brodsky

Taplinger Publishing Company / New York

SECOND PRINTING

Published in the United States in 1975 by
TAPLINGER PUBLISHING CO., INC.
New York, New York

Grateful acknowledgment is made to the following for quotations from
copyright material:

From *The Art of Loving* by Erich Fromm.
Copyright © 1956 by Erich Fromm. Published by Harper & Row: New York, 1956.

From *Beloved Infidel* by Sheilah Graham and Gerold Frank.
Copyright © 1958 by Sheilah Graham and Gerold Frank. Published by
Holt, Rinehart & Winston: New York, 1958.

From *The Female Eunuch* by Germaine Greer.
Copyright © 1971 by Germaine Greer. Published by the McGraw-Hill Book Company:
New York, 1971.

From *Women in Love* by D. H. Lawrence.
Copyright 1920, 1922 by David Herbert Lawrence; copyright renewal
1948, 1950 by Frieda Lawrence. Reprinted by permission of The Viking Press, Inc.,
and of Lawrence Pollinger Ltd. and the Estate of Frieda Lawrence.

Published simultaneously in the Dominion of Canada by
Burns & MacEachern, Ltd, Ontario

Library of Congress Catalog Card Number: 74-5818

ISBN 0-8008-5041-6

Designed by Mollie M. Torras

*There are more spells
than your commonplace magicians
ever dreamed of.*

—JOSEPH CONRAD, *Victory*

Acknowledgments

Archie and I would especially like to thank two people whose involvement with this book has been almost as deep and longstanding as our own. Mary Arnold has contributed sensitive editorial suggestions, participated in our inner and outer lives, and helped create an atmosphere in which we could try to realize in life the ideals of the book. Donna Gertler has worked with us on many, many versions of the manuscript, researched and traveled with us, and shared the ups and downs of our effort.

We appreciate, too, the sympathetic and useful comments made by several other readers of the manuscript: Barbara DuBois, Ruth Karei, Stanley Sagov, and Julia Vellacott, as well as readers of individual chapters who are too numerous to list here. There are also two friends who have supported our work through their hospitality, practical help, and advice: Michael Gross and Stanley Morse. Time, space, and structure have been provided us by our consulting company, Fred's Firm, Inc.

Finally, we owe much to our publisher, Terry Taplinger, and our editor, Bobs Pinkerton. Their faith and their investment in this book have helped give it a form and enabled it to reach those we want to speak to. Here it is.

S.P.

Contents

Introduction 13

1 'Til Death Do Us Part 21

2 What Addiction Is, and
What It Has to Do with Drugs 29

3 A General Theory of Addiction 55

4 "Love" as an Addiction 71

5 Addicted Lovers Together 91

6 Growing Up Addicted 115

7 The Addicted Society 141

8 Addicted Lovers Apart 171

9 Society and Personal Growth 199

10 Getting Ourselves Together 217

11 From Addiction to Love 241

Appendix 261

Bibliography 269

Index 277

LOVE and ADDICTION

Introduction

"Love" and "addiction": the juxtaposition seems strange. Yet it shouldn't, for addiction has as much to do with love as it does with drugs. Many of us are addicts, only we don't know it. We turn to each other out of the same needs that drive some people to drink and others to heroin. And this kind of addiction is just as self-destructive as—and a lot more common than—those other kinds.

Ideally, love and addiction do not have anything at all to do with one another. They are polar opposites. Nothing could be further removed from genuine love—conceived as a commitment to mutual growth and fulfillment—than the desperate self-seeking dependency which, with drugs, we call addiction. Yet in practice, we tend to get them confused. We often say "love" when we really mean, and are acting out, an addiction—a sterile, ingrown dependency relationship, with another person serving as the object of our need for security. This interpersonal dependency is not *like* an addiction, not something analogous to addiction; it *is* an addiction. It is every bit as much an addiction as drug dependency.

13

This is in some ways a personal book. I began to write it when I observed the destructive consequences, psychological and moral, of many love relationships. I concluded that these relationships did not measure up either to the lovers' self-proclaimed ideal of love, or to what I understood love to be. As the book has broadened in scope, I have developed the theme wherever possible in the form of psychological vignettes. These are fictional accounts, inspired not so much by clinical observation as by normal experience. Although fictional, the characters in these accounts are in a sense familiar to us all. As composite portraits of commonly observed patterns of behavior, they do not represent actual living individuals, but instead are images of people who are trapped in addictive relationships, and people who are growing mature enough to love out of strength rather than need.

These stories depict the experience of being young in post-World War II America. They are about how the insularity of our family lives in childhood—along with the mania of our era for finding boyfriends and girlfriends, husbands and wives—conditions us to be dependent on other people. Such is the fate of mainstream Americans. True, poverty may be a cause of addiction, but in the middle-class young we see that material comfort, too, may contribute to addiction. Addiction can be inescapable, when a person is denied the means to resolve his problems. It can also stem from the protection from reality that an overly supportive environment provides. In this regard, it is not accidental that many of the stories in these pages are about relatively privileged people whose maturation was delayed by long years of schooling. As much as anything else, this is a book about growing up.

In today's uncertain world, there are many people who can identify with the experience of unwise or desperate love. And there are many people who can identify with the experiences of aimlessness and self-doubt, fear and escapism. Some of these readers may find that this broadened concept of addiction gives them a concrete way to interpret their experiences. In this sense, too, *Love and Addiction* is a personal book, one whose relevance can only be accurately interpreted by each individual.

This is a book about addiction which focuses on interpersonal relationships. Its main purpose is to explore what addiction really is, psychologically, socially, and culturally. It does this in two ways—first, by showing what really happens when a person becomes dependent (or resists becoming dependent) on a drug; second, by showing how the same process may occur in other areas of our everyday lives, especially our relationships with those with whom we are most intimately involved.

The first part of this exploration is relatively straightforward, since much of it has already been done. Drug researchers like Isidor Chein, Charles Winick, and Norman Zinberg have shown convincingly that it is not drugs that addict people, but people who addict themselves. Heroin and morphine do not always produce the "physical" symptoms that we associate with addiction, while these symptoms can and do occur with other drugs such as cigarettes and coffee, depending on the user's cultural background, expectations, mood, and emotional needs. Once we have reviewed this research, all that remains is to interpret the addiction process to bring out its relevance to love and other human involvements.

For if addiction is now known *not* to be primarily a matter of drug chemistry or body chemistry, and if we therefore have to broaden our conception of dependency-creating objects to include a wider range of drugs, then why stop with drugs? Why not look at the whole range of things, activities, and even people to which we can and do become addicted? We must, in fact, do this if addiction is to be made a viable concept once again. At present, addiction as a scientific notion is falling into disuse because of the mass of contradictory data about drugs and their effects. Since people who take narcotics often do not get addicted, scientists are beginning to think that addiction does not exist. Yet, more casually, we find the word being used in an increasing number of contexts—"addicted to work," "addicted to gambling"—because it describes something real that happens to people.

Addiction does exist, and it is a large issue in human psychology. An understanding of addiction will help answer the question of why we repeatedly return to things we have done before—the question of habit. Addiction can be considered a pathological habit. It occurs with human necessities, such as food and love, as well as with things which people can do without, such as heroin and nicotine.

In other words, addiction is not something mysterious, something about which our ordinary experience has nothing to say. It is a malignant outgrowth, an extreme, unhealthy manifestation, of normal human inclinations. We can recognize examples of addiction in ourselves even when we would not characterize ourselves entirely, or even basically, as addicts. This is why the idea of addiction can be an important tool in our self-understanding. But for its value to be realized, it must be redefined. There has to be a fundamental change in the way we think about addiction.

If we want to reformulate the concept of addiction, we have to start where the concept is commonly and traditionally applied—that is, with drugs. This is a very different kind of book from, say, Wayne Oates's *Confessions of a Workaholic,* which accepts a conventional theory of drug addiction and goes on to draw an informal, semihumorous analogy to compulsive work patterns. Such a book is useful, if for no other reason than that it shows that people are beginning to use the notion of addiction to explain diverse areas of their experience. But Oates does not examine the implications of the analogy he draws. What we want to do here is not to apply an existing concept of addiction to love relationships, but to *change* the concept. This means starting by showing how drugs really work. If we seek to establish that addiction is just as real, just as concrete when a person is the object as when a drug is the object, then we must first confront the old stereotypes of "physical addiction" and "drug addiction" that are so deeply ingrained in our thinking.

As a social psychologist dealing mainly with human relations, I first became interested in drugs when I began to see how people were misconstruing human problems as physical or biochemical problems. It soon became clear to me that our attitudes about drugs are very revealing about ourselves. This is an area where our society's uneasiness about individual autonomy is most plainly exposed. A fear of external control over people's minds and souls is at the center of our anxieties. This fear is present in all Western countries where drug use is viewed as a social problem. But America has exhibited a more extreme response to drugs, especially the opiates, than any other country in the world, precisely because it feels the severest conflict over the impossibility of living out a traditional ideal of personal initiative.

What we think drugs do influences what they can do, and so by studying drugs we learn about our attitudes toward ourselves. Questions of self-mastery and mastery over the environment provide the key to the susceptibility to addiction; when we think of drugs as overpowering, it is because we doubt our own psychological strength. The social history of America's evolving reactions to mind-altering drugs, even drugs such as marijuana and LSD which are not regarded as "addictive," tells us a lot about how we view our own strength as individuals and as a society. It tells us, in other words, about our predisposition to give ourselves over to addiction—to drugs, to people, to anything.

Interpersonal addiction—love addiction—is just about the most common, yet least recognized, form of addiction. Highlighting it helps us break down the stereotype of the "drug addict" and arrive at a better understanding of the way addiction affects us all. On the other side, the antithesis of addiction is a true relatedness to the world, and there is no more powerful expression of that relatedness than love, or true responsiveness to another person. The issue of love versus addiction is one that is very close to our lives, and thus one that we can do something about as individuals.

The environment that is most important to us is the human one. This is why, when we get addicted, we tend to get addicted to people. Similarly, our best hope of breaking out of addiction is by learning better ways of dealing with people. This is true not only for romantic involvements but also for family ties and friendships.

Our families have a tremendous impact on our addictive, or non-addictive, potential, since they teach us either self-confidence or helplessness, self-sufficiency or dependency. Outside the family, much of our modern social environment takes the form of organizations, such as schools. Our experiences with such institutions can instill in us serious doubts about our capacity to manage our own lives, let alone to interact creatively with the rest of the world. And in reality, they may keep us from developing that capacity to the fullest. Here is where the impulse toward escape and dependency arises. One of the best things we can do to safeguard ourselves against addiction, therefore, is to understand how our social environment affects us and to develop the internal strength to become something more than creatures of society.

Addiction is not a chemical reaction. Addiction is an *experience*—one which grows out of an individual's routinized subjective response to something that has special meaning for him—something, anything, that he finds so safe and reassuring that he cannot be without it. If we want to come to terms with addiction, we have to stop blaming drugs and start looking at people, at ourselves, and at what makes us dependent. We will find that we learn habits of dependence by growing up in a culture which teaches a sense of personal inadequacy, a reliance on external bulwarks, and a preoccupation with the negative or painful rather than the positive or joyous.

Addiction is not an abnormality in our society. It is not an aberration from the norm; it is itself the norm. The dependency which is addiction is a mirror-image of more basic dependencies that we learn at home and in school. The addict's search for a superficial, external resolution of life (whether through drugs or so-called "love") follows directly from the superficial, external relationships we are led to have with each other, with our own minds and bodies, with the physical world, with learning and work and play. Those young people who suddenly repudiate convention and seek solace in drugs, or a religious commune, are only expressing tendencies that were always present in acceptable guises in their home and school lives.

Excessive parental supervision, artificial criteria for learning, and a reverential attitude toward established institutions, such as organized medicine—along with other cultural influences—combine to leave us without moorings in our direct daily experience. What can be done to combat this widespread addictive drift? We can start by gathering tools of self-analysis, developing criteria for assessing our personal involvements, and raising questions that may not ordinarily occur to us. Asking whether a certain kind of "love" may in fact be an addiction can be the first step toward reexamining and restructuring a life.

The progression of this book moves outward from the small to the large: from the effects of drugs to a portrait of the addict as a person, then to relationships between two people, then to the social causes of addiction, and finally to the possibilities for personal growth and social change. Our aim is greater self-awareness and self-realization. By its very nature, addiction is easier to diagnose than to cure. Since a reliance on simple, universal solutions to life is the problem we are dealing with, any resort to a similar program for curing it would just amount to replacing one addiction with another, something addicts do all the time. Since the problem stems from a lack of secure underpinnings in life—from a paucity of life experience, contentment, and self-fulfillment—any real solution will of necessity be a complex one. Such a solution will certainly entail the development of internal capacities—interests, joys, competencies—to counteract the desire for escape and self-obliteration. It means wanting, and having, something to offer another person. For love is made possible by an integrity of being in two individuals who come together to share, not out of passive dependence but out of surety and strength.

I need your love to survive
Without it I'm just half alive . . .
. . . I'm forgetting all my pride
I couldn't leave you, girl, if I tried
Before I love someone else
I'd rather be by myself

Baby, I've got to have you Baby

—AL HAMILTON, HERMON WEEMS, WILLIAM GARRETT, *I've Got to Have You*

1

'Til Death Do Us Part

Several years ago I began to think that what people call love can sometimes be an addiction. It was my way of making sense of some observations about drugs and about people. This was in the late 1960s, at the height of the drug explosion, when reports on acid-tripping and speed-freaking (along with the use of marijuana and heroin) were widely broadcast. At that time, newspapers and magazines began to print tables of drugs to enlighten the public about what effects these drugs had. Two things struck me in reading these tables—first, how many misconceptions I and the people I knew had about drugs, and second, how much inexact information the tables themselves contained. The assumptions I and others were making about the power of psychoactive drugs did not seem justified by any existing evidence. To me this signaled a large undefined area where the motivations and attitudes of people who took drugs could come into play. It also indicated basic fears and irrationalities in our society about drugs and what they could do.

At about the same time, though for unrelated reasons, I was beginning to look more critically at the concept of romantic love with which I had grown up. In today's open society, many varieties of male-female relationships can readily be observed in life, in motion pictures, in novels, in song lyrics. What I saw in these contexts was often disconcerting. Relationships which supposedly entailed some notion of growing together were really based mostly on security and the comfort of spending as much time as possible with someone totally sensitized to one's needs. In those cases, loving another person actually seemed to bring about a contraction in the scope of one's life. What made such relationships stand out for me was the feeling that there was something fundamental in their nature that made them this way. I could think of only one word to describe it: addiction. The individuals involved were hooked on someone whom they regarded as an object; their need for the object, their "love," was really a dependency.

At first this idea was only a metaphor to me. I didn't try to apply it seriously until I read an account of the daily lives of three married couples. In its lighthearted way, the account indicates that the writer was thinking along much the same lines as I was:

> It's amazing how marriage affects people's use of the telephone. First off, there's Mike and Betty. Whenever I call Mike, even on what amounts to a business matter, I have to endure long silences, stretching the conversation to twice the length that would otherwise be necessary, while he fills Betty in on what I have just said. Still, hers is a benign form of interference. Betty thinks of herself as a friend of mine too, and she might reasonably be said to be expressing an interest in my welfare when she jumps up and down in front of the phone screaming, "What's he saying?" The kind of thing I'm talking about becomes malignant when you try to talk to Herman. We all know that Herman's wife hardly ever lets him go to a basketball game, and that when she does let him go she goes with him and makes him reserve seats far away from his friends. But lately he can't even carry on a phone conversation without muffling the receiver each time you say something and repeating the message verbatim to his wife, so that she can tell him what to say.
>
> Janet, too, has her own style of relating over the phone. On the rare occasions when Arnold is absent for more than an hour or two in the evening, she will call me and keep a long, aimless conversation going so as to avoid having to find something to do on her own. (Often, in her desperation to find a substitute, she will get stoned—a bad move, since it makes three hours without Arnold seem like six.) But should Arnold re-

turn, even if we've been talking only a short time, or we're in the middle of an important topic, Janet will scream out his name as soon as she hears the key in the door and hang up before I can even say goodbye.

He continues with a description of the study habits of two of these couples:

Janet and Arnold have worked out a modus operandi for studying which contrasts interestingly in its elaborated rigor with Mike and Betty's primitive approach to the same problem. Mike, you see, is known not to resist distractions very well. Even so, Betty does not feel any responsibility to avoid disturbing him while he's studying for finals. So incapable is she of passing time in their apartment without talking to him that she just goes on offering him distractions, and this makes him angry at her. It is a long way from this situation-comedy atmosphere to Janet and Arnold's assembly-line efficiency. These two have a set of rules whereby when one has exams at a time when the other has nothing of comparable urgency, all normal life (work, acquaintances, freedom of movement) is suspended for the second partner, who *must,* at all times when the first is actually studying, be (a) in the apartment, (b) awake, and (c) in the same room as the first, though silent, so as to be available to meet the slightest request.

My God, what is wrong with all these people? Don't they have any notion of two people eating and sleeping and having fun and doing worthwhile things together while maintaining at least some separate studies and interests and separate places in which to carry them out? Or at least while having dignified telephone conversations separately?

What comes through in the writer's exasperated tone is a sense of waste—of seeing individual identities distorted, and individual possibilities circumscribed, by an intensely felt pressure to seek security in one other person. It is a universal pattern, expressed in a variety of personal styles. My reaction eventually was to consider just how closely this pattern fit the addiction model. As an illustration, I have put together a composite case which conveys the essence of relationships like the three that have been described. Since this is meant to be a straightforwardly schematic example of addiction, I have deliberately kept it free of distracting detail and complicated motivations. In it there is none of Mike and Betty's chaotic loving conflict and comical domesticity, none of the coercion worked by Herman's wife, none of Janet and Arnold's bizarre regimentation. Bruce and

Vicky's relationship is smooth and harmonious, its terms mutually agreeable.

AN *EGOISME A DEUX*

Vicky and Bruce are individual human beings in body only; they are constantly struggling to overcome the separation of skin that is the one barrier to their total union. Their backgrounds explain some of the story. Both of them grew up, comfortable and protected, in a suburb of Los Angeles. From an early age they thought in terms of professional careers and a domestic existence. Bruce, who graduated from high school a year ahead of Vicky, turned down a scholarship to an Ivy League university he had always dreamed of attending. Instead, unwilling to leave Vicky, he went to a university in the Los Angeles area. Vicky followed him there a year later. She hadn't wanted to go too far from her parents, and in fact she lived at home rather than on campus, just as Bruce had done the year before so that he could be near her. The couple made the hour-long trip to and from school every day together, and they continued to see each other in the comfortable settings of their old neighborhood and their parents' homes. It was as if they were biding time, waiting simply to reach an age when they could marry without arousing comment. Their lack of experience with other people at college naturally did not give them a chance to gain a very accurate impression of themselves as others saw them. The result was that they didn't develop adult qualities that might have made them attractive to people who didn't already know and love them.

And there you have it. Two people reluctant to leave the security of their high school relationship, probably as much from a fear of disappointing each other, and of never finding anything better for themselves, as from inherent desire, had joined themselves together " 'til death do us part." In the meantime, they had missed the opportunity to live away from home, an experience their upper-middle-class parents would willingly have subsidized. The price they extracted from each other for the sacrifices involved in maintaining the relationship was the constant reassurance of each other's company. Having spent so much of themselves simply to stay together, they both felt the relationship owed them a great deal. And, to justify this commitment, they steadily inflated each other's worth to the point where nothing else seemed of any consequence to them.

They soon gave up whatever independent interests they had. Vicky discarded the idea of joining the college drama club because it would have taken too much of her time from Bruce. They did not see much of their old friends, most of whom had gone away to college. Nor did they make new friends at the university, except a few classroom friends. They talked about courses and teachers with these people, and together went to occasional parties with them, but because so little of their free time was spent on campus, these outside relationships didn't amount to anything. The couple grew more and more clinging, turned to each other for more and more of what they wanted, and gradually severed all connections with the rest of the world except for school and their parents.

Vicky and Bruce got married upon Bruce's graduation. Together, they decided to move to San Francisco for their graduate training. Bruce was to go to law school, while Vicky planned to take her Ph.D. in history after completing her senior year at a college in the area. Not that she had any intention of being a historian. She found her history courses boring and, worse, tremendously stressful. Constrained but not inspired by the curriculum during her undergraduate years, she had made her way through with the help of stimulants and tranquilizers. One may wonder why she didn't rise up against this agony and get off the academic treadmill, but it is not surprising that a person so little disposed to question the security of her family home and her marriage would not seek something more purposeful than continued, meaningless academic activity. In fact, she saw no alternative for herself while her husband was in law school.

Vicky and Bruce were concerned about moving so far away from their families. However, they enjoyed regular weekend visits from their parents. They frequently returned these visits, carefully dividing their time between the two families, as well as bringing them together for joint gatherings. And they had hardly arrived in San Francisco before they began making detailed plans for their eventual return to Los Angeles, where they would buy a house near both families once Bruce was earning a lawyer's income and their San Francisco "bohemian" period had come to an end.

At this point they settled into the kind of married life described in the account at the beginning of this chapter. Marriage gave their relationship, blessed with parental indulgence from the beginning, the added comforts of a home life. Occasionally they roused themselves to attend an evening lecture or other university cultural event. However, their penetration into San Francisco never went much deeper than that. With few friends, their social life was as limited and superficial as it had been in college, and although they espoused topical viewpoints, they were certainly not part of the new West Coast scene.

Thus two underdeveloped egos merged into what D. H. Lawrence called an *égoisme à deux:* two people banded together, not because of love or an increasing understanding of each other, but rather because of their overentanglement and mutual self-deprivation. With each step in their growing interdependence, Bruce and Vicky broke a few more of the ties they had had with other people, things, and activities. And as these disappeared, they hung on to each other that much more frantically to bolster themselves against an increasingly alien environment.

We can partially trace the genesis of these addictive personalities in Vicky's and Bruce's upbringing. Neither of them had broken from a childhood dependence on their parents. They approached all experience outside the family as somehow external to themselves. Although they were both successful students, and both accepted the yoke of school's demands, their schoolwork had little meaning for them, and they spoke of it cynically. Nor were they capable of forming relationships outside the family, but for one—with each other. It was as though this isolated excursion drained them of all the energy they might have applied toward knowing other people.

Their parents had been so generous, so quick to bend the environment to Bruce and Vicky's needs, that they could not realize how they were limiting their children's experience. When Vicky became involved with Bruce, her parents, with his parents' blessing, turned over their beach house to the young lovers, and rented a smaller place at Lake Arrowhead. The couple could go to the beach house and be together without interference. Except, of course, it was total interference, for the young people were never allowed to develop distinct wills of their own. Vicky had no reason to go out into the world when her mother and father were so attentive to her needs, so appreciative of her charm and intelligence, that she could not have hoped to find better treatment anywhere else. Moving straight from her parents' home to her husband's, this woman never had the experience of living alone, on her own emotional resources, and probably never will. In this way, Vicky's and Bruce's parents incorporated every stage of their children's growth except for the last stage, independence—not only a healthy separation from the home, but a true psychological independence; something a person carries with him or her for all time. And it is this kind of self-completion which instills the integrity that every real coming together of two or more individuals presupposes.

THE PARALLEL WITH OPIATE ADDICTION

How does this story resemble the more familiar pattern of addiction we see in habitual drug users? Showing just how deep the resemblance goes is what this book is about. The addict is a person who never learns to come to grips with his world, and who therefore seeks stability and reassurance through some repeated, ritualized activity. This activity is reinforced in two ways—first, by a comforting sensation of well-being induced by the drug or other addictive object; second, by the atrophy of the addict's other interests and abilities and the general deterioration of his life situation while he is preoccupied with the addiction. As alternatives grow smaller, the addiction grows larger, until it is all there is. A true addict progresses into a monomania, whether the object of addiction is a drug or a lover. Vicky and Bruce's sheltered childhoods denied them the self-confidence and the well-formed enthusiasms that a complete life is built on. As a result, they fastened on each other as a daily habit, and this habit became the *raison d'être* of their existence.

It is important to note the vicious cycle at work here. The addict's lack of internal direction or purpose creates the need for ritualized escape in the first place, and is in turn exacerbated by exclusive involvement with the addiction and abandonment of the substance of a normal life. Operating on the personal malaise an addict feels, drugs give him an artificial sense of self-sufficiency that removes what small motivation he has for complicated or difficult pursuits. Similarly, Vicky and Bruce came to each other originally in a state of ennui, without interests that extended deep enough to engage them. Once they found each other, they became even less motivated to cultivate friends or apply themselves to their work in any but the most external way. Their dependency, like the drug addict's, could only increase as other concerns dropped off.

The one major feature of the addiction cycle that the case of Vicky and Bruce does not directly illustrate is withdrawal—the addict's anguished reaction to an interruption of his supply. Vicky and Bruce organized their environment so totally around each other that there never was the slightest threat of a breakup. The couple had at some cost resisted even temporary separations, as when Bruce resigned himself to a school he didn't like in order to stay with his fiancée. Lovers often do suffer withdrawal symptoms when breakups occur. With Vicky and Bruce, the passion for staying together was in large part a fear and avoidance of withdrawal. Vicky and Bruce are like the well-to-do, respectable opiate addict who is able to guarantee that he will never have to feel the pain of withdrawal.

Addiction to a person is just an extension of the social side of all addictions. People who share an addiction form a private world for themselves. For example, a group of people who are addicted to the same drug tend to give their experience a collective interpretation which is incomprehensible to those outside the group. They are not concerned with this discrepancy because only the approval of other group members matters to them. The same is true for Vicky and Bruce, with their family and household rituals, their exclusive concern to please each other, and their inflated estimation of themselves. In fact, an addictive romantic relationship like theirs is the smallest, most isolated group possible.

But it is not enough simply to make the description of two things sound alike. In order to show why and how the parallel is a real one, we have to confront the question of what addiction is and how it works—both with drugs and elsewhere. Then we will see that certain interpersonal attachments can genuinely be called addictions.

Breuer preferred what might be called a physiological theory: he thought that the processes which could not find normal outcome were such as had originated during unusual, hypnoid, mental states. This opened the further question of the origin of these hypnoid states. I, on the other hand, was inclined to suspect the existence of an interplay of forces and the operation of intentions and purposes such as are to be observed in normal life. —SIGMUND FREUD, *An Autobiographical Study*

2

What Addiction Is, and What It Has to Do with Drugs

When we talk about addictive love relationships, we are not using the term in any metaphorical sense. Vicky's relationship with Bruce was not *like* an addiction; it *was* an addiction. If we have trouble grasping this, it is because we have learned to believe that addiction takes place only with drugs. In order to see why this is not the case— to see how "love" can also be an addiction—we have to take a new look at what addiction is, and what it has to do with drugs.

To say that people like Vicky and Bruce are genuinely addicted to each other is to say that addiction to drugs is something other than what most people take it to be. Thus, we must reinterpret the process by which a person becomes dependent on a drug, so that we can trace the inner, psychological experience of drug addiction, or any addiction. That subjective experience is the key to the true meaning of addiction. It is conventionally believed that addiction happens automatically whenever someone takes sufficiently large and frequent doses of certain drugs, particularly the opiates. Recent

29

research that we will cite in this chapter has shown that this assumption is false. People respond to powerful drugs, even regular doses of them, in different ways. At the same time, people respond to a variety of different drugs, as well as experiences that have nothing to do with drugs, with similar patterns of behavior. The response people have to a given drug is determined by their personalities, their cultural backgrounds, and their expectations and feelings about the drug. In other words, the sources of addiction lie within the person, not the drug.

While addiction is only tangentially related to any particular drug, it is still useful to examine people's reactions to the drugs which are commonly believed to produce addiction. Because these drugs are psychoactive—that is, they can alter people's consciousness and feelings—they have a strong appeal for individuals who are desperately looking for escape and reassurance. Drugs are not the only objects which serve this function for people who are predisposed to addiction. By seeing what it is about some drugs, such as heroin, that draws the addict into a repetitive and eventually total involvement with them, we can identify other experiences, such as love relationships, that potentially have the same effect. The dynamics of drug addiction can then be used as a model for understanding these other addictions.

We will see that more than anywhere else in the world, addiction is a major issue in America. It grows out of special features of the culture and history of this country, and to a lesser extent, of Western society generally. In asking why Americans have found it necessary to believe in a false relationship between addiction and the opiates, we discover a major vulnerability in American culture that mirrors the vulnerability of the individual addict. This vulnerability is close to the heart of the very real and very large significance of addiction—drug and otherwise—in our time. Consider our image of the drug addict. The Federal Bureau of Narcotics and fiction like *The Man with the Golden Arm* have taught us to visualize the "dope fiend" as a criminal psychopath, violently destructive to himself and others, as his habit leads him inexorably toward death. In reality, most addicts are not at all like this. When we look at the addict in human terms, when we try to figure out what is going on inside him, we see more clearly why he acts as he does—with or without drugs. We see something like this portrait of Ric, an on-again off-again addict, from an account given by a friend of his:

> I helped Ric, now off his probation period, move out of his parents' house yesterday. I didn't mind the work, since Ric is such a nice guy and has offered to help put new linoleum down in my kitchen. So I set in to do the wall-washing, vacuuming, floor-sweeping, etc., in his room with good spirits. But these were quickly turned into feelings of depression and paralysis by Ric's inability to do anything in a reasonably complete and efficient manner, and by my seeing him, at the age of 32, moving in and out of his parents' house. It was the *reductio ad absurdum* of all the inadequacies and problems we see around us, and it was goddamned depressing.
>
> I realized that the struggle for life is never done, and that Ric has blown it badly. And he knows it. How could he fail to realize it with his father telling him that he wasn't a man yet and with his mother not wanting to let us take their vacuum cleaner to clean his new apartment? Ric argued, "What do you think I'm going to do—pawn it or something?" which has probably been a real possibility on many occasions, if not this time. Ric was sweating in the morning chill, complaining about that fucking methadone, when it was probably his needing a fix sooner or later and his father noticing and knowing and saying that he couldn't take a little work—that he wasn't a man yet.
>
> I started right in cleaning—Ric said it would be about half an hour's work—because he had been an hour late picking me up and because I wanted to get it over with so as to get away from him and that place. But then he got a phone call and went out, saying he'd be back in a little while. When he returned he went into the john—presumably to fix. I kept on cleaning; he came out, discovered that he didn't have the garbage bags he needed for packing, and went out again. By the time he got back, I had done everything I could, and he finally set into packing and throwing things out to the point where I could help him.
>
> We started to load up Ric's father's truck, but it was bad timing, since his father had just come back. The whole time we carried things down and placed them in the truck, he complained about how he needed it himself. Once, as he and Ric carried down a horrendously heavy bureau, he started in on how it and the rest of the things we were carrying should have stayed where they belonged in the first place, and not been moved in and out. Like Ric stepping out into the world, to love, to work, only to retreat; to be pushed or pulled back inside, to go back in again behind

drugs, or jail, or momma or papa—all the things that have safely limited Ric's world for him.

It is not likely that Ric will die of his habit, or kill for it. It is not likely that his body will rot and that he will be reduced to a disease-ridden degenerate. We can see, however, that he is severely debilitated, though not primarily, or initially, by drugs. What makes a heroin addict? The answer lies in those aspects of a person's history and social setting which leave him in need of outside help in order to cope with the world. Ric's addiction stems from his weakness and incompetence, his lack of personal wholeness. Heroin reflects and reinforces all his other dependencies, even as he uses it to forget them. Ric is an addict, and he would be one whether he were dependent on drugs or love or any of the other objects that people turn to repeatedly under the stress of an incomplete existence. The choice of one drug over another—or of drugs at all—has to do primarily with ethnic and social background and circles of acquaintance. The addict, heroin or otherwise, is addicted not to a chemical, but to a sensation, a prop, an experience which structures his life. What causes that experience to become an addiction is that it makes it more and more difficult for the person to deal with his real needs, thereby making his sense of well-being depend increasingly on a single, external source of support.

ADDICTION AND DRUGS

No one has ever been able to show how and why "physical dependence" occurs when people take narcotics (i.e., the opiates: opium, heroin, and morphine) regularly. Lately it has become clear that there is no way to measure physical dependence. In fact, nothing like it occurs with a surprising number of narcotic users. We know now that there is no universal or exclusive connection between addiction and the opiates (universal, in the sense that addiction is an inevitable consequence of opiate use; exclusive, in the sense that addiction occurs only with the opiates as opposed to other drugs). Supporting this conclusion is a wide range of evidence which we will review briefly here. An Appendix has been provided for those who want to explore further the scientific basis of the findings about drugs which are reported in this chapter. The reader may also want to consult some excellent recent books such as Erich Goode's *Drugs in American Society,* Norman Zinberg and John Robertson's *Drugs and the Public,* and Henry Lennard's *Mystification and Drug Misuse.* These books reflect the consensus among well-informed observers that the effects of drugs are relative to the people who take them and the settings in which they are taken. As Norman Zinberg and David Lewis concluded a decade ago after an in-depth study of 200 narcotic users, "most of the problems of narcotic use do not fall into the classic definition of addiction . . . [i.e., craving, tolerance, and withdrawal]. Indeed, the range of cases that do not fit the stereotype of the narcotic addict is very wide. . . ."

In the first place, exactly what are the withdrawal symptoms we hear so much about? The most commonly observed symptoms of severe withdrawal distress call to mind a case of the flu—rapid respiration, loss of appetite, fever, sweating, chills, rhinitis, nausea, vomiting, diarrhea, abdominal cramps, and restlessness together with lethargy. That is to say, withdrawal isn't a unique, definite syndrome that can be precisely distinguished from many other cases of bodily discomfort or disorientation. Whenever the body's internal balance is upset, whether through withdrawal from a drug or an attack of illness, it can manifest these signs of physical and psychological distress. Indeed, the most intensely felt symptom of withdrawal, one that we know about only from the statements of addicts themselves, is not chemical at all. It is an agonizing sense of the absence of well-being, a sense of some terrible deficiency inside oneself. This is the major, personal upheaval that results from the loss of a comfortable buffer against reality, which is where the real wallop of narcotic addiction comes from.

Tolerance, the other major identifying mark of addiction, is the tendency for a person to adapt to a drug, so that a larger dose is required to produce the same effect that resulted initially from a smaller dose. There are limits to this process, however; both monkeys in the laboratory and human addicts soon reach a ceiling point where their usage level is stabilized. Like withdrawal, tolerance is something we know about from observing people's behavior and listening to what they tell us. People show tolerance for all drugs, and individuals vary greatly in the tolerance they show for a given drug.

Just how much variation there can be in withdrawal and tolerance effects stemming from the use of opiates and other drugs is revealed by the following studies and observations of different groups of users:

1. *Vietnam veterans, hospital patients.* After it became known that perhaps one-fourth of all American soldiers in Vietnam were using heroin, there was widespread concern that returning veterans would trigger an epidemic of addiction in the United States. Nothing of the sort happened. Jerome Jaffe, the physician who headed the Government's rehabilitation program for drug-dependent veterans, explained why in an article in *Psychology Today* entitled "As Far as Heroin Is Concerned, the Worst Is Over." Dr. Jaffe found that most of the G.I.s used heroin in response to the unbearable conditions they faced in Vietnam. As they prepared to return to America, where they would be able to resume their normal lives, they withdrew from the drug with little difficulty and apparently showed no further interest in it. Dr. Richard S. Wilbur, then Assistant Secretary of Defense for Health and Environment, said that this conclusion to the heroin experience in Vietnam amazed him, and caused him to revise the notions about addiction that he had learned in medical school, where he "was taught that anyone who ever tried heroin was instantly, totally, and perpetually hooked."

Similarly, hospital patients often receive morphine for relief of pain without becoming addicted. Norman Zinberg interviewed 100 patients who had received an opiate regularly (at higher than street-level doses) for ten days or longer. Only one recalled having felt any desire for more injections once the pain had ceased.

2. *Controlled users.* Hospital patients and Vietnam veterans are accidental or temporary opiate users. There are also people who take regular doses of powerful drugs as part of their normal life routine. They do not experience tolerance, or physical or mental deterioration. These individuals are called "controlled users." Controlled use is a more widely recognized phenomenon with alcohol, but there are also controlled users of opiates. Many of them are prominent, successful people who have the wherewithal to maintain their habit and keep it secret. One example is provided by Clifford Allbutt and W. E. Dixon, eminent British authorities on drugs around the turn of the century:

A patient of one of us took a grain of opium in a pill every morning and every evening of the last fifteen years of a long, laborious and distinguished career. A man of great force of character, concerned in affairs of weight and of national importance, and of stainless character, he persisted in this habit, as being one . . . which toned and strengthened him for his deliberations and engagements.

(quoted by Aubrey Lewis in Hannah Steinberg, ed., *Scientific Basis of Drug Dependence*)

Doctors are the best-known single group of controlled drug users. .Historically, we can cite Sir Arthur Conan Doyle's cocaine habit and the distinguished surgeon William Halsted's daily use of morphine. Today, estimates of the number of physicians taking opiates run to about one in every hundred. The very circumstance that prompts many doctors to use narcotics—their ready access to such drugs as morphine or the synthetic narcotic Demerol—makes such users difficult to uncover, especially when they remain in control of their habit and of themselves. Charles Winick, a New York physician and public health official who has investigated many aspects of opiate use, studied physician users who had been publicly exposed, but who were not obviously incapacitated, either in their own eyes or in the eyes of others. Only two out of the ninety-eight doctors Winick questioned turned themselves in because they found they needed increasing dosages of the narcotic. On the whole, the doctors Winick studied were more successful than average. "Most were useful and effective members of their community," Winick notes, and continued to be while they were involved with drugs.

It is not only middle-class and professional people who can use narcotics without meeting the fate which supposedly awaits addicts. Both Donald Louria (in Newark) and Irving Lukoff and his colleagues (in Brooklyn) have found evidence of controlled heroin' use in the lower class. Their studies show that heroin users in these ghetto communities are more numerous, better off financially, and better educated than was previously supposed. In many cases, in fact, heroin users are doing better economically than the average ghetto resident.

3. *Ritualistic drug use.* In *The Road to H*, Isidor Chein and his co-workers investigated the variety of heroin usage patterns in the ghettos of New York. Along with regular, controlled users, they

found some adolescents who were taking the drug irregularly and without withdrawal, and others who were drug-dependent even when they were getting the drug in doses too weak to have any physical effect. Addicts in the latter circumstances have even been observed to go through withdrawal. Chein believes that people like these are dependent not on the drug itself, but on the ritual of obtaining and administering it. Thus a large majority of the addicts interviewed by John Ball and his colleagues rejected the idea of legalized heroin, because that would eliminate the secretive and illicit rituals of their drug use.

4. *Maturing out of addiction.* By going over the Federal Bureau of Narcotics' lists of addicts, and comparing the names which appeared on the lists at five-year intervals, Charles Winick discovered that street addicts commonly grow out of their dependency on heroin. In his study, entitled "Maturing Out of Narcotic Addiction," Winick demonstrated that one-fourth of all known addicts become inactive by the age of 26, and three-fourths by 36. He concluded from these findings that heroin addiction is largely an adolescent habit, one which most people get over at some point in their adulthood.

5. *Reactions to a morphine placebo.* A placebo is a neutral substance (like sugared water) which is given to a patient in the guise of an active medication. Since people can show moderate or practically nonexistent reactions to morphine, it is not surprising that they also may experience the effects of morphine when they simply imagine that they are receiving the drug. In a classic study of the placebo effect, Louis Lasagna and his co-workers found that 30 to 40 percent of a group of postoperative patients couldn't tell the difference between morphine and a placebo that they were told was morphine. For them, the placebo relieved pain as well as the morphine did. The morphine itself worked only 60 to 80 percent of the time, so that although it was somewhat more effective than the placebo as a painkiller, it too was not infallible (see Appendix A).

6. *Addictions transferred from one drug to another.* If the action of a powerful drug can be simulated by an injection of sugared water, then we should certainly expect people to be able to substitute one drug for another when the effects of the drugs are similar. For example, pharmacologists consider barbiturates and alcohol to be cross-dependent. That is, a person who is addicted to either of them

can suppress the withdrawal symptoms that result from not getting the one drug by taking the other. Both of these drugs also serve as substitutes for the opiates. The historical evidence, presented by Lawrence Kolb and Harris Isbell in the anthology *Narcotic Drug Addiction Problems,* shows that the fact that all three substances are depressants makes them roughly interchangeable for the purposes of addiction (see Appendix B). When there is a shortage of available heroin, addicts typically resort to barbiturates, as they did in World War II when the normal channels for importation of heroin were cut off. And many of the Americans who became opiate users in the nineteenth century had been heavy drinkers before the arrival of opium in this country. Among heroin addicts whom John O'Donnell surveyed in Kentucky, those who were no longer able to obtain the drug tended heavily to become alcoholics. This shift to alcoholism by narcotic users has been commonly observed in many other settings.

7. *Addiction to everyday drugs.* Addiction occurs not only with strong depressant drugs like heroin, alcohol, and barbiturates, but with mild sedatives and pain-relievers like tranquilizers and aspirin. It also appears with commonly used stimulants like cigarettes (nicotine) and coffee, tea, and cola (caffeine). Imagine someone who begins smoking a few cigarettes a day and works up to a stable daily habit of one or two or three packs; or a habitual coffee drinker who eventually needs five cups in the morning to get started and several more during the day to feel normal. Think how uncomfortable such a person gets when there are no cigarettes or coffee in the house, and to what lengths he or she will go to obtain some. If an inveterate smoker can't get a cigarette, or tries to give up smoking, he may show the full symptoms of withdrawal—shaking nervously, becoming uncomfortable, agitated, uncontrollably restless, and so on.

In the Consumers Union report, *Licit and Illicit Drugs,* Edward Brecher states that no essential difference exists between the heroin and nicotine habits. He cites cigarette-deprived, post-World War II Germany, where proper citizens begged, stole, prostituted themselves, and traded off precious commodities—all in order to obtain tobacco. Closer to home, Joseph Alsop devoted a series of newspaper columns to the problem many ex-smokers have in concentrating on their work after giving up their habit—a difficulty heroin treatment programs traditionally have had to deal with in addicts. Alsop wrote that the first of these articles "brought in scores of readers' letters saying in effect, 'Thank God you wrote about not being able to work. We've told the doctors again and again, and they won't believe it.' "

SOCIAL AND CULTURAL VARIATIONS
IN DRUG EFFECTS

If many drugs can addict, and if not everyone gets addicted to any particular drug, then there can be no single physiological mechanism which explains addiction. Something else has to account for the variety of reactions people have when different chemicals are introduced into their bodies. The signs which are taken as indicators of addiction, withdrawal and tolerance, are affected by a host of situational and personal variables. The way people respond to a drug depends on how they view the drug—that is, what they expect from it—which is called their "set," and on the influences they feel from their surroundings, which comprise the setting. Set and setting are in turn shaped by the underlying dimensions of culture and social structure.

Lasagna's placebo experiment demonstrated that people's reactions to a drug are determined as much by what they think the drug is as by what it actually is. An important study that showed people's expectations working in combination with pressures from the social environment was conducted by Stanley Schachter and Jerome Singer. In it, individuals who were given a shot of adrenalin responded to the drug in entirely different ways, depending on whether they knew ahead of time to anticipate the effects of the stimulant, and on what mood they observed being acted out by someone else in the same situation. When they weren't sure what they were getting in the injection, they looked to see how the *other* person was acting in order to know how *they* should feel (see Appendix C). On a larger scale, this is how drugs are defined as being addictive or nonaddictive. People model their response to a given drug on the way they see other people responding, either in their social group or in the society as a whole.

A striking example of this social learning is provided by Howard Becker's study (in his book *Outsiders*) of the initiation of novice marijuana smokers into groups of experienced smokers. The novice has to be taught first that feeling certain sensations means that he is high, and then that these sensations are pleasurable. Similarly, groups of people who took LSD together in the 1960s were often known as tribes. These groups had widely differing experiences with the drug, and people who joined a tribe quickly learned to experience whatever it was that the rest of the group encountered in a trip. In the case of heroin, Norman Zinberg reports in his December, 1971, *New York Times Magazine* article, "G.I.'s and O.J.'s in Vietnam," that army units each developed their own specific withdrawal symptoms. The symptoms tended to be uniform within a unit, but varied greatly among units. In *Drugs and the Public,* Zinberg and John Robertson also note that withdrawal was consistently milder at the Daytop Village addiction treatment center than it was, for the same addicts, in jail. The difference was that the social atmosphere at Daytop did not allow severe withdrawal symptoms to appear because they could not be used as an excuse for not doing one's work.

Whole societies, too, teach specific lessons about drugs in line with their attitudes toward them. Historically, the drugs which other cultures have considered dangerous often have not been the same ones that we, in our culture, think of in such a light. In *The Soul of the Ape,* for example, Eugene Marais describes the devastating effects of our ordinary smoking tobacco on the Bushmen and Hottentots of nineteenth-century South Africa, who were familiar and moderate users of *dagga* (marijuana). Opium, which has been taken as a pain-killer since antiquity, was not regarded as a special drug menace before the late nineteenth century, and it was only then, according to Glenn Sonnedecker, that the term "addiction" began to be applied to this drug alone with its present meaning. Previously, the negative side effects of opium were lumped together with those of coffee, tobacco, and alcohol, which, according to the data compiled by Richard Blum in *Society and Drugs,* were often objects of greater concern. China banned tobacco-smoking a century before it prohibited opium in 1729. Persia, Russia, parts of Germany, and Turkey all at some time made the production or use of tobacco a capital offense. Coffee was outlawed in the Arab world around 1300 and in Germany in the 1500s.

Consider the following description of drug dependence: "The

sufferer is tremulous and loses his self-command; he is subject to fits of agitation and depression. He has a haggard appearance. . . . As with other such agents, a renewed dose of the poison gives temporary relief, but at the cost of future misery." The drug in question is coffee (caffeine), as seen by the turn-of-the-century British pharmacologists Allbutt and Dixon. Here is their view of tea: "An hour or two after breakfast at which tea has been taken . . . a grievous sinking . . . may seize upon a sufferer, so that to speak is an effort. . . . The speech may become weak and vague. . . . By miseries such as these, the best years of life may be spoilt."

What seems dangerous and uncontrollable at one time or in one place becomes natural and comfortable to deal with in another setting. Although tobacco has been proved to be injurious to health in any number of ways, and recent investigations suggest that coffee may be equally harmful, Americans do not, by and large, strongly mistrust either substance (see Appendix D). The ease we feel in handling the two drugs has led us to underestimate or disregard their chemical potency. Our sense of being psychologically secure with tobacco and coffee stems, in turn, from the fact that energizing, stimulant drugs closely fit the ethos of American and other Western cultures.

A culture's reaction to a drug is conditioned by its image of that drug. If the drug is seen as mysterious and uncontrollable, or if it stands for escape and oblivion, then it will be widely misused. This usually happens when a drug is newly introduced to a culture on a large scale. Where people can readily accept a drug, then dramatic personal deterioration and social disruption will not result from its use. This is usually the case when a drug is well-integrated into life in a culture. For instance, studies by Giorgio Lolli and Richard Jessor have shown that Italians, who have a long and settled experience with liquor, do not think of alcohol as possessing the same potent ability to console that Americans ascribe to it. As a result, Italians manifest less alcoholism, and the personality traits which are associated with alcoholism among Americans are not related to drinking patterns among Italians.

Based on Richard Blum's analysis of alcohol, we can develop a set of criteria for whether a drug will be used addictively or nonaddictively by a particular culture. If the drug is consumed in connection with prescribed patterns of behavior and traditional social customs and regulations, it is not likely to cause major problems. If, on the other hand, either the use or control of the drug is introduced without respect to existing institutions and cultural practices, and is associated either with political repression or with rebellion, excessive or asocial usage patterns will be present. Blum contrasts the American Indians, in whom chronic alcoholism developed in the wake of the white man's disruption of their cultures, with three rural Greek villages where drinking is so fully integrated into a traditional way of life that alcoholism as a social problem is not even conceived of.

The same relationships hold true for the opiates. In India, where opium has long been grown and is used in folk medicine, there has never been an opium problem. In China, however, where the drug was imported by Arab and British traders and was associated with colonial exploitation, its use got out of hand. But not even in China has opium been as disruptive a force as in America. Brought to America by Chinese laborers in the 1850s, opium caught on quickly here, first in the form of morphine injections for wounded soldiers in the Civil War, and later in patent medicines. Nonetheless, according to accounts by Isbell and Sonnedecker, doctors and pharmacists did not regard opiate addiction as a problem different from other drug dependencies until the two decades between 1890 and 1909, when opium importation increased dramatically. It was during this period that the most concentrated opiate, heroin, was first produced from morphine. Since then, narcotic addiction in America has grown to unprecedented proportions, despite—or perhaps in part due to—our determined attempts to ban the opiates.

ADDICTION, THE OPIATES, AND OTHER DRUGS IN AMERICA

The belief in addiction encourages a susceptibility to addiction. In *Addiction and Opiates,* Alfred Lindesmith states that addiction is more regularly a consequence of heroin use now than in the nineteenth century, because, he argues, people now "know" what to expect from the drug. In that case, this new knowledge we have is a dangerous thing. The very concept that one can be addicted to a drug, especially heroin, has been put into people's minds by society's belaboring of that idea. By convincing people that such a thing as physiological addiction exists, that there are drugs which can take control of one's mind and body, society makes it easier for people to relinquish themselves to a drug's power. In other words, the American conception of drug addiction is not just a mistaken interpretation of the facts, it is itself part of the problem—part of what addiction is about. Its effects go beyond drug dependencies per se to the whole issue of personal competence and the ability to control one's destiny in a confusing, technologically and organizationally complex world. So it is important that we ask why Americans have believed in addiction so strongly, feared it so much, and linked it so erroneously with one class of drugs. What characteristics of American culture account for such outsized misunderstanding and irrationality?

In his essay entitled "On the Presence of Demons," Blum attempts to explain the American hypersensitivity to drugs, which he describes this way:

> Mind-altering drugs have been invested by the public with qualities which are not directly linked to their visible or most probable effects. They have been elevated to the status of a power deemed capable of tempting, possessing, corrupting, and destroying persons without regard to the prior conduct or condition of those persons—a power which has all-or-none effects.

Blum's thesis is that Americans are especially threatened by the psychoactive properties of drugs because of a unique Puritan heritage of insecurity and fear, including the special fear of possession by spirits that was apparent in the Salem witch trials. This interpretation is a good start toward understanding the problem, but ultimately it breaks down. For one thing, the belief in witchcraft also existed throughout Europe. For another, it cannot be said that Americans, compared to people in other countries, have an inordinately strong sense of their own powerlessness before outside forces. On the contrary, America has traditionally placed more stock in internal strength and personal autonomy than have most cultures, both because of its Protestant roots and the open opportunities it offered for exploration and initiative. We must start, in fact, with America's ideal of individualism if we are to understand why drugs have become such a sensitive issue in this country.

America has been faced with a perplexing conflict over its inability to live out the Puritan principle of inner vision and the pioneer spirit which are part of its ethos. (This conflict has been analyzed from different angles in works like Edmund Morgan's *Visible Saints,* David Riesman's *The Lonely Crowd,* and David McClelland's *The Achieving Society.*) That is, because they idealized the individual's integrity and self-direction, Americans were especially hard hit by evolving conditions of modern life that assaulted those ideals. Such developments included the institutionalization of work within large industries and bureaucracies in the place of farming, craftsmanship, and small enterprises; the regimentation of education through the public school system; and the disappearance of free land to which the individual could migrate. All three of these processes came to a head in the latter half of the nineteenth century, just when opium was being introduced to America. For example, Frederick Jackson Turner dated the closing of the frontier—and the profound social changes he attached to that event—at 1890, the beginning of the period of most rapid growth in opium importation.

This radical transformation of American society, with its undermining of the potential for individual effort and enterprise, left Americans unable to control their destinies as much as, in keeping with their beliefs, they felt they should. The opiates appealed to Americans because these drugs act to assuage the consciousness of personal deficiencies and impotence. But at the same time, because they contribute to this impotence by making it more difficult for a person to cope effectively, the opiates came to symbolize the feelings of loss of control that also appeared in this era. It is at this point in American history that the concept of addiction emerged with its contemporary meaning; earlier, the word merely stood for the idea of a bad habit, a vice of some kind. Now narcotics began to evoke a magical awe in people's minds, and to assume a farther-reaching power than they had ever had.

Thus, through their introduction into the United States at this time, heroin and the other opiates became a part of a larger conflict within the society. As one more form of control that lay outside the individual, they aroused the fear and defensiveness of people already troubled by these issues. They also drew the ire of the bureaucratic institutions which were growing up alongside of opiates in

America—institutions which exercised a similar type of power psychologically to that of the narcotics, and with which, therefore, the drugs were essentially competing. This atmosphere spawned the fervent organized and official efforts that were made to combat opiate use. Because opiates had become the focus for America's anxieties, they provided a means to direct attention away from the deeper reality of addiction. Addiction is a complex and wide-ranging reaction in society to the constriction and subjugation of the individual psyche. The technological and social change that created it has been a worldwide phenomenon. By a combination of factors, including historical accident and other variables which no one analysis can take into account, this psychological process has been linked especially strongly to one class of drugs in America. And the arbitrary association persists to this day.

Because of their misconceptions and their desire to establish themselves as final arbiters over what drugs were proper for regular consumption by Americans, two organizations—the Federal Bureau of Narcotics and the American Medical Association—launched a propaganda campaign against the opiates and their users, exaggerating both the extent and the severity of the problem at that time. Both of these institutions were intent on consolidating their own power over drugs and related matters in the society, the Narcotics Bureau branching out from collecting drug taxes within the Treasury Department, and the AMA striving to reinforce its position as the certifying body for physicians and approved medical practices. Together, they had a powerful influence on American policy and attitudes toward narcotics in the early twentieth century.

Lawrence Kolb, in Livingston's *Narcotic Drug Addiction Problems,* and John Clausen, in Merton and Nisbet's *Contemporary Social Problems,* have recounted the destructive consequences of this policy, consequences which are still with us today. The Supreme Court gave a controversial, prohibitionist interpretation to the Harrison Act of 1914, which originally had provided only for the taxation and registration of persons handling drugs. This decision was part of a decisive shift in popular opinion by which the regulation of narcotics use was taken out of the hands of the individual addict and his physician and given over to the government. The major impact of this move, in fact, was to make the criminal underworld the agency largely responsible for the propagation of drugs and drug habits in the United States. In England, where the medical community has retained control over opiate distribution and the maintenance of addicts, addiction has been a mild phenomenon, with the number of addicts remaining constant at a few thousand. Addiction there has also been largely unconnected with crime, and most of the addicts lead stable, middle-class lives.

One important effect of the official war against narcotics carried out in America was to banish the opiates from respectable society and consign them to the lower class. The image that was created of the heroin addict as an uncontrolled, criminal degenerate made it difficult for middle-class people to become involved with the drug. As the heroin user was made into a social outcast, public disgust influenced his own conception of himself and his habit. Before 1914, opiate takers had been mainstream Americans; now addicts are concentrated in various minority groups, especially blacks. Meanwhile, society has provided the middle class with different addictions—some representing social and institutional attachments, others merely consisting of dependencies on different drugs. For example, the "bored housewife" syndrome created many opiate users in the nineteenth century out of women who no longer had an energetic role to play at home or in independent family enterprises. Today these women drink or take tranquilizers. Nothing is more indicative of the unresolved problem of addiction than the wistful search for a nonaddicting anodyne. Since the advent of morphine, we have welcomed hypodermic injections, heroin, the barbiturates, Demerol, methadone, and various sedatives as offering the chance to escape pain without causing us to become addicted. But the more effective at its purpose each drug has been, the more clearly its addictiveness has been established.

The persistence of our addictive susceptibilities is also evident in our conflicting and irrational attitudes toward other popular drugs. Alcohol, like opium a depressant drug with soothing effects, has been regarded with ambivalence in this country, even though a longer familiarity has prevented reactions quite as extreme as the sort opium aroused. Throughout the period from 1850 to 1933, attempts at prohibition of alcohol were repeatedly made at the local, state, and national levels. Today, alcoholism is considered our

largest-scale drug problem. Explaining the reasons for alcohol misuse, David McClelland and his colleagues discovered in *The Drinking
Man* that heavy, uncontrolled drinking occurs in cultures which explicitly value personal assertiveness while at the same time suppressing its expression. This conflict, which alcohol eases by offering its
users the illusion of power, is precisely the conflict which gripped
America during the period when opiate use grew and was outlawed,
and when our society had such a hard time deciding what to do
about alcohol.

Another instructive example is marijuana. As long as this drug
was novel and threatening and was associated with deviant minorities, it was defined as "addictive" and classed as a narcotic. That definition was accepted not only by the authorities, but by those who
used the drug, as in the Harlem of the 1940s evoked in Malcolm X's
autobiography. In recent years, however, middle-class whites have
discovered that marijuana is a relatively safe experience. Although
we still get sporadic, alarmist reports on one or another harmful
aspect of marijuana, respected organs of society are now calling for
the decriminalization of the drug. We are near the end of a process
of cultural acceptance of marijuana. Students and young professionals, many of whom lead very staid lives, have become comfortable with it, while still feeling sure that people who take heroin
become addicted. They do not realize they are engaging in the cultural stereotyping which currently is removing marijuana from the
locked "dope" cabinet and placing it on an open shelf alongside
alcohol, tranquilizers, nicotine, and caffeine.

A more potent hallucinogen than marijuana, LSD has aroused
the intense aversion reserved for strong drugs like heroin, even
though it has never been regarded as addictive. Before it became
both popular and controversial in the 1960s, LSD was used in medical research as an experimental means of inducing temporary psy-
chosis. In 1960, while the drug was still known only to a few doctors
and psychologists, Sidney Cohen surveyed these researchers on the
incidence of serious complications from LSD use among experimental volunteers and psychiatric patients. The rate of such complications (suicide attempts and prolonged psychotic reactions) was
minuscule. It seems that without prior public knowledge, long-term

LSD effects were about as minor as those resulting from the use of any other psychoactive drug.

Since then, however, anti-LSD propaganda and rumors spread by people in and around the drug-using subculture have made it impossible for observers and potential users to assess the drug's properties objectively. Even users can no longer give us an unbiased picture of what their trips have been like, since their experiences with LSD are governed by their own group's preconceptions, as well as by a larger cultural set defining the drug as dangerous and unpredictable. Now that people have been taught to fear the worst, they are ready to panic when a trip takes a bad turn. An entirely new dimension has been added to the LSD trip by the evolution of cultural perspectives on that drug.

As the psychological consequences of LSD use began to look more threatening, the majority of people—even among those who considered themselves in the cultural vanguard—became reluctant to expose themselves to the self-revelations that an LSD trip entailed. This is understandable, but the way they opted out was by sanctifying an entirely fallacious report of the effects of LSD use. The study, published by Maimon Cohen and others in *Science* in 1967, stated that LSD caused an increased breakage rate in human chromosomes, and thus raised the specter of genetic mutations and birth defects. The newspapers seized upon these findings, and the chromosome scare had a great impact within the drug scene. In fact, though, the study began to be refuted almost as soon as it was published, and it was eventually discredited. A review of LSD research by Norman Dishotsky and others which was published in *Science* four years later showed that Cohen's findings were an artifact of laboratory conditions, and concluded that there was no reason to fear LSD on the grounds originally put forward—or at least no more reason to fear LSD than aspirin and caffeine, which caused chromosome breakage at approximately the same rate under the same conditions (see Appendix E).

It is unlikely that a chromosome scare would induce many users of aspirin, coffee, or Coca-Cola to give up those drugs. But the users and potential users of LSD turned away from it almost in relief. To this day, many people who refuse to have anything to do with LSD justify their position by citing that now-invalidated piece of research. This could happen, even among drug-sophisticated young people, because LSD doesn't fit into a comfort-seeking approach to drugs. People who didn't want to admit that this was why they were avoiding the drug were handed a convenient rationalization by the selective reports that newspapers printed, reports which didn't reflect the body of scientific knowledge about LSD. Turning down experimental psychic journeys (which it was their privilege to do), these people found it necessary to defend their reluctance with spurious testimony.

Such recent instances of fear and irrationality with regard to psychoactive drugs show that addiction is still very much with us as a society: addiction, in the sense of an unsureness of our own strength and power, coupled with a need to find scapegoats for our uncertainties. And while we are distracted with questions of what drugs can do to us, our misunderstanding of the nature and causes of addiction makes it possible for addictions to slip in where we least expect to find them—in safe, respectable places like our love relationships.

A NEW CONCEPT OF ADDICTION

At present, the general confusion about drugs and their effects is a reflection of a similar confusion felt by scientists. Experts throw up their hands when confronted with the wide range of reactions people can have to the same drugs, and the wide range of substances which can produce addiction in some people. This confusion is expressed in *Scientific Basis of Drug Dependence,* a report on a British colloquium of the world's leading authorities on drugs. Predictably, the participants gave up trying to talk about addiction altogether, and addressed themselves instead to the broader phenomenon of "drug dependence." After the discussions the chairman, Professor W. D. M. Paton of the Department of Pharmacology at Oxford, summarized the major conclusions which had been reached. First, drug dependence is no longer equated with the "classical withdrawal syndrome." In its place, "the central issue of drug dependence has shifted elsewhere and seems to lie in the nature of the primary 'reward' which the drug provides." That is, the scientists have begun to think of drug dependence in terms of the benefits which habitual users get from a drug—its making them feel good, or helping them forget their problems and pain. Along with this change in emphasis has come a less exclusive concentration on the opiates as addicting drugs, and also a greater recognition of the importance of cultural factors in drug dependence.

These are all constructive steps toward a more flexible, people-centered definition of addiction. But they also reveal that in abandoning the old idea of narcotic addiction, the scientists have been left with a mass of unorganized facts about different drugs and different ways of using drugs. In a misguided effort to catalogue these facts in something resembling the old familiar way, pharmacologists have simply replaced the term "physical dependence" with "psychic dependence" in their classifications of drugs. With the discovery or popularization of many new drugs in recent years, a new concept was needed to explain this diversity. The notion of psychic dependence could be applied to more drugs than could addiction, since it was even less precisely defined than addiction. If we go by a table of drugs prepared by Dale Cameron under the aegis of the World Health Organization, there is not one commonly used psychoactive drug that does not produce psychic dependence.

Such an assertion is the *reductio ad absurdum* of drug classification. For a scientific concept to have any value, it has to distinguish between some things and others. With the shift to the category of psychic dependence, pharmacologists have lost whatever meaning the earlier concept of physical dependence might have had, since, looked at on their own, drugs could only bring about a dependence of chemical origin. And if dependence does not stem from any specific properties of the drugs themselves, then why single out drugs as dependency-producing objects at all? As Erich Goode puts it, to say that a drug like marijuana creates psychic dependence is to say merely that some people have reason regularly to do something of which you disapprove. Where the experts have gone wrong, of course, is in conceiving of the creation of dependence as an attribute of drugs, whereas in reality it is an attribute of people. There is such a thing as addiction; we just haven't known where to look for it.

We need a new concept of addiction to make understandable the observed facts that have been left in a theoretical limbo by the breakdown of the old concept. In their recognition that drug use has many causes and takes many forms, drug experts have reached that critical point in the history of a science where an old idea has been discredited, but where there is not yet a new idea to take its place. Unlike these experts, however—unlike even Goode and Zinberg, the most informed investigators in the field—I believe we do not have to stop short by acknowledging that drug effects can vary almost without limit. Rather, we can understand that some types of drug use are dependencies, and that there are equivalent dependencies of many other sorts. To do this, we need a concept of addiction that emphasizes the way people interpret and organize their experience. As Paton says, we have to start with people's needs, and then ask how drugs fit into those needs. What psychological benefits does a habitual user seek from a drug? (See Appendix F.) What does the fact that he needs this type of gratification say about him, and what are the consequences for him of obtaining it? Finally, what does this tell us about the possibilities for addiction to things other than drugs?

First, drugs do have real effects. Although these effects can be mimicked or masked by placebos, drug-using rituals, and other means of manipulating people's expectations, ultimately there are specific actions which drugs have and which differ from one drug to another. There will be times when nothing but the effects of a particular drug will do. For example, in demonstrating that cigarette-smoking is a genuine drug addiction (rather than an addiction to the activity of smoking), Edward Brecher cites studies where people were observed to puff harder on cigarettes which contained a lower concentration of nicotine. Similarly, given that the mere name of heroin is enough to trigger strong reactions in individuals who are exposed only to a placebo or the injection ritual, there must be something about heroin that inspires the addictive reactions of varying severity that large numbers of people have to it. Clearly, the real effects of heroin—or nicotine—produce a state of being that a person desires. At the same time, the drug also symbolizes this state of being even when, as Chein found among New York addicts, there is little or no direct effect from the drug. In this state of being, whatever it is, lies the key to understanding addiction.

Narcotics, barbiturates, and alcohol suppress the user's consciousness of things he wants to forget. In terms of their chemical action, all three drugs are depressants. For example, they inhibit reflexes and sensitivity to outside stimulation. Heroin in particular detaches a person from feelings of pain, lessening the awareness of physical and emotional discomfort. The heroin user experiences what is called "total drive satiation"; his appetite and sex drive are suppressed, and his motivation to achieve—or his guilt at not achieving—likewise disappear. Thus, opiates remove memories and worries about unresolved issues and reduce life to a single striving. The heroin or morphine high is not one which in itself produces ecstasy for most people. Rather, opiates are desired because they bring welcome relief from other sensations and feelings which the addict finds unpleasant.

The dulling of sensibility, the soothing feeling that all is well, is a powerful experience for some people, and it may be that few of us are entirely immune to its appeal. Those who depend totally on such an experience do so because it gives their lives a structure and secures them, at least subjectively, against the press of what is novel and demanding. This is what they are addicted to. In addition, since heroin diminishes mental and physical performance, it reduces the habituated user's ability to cope with his world. In other words, while he is involved with the drug and feeling relief from his problems, he is even less able to deal with these problems, and thereby becomes less prepared to confront them than he was before. So naturally, when he is deprived of the sensations which the drug provides, he feels inwardly threatened and disoriented, which exacerbates his reactions to the physical symptoms that removal from a course of drugs invariably produces. This is the extremity of withdrawal that is sometimes noted among heroin addicts.

The hallucinogens, such as peyote and LSD, are not generally addictive. It is possible, however, for an individual's self-image to become based upon notions of special perception and intensified experience that the regular use of hallucinogens encourages. In this occasional case, the person will be dependent on a hallucinogen for his feelings that he has a secure place in the world, will seek the drug out regularly, and will be correspondingly traumatized when he is deprived of it.

Marijuana, as both a mild hallucinogen and sedative, can be used addictively, although such use is less common now that the drug is generally accepted. But with the stimulants—nicotine, caffeine, amphetamines, cocaine—we do find widespread addiction in our society, and the parallel with the depressants is striking. Paradoxically, the excitation of the nervous system by a stimulant drug serves to shield the habituated user from the emotional impact of external events. Thus the stimulant taker cloaks the tension that dealing with his environment causes him, and imposes an overriding constancy of sensation in its place. In a study of "Chronic Smoking and Emotionality," Paul Nesbitt found that while cigarette smokers are more anxious than nonsmokers, they feel more calm when they are smoking. With the constant elevation of their heart rate, blood pressure, cardiac output, and blood sugar level, they are inured to variations in outside stimulation. Here, as with the depressants (but not hallucinogens), an artificial sameness is the keynote of the addictive experience.

The primary action of a stimulant is to give a person the illusion of being energized through the freeing of stored energy for immediate use. Since that energy is not being replaced, the chronic stimulant taker is living on borrowed energy. Like the heroin user, he is doing nothing to build up his basic resources. His true physical or emotional state is hidden from him by the artificial boosts he gets from the drug. If he is withdrawn from the drug, he experiences all at once his actual, now very depleted condition, and he feels wrecked. Again, as with heroin, addiction is not an unrelated side effect, but stems from the intrinsic action of the drug.

People imagine that heroin soothes, and it *also* addicts; that nicotine or caffeine energizes, and it *also* keeps you coming back for more. That misconception, which separates what in reality are two sides of the same thing, lies behind the futile search for a nonaddictive pain-killer. Addiction is not a mysterious chemical process; it is the logical outgrowth of the way a drug makes a person feel. When we understand this, we can see how natural (though unhealthy) a process it is (see Appendix G). A person repeatedly seeks artificial infusions of a sensation, whether it be one of somnolence or vitality, that is not supplied by the organic balance of his life as a whole. Such infusions insulate him from the fact that the world he perceives psychologically is becoming farther and farther removed from the real state of his body or his life. When the dosages are stopped, the addict is made painfully aware of the discrepancy, which he must now negotiate unprotected. This is addiction, whether it be a socially approved addiction or an addiction whose consequences are aggravated by social disapproval.

The insight that both stimulants and depressants have aftereffects which destroy the immediate sensations they offer is the starting point for a comprehensive theory of motivation proposed by the psychologists Richard Solomon and John Corbit. Their approach explains drug addiction as just one of a set of basic human reactions. According to Solomon and Corbit, most sensations are followed by an opposite aftereffect. If the original sensation is unpleasant, the aftereffect is pleasant, as in the relief one feels when pain lets up. With repeated exposures the aftereffect grows in intensity, until it is dominant almost from the outset, neutralizing even the immediate effect of the stimulus. For example, the novice parachute jumper begins his first jump in terror. When it is over, he is too stunned to feel much positive relief. As he becomes practiced at jumping, however, he makes his preparations with a tense alertness which he no longer experiences as agony. After jumping, he is overwhelmed with exhilaration. This is how a positive aftereffect overcomes initially negative stimulation.

Using this model, Solomon and Corbit demonstrate a fundamental similarity between opiate addiction and love. In both cases, a person repeatedly seeks out a kind of stimulation which is intensely pleasurable. But as time goes on, he finds that he needs it more even as he enjoys it less. The heroin addict gets less and less of a positive kick from the drug, yet he must return to it to counteract the insistent pain caused by its absence. The lover is no longer so excited by his or her partner, but is more and more dependent on the comfort of the partner's continued presence, and is less able to handle a separation. Here the negative aftereffect overcomes initially positive stimulation.

Solomon and Corbit's "opponent-process" theory is a creative demonstration that addiction is not a special reaction to a drug, but a primary and universal form of motivation. The theory, however, does not really explain the psychology of addiction. In its abstractness it doesn't explore the cultural and personality factors—the when, where, and why—in addiction. What accounts for the differences in human consciousness that enable some people to act on the basis of a larger and more varied set of motivations, while others have their entire lives determined by the mechanistic effects of the opponent process? After all, not everyone becomes mired down in a once positive experience which has gone sour. Thus, this model doesn't deal with what sets some drug users apart from other drug users, some lovers from other lovers—i.e., the addict from the person who is not addicted. It doesn't leave room, for example, for a kind of love relationship that counteracts encroaching boredom by constantly introducing challenge and growth into the relationship. These latter factors make the difference between experiences which are not addictions and those which are. To identify these essential differences in human involvements, we must consider the nature of the addict's personality and outlook.

I hate its weakness more than I like its pleasant futility. I hate it and myself in it all the time I'm dwelling on it. I hate it as I'd hate a little drug habit fastened on my nerves. Its influence is the same but more insidious than a drug would be, more demoralizing. As feeling fear makes one afraid, feeling more fear makes one more afraid.   —MARY MacLANE, *I, Mary MacLane: A Diary of Human Days*

3

A General Theory of Addiction

With our new model of addiction in mind, we need no longer think of addiction exclusively in terms of drugs. We are concerned with the larger question of why some people seek to close off their experience through a comforting, but artificial and self-consuming relationship with something external to themselves. In itself, the choice of object is irrelevant to this universal process of becoming dependent. Anything that people use to release their consciousness can be addictively misused.

As a starting point for our analysis, however, addictive drug use serves as a convenient illustration of the psychological whys and hows of addiction. Since people usually think of drug dependencies in terms of addiction, who becomes addicted and why is best understood in that area, and psychologists have come up with some fairly good answers to these questions. But once we take account of their work and its implications for a general theory of addiction, we must move beyond drugs. It is necessary to transcend the culture-bound, class-bound definition that has enabled us to dismiss addiction as

55

somebody else's problem. With a new definition, we can look directly at our own addictions.

PERSONALITY CHARACTERISTICS OF ADDICTS

The first researcher to take a serious interest in the personalities of addicts was Lawrence Kolb, whose studies of opiate addicts at the U.S. Public Health Service in the 1920s are collected in a volume entitled *Drug Addiction: A Medical Problem*. Discovering that the psychological problems of addicts existed prior to addiction, Kolb concluded, "The neurotic and the psychopath receive from narcotics a pleasurable sense of relief from the realities of life that normal persons do not receive because life is no special burden to them." At the time, Kolb's work offered a note of reason amidst the hysteria about the personal deterioration that the opiates in themelves supposedly caused. Since then, however, Kolb's approach has been criticized as being too negative toward drug users and ignoring the range of motivations that contribute to drug use. If drug users per se are what we are concerned with, then the criticism of Kolb is well-taken, for we know now that there are many varieties of drug users besides those with "addictive personalities." But in its having pinpointed a personality orientation that often reveals itself in self-destructive drug use, as well as in many other unhealthy things that people do, Kolb's insight remains sound.

Later personality studies of drug users have expanded upon Kolb's discoveries. In their study of reactions to a morphine placebo among hospital patients, Lasagna and his colleagues found that patients who accepted the placebo as a pain-killer, as compared with those who did not, were also more likely to be satisfied with the effects of morphine itself. It seems that certain people, as well as being more suggestible about an innocuous injection, are more vulnerable to the actual effects of a potent analgesic like morphine. What characteristics distinguish this group of people? From interviews and Rorschach tests, some generalizations emerged about the placebo reactors. They all considered hospital care "wonderful," were more cooperative with the staff, were more active churchgoers, and used conventional household drugs more than the nonreactors. They were more anxious and more emotionally volatile, had less control

over the expression of their instinctual needs, and were more dependent on outside stimulation than on their own mental processes,
which were not as mature as those of nonreactors.

These traits yield a distinct picture of the people who respond
most strongly to narcotics (or placebos) in hospitals as being pliable,
trusting, unsure of themselves, and ready to believe that a drug
given them by a doctor must be beneficial. Can we draw a parallel
between these people and street addicts? Charles Winick gives the
following explanation for the fact that many addicts become addicted in adolescence, only to "mature out" when they become older
and more stable:

> . . . they [the addicts] began taking heroin in their late teens or early
> twenties as their method of coping with the challenges and problems of
> early adulthood. . . . The use of narcotics may make it possible for the
> user to evade, mask, or postpone the expression of these needs and
> these decisions [i.e., sex, aggression, vocation, financial independence
> and support of others]. . . . On a less conscious level, he may be antici-
> pating becoming dependent on jails and other community resources.
> . . . Becoming a narcotics addict in early adulthood thus enables the ad-
> dict to avoid many decisions. . . .

Here again, we see that lack of self-assurance and related dependency needs determine the pattern of addiction. When the addict ar-
rives at some resolution of his problems (whether by permanently
accepting some other dependent social role or by finally gathering
the emotional resources to attain maturity), his addiction to heroin
ceases. It no longer serves a function in his life. Stressing the importance of fatalistic beliefs in the addiction process, Winick concludes
that addicts who fail to mature out are those "who decide that they
are 'hooked,' make no effort to abandon addiction, and give in to
what they regard as inevitable."

In their portrait of the day-to-day existence of the street heroin
user in *The Road to H,* Chein and his colleagues emphasize the addict's need to compensate for his lack of more substantial outlets. As
Chein puts it in a later article:

> From almost his earliest days, the addict has been systematically edu-
> cated and trained into incompetence. Unlike others, therefore, he could
> not find a vocation, a career, a meaningful, sustained activity around

which he could, so to say, wrap his life. The addiction, however, offers an answer to even this problem of emptiness. The life of an addict constitutes a vocation—hustling, raising funds, assuring a connection and the maintenance of supply, outmaneuvering the police, performing the rituals of preparing and of taking the drug—a vocation around which the addict can build a reasonably full life.

Although Chein doesn't say so in quite these terms, the substitute way of life is what the street user is addicted to.

Exploring why the addict needs such a substitute life, the authors of *The Road to H* describe the addict's constricted outlook and his defensive stance toward the world. Addicts are pessimistic about life and preoccupied with its negative and dangerous aspects. In the ghetto setting studied by Chein, they are emotionally detached from people, and are capable of seeing others only as objects to be exploited. They lack confidence in themselves and are not motivated toward positive activities except when pushed by someone in a position of authority. They are passive even as they are manipulative, and the need they feel most strongly is a need for predictable gratification. Chein's findings are consistent with Lasagna's and Winick's. Together, they show that the person predisposed to drug addiction has not resolved childhood conflicts about autonomy and dependence so as to develop a mature personality.

To understand what makes a person an addict, consider the controlled users, the people who do not become addicts even though they take the same powerful drugs. The doctors Winick studied are aided in keeping their use of narcotics under control by the relative ease with which they can obtain the drugs. A more important factor, however, is the purposefulness of their lives—the activities and goals to which drug use is subordinated. What enables most physicians who use narcotics to withstand dominance by a drug is simply the fact that they must regulate their drug-taking in line with its effect on the performance of their duties.

Even among people who do not have the social standing of doctors, the principle behind controlled use is the same. Norman Zinberg and Richard Jacobson unearthed many controlled users of heroin and other drugs among young people in a variety of settings. Zinberg and Jacobson suggest that the extent and diversity of a person's social relationships are crucial in determining whether the person will become a controlled or compulsive drug user. If a person is acquainted with others who do not use the drug in question, he is not likely to become totally immersed in that drug. These investigators also report that controlled use depends on whether the user has a specific routine which dictates when he will take the drug, so that there are only some situations where he will consider it appropriate and others—such as work or school—where he will rule it out. Again, the controlled user is distinguished from the addict by the way drugs fit into the overall context of his life.

Considering the research on controlled users in conjunction with that on addicts, we can infer that addiction is a pattern of drug use that occurs in people who have little to anchor them to life. Lacking an underlying direction, finding few things that can entertain or motivate them, they have nothing to compete with the effects of a narcotic for possession of their lives. But for other people the impact of a drug, while it may be considerable, is not overwhelming. They have involvements and satisfactions which forestall total submission to something whose action is to limit and deaden. The occasional user may have need for relief or may only use a drug for specific positive effects. But he values his activities, his friendships, his possibilities too much to sacrifice them to the exclusion and repetition which is addiction.

The absence of drug dependencies in people who have been exposed to narcotics under special conditions, such as hospital patients and the G.I.'s in Vietnam, has already been noted. These people use an opiate for solace or relief from some sort of temporary misery. In normal circumstances, they do not find life sufficiently unpleasant to want to obliterate their consciousness. As people with a normal range of motivations, they have other options—once they have been removed from the painful situation—which are more attractive than unconsciousness. Almost never do they experience the full symptoms of withdrawal or a craving for drugs.

In *Addiction and Opiates,* Alfred Lindesmith has noted that even when medical patients do experience some degree of withdrawal pain from morphine, they are able to protect themselves against prolonged craving by thinking of themselves as normal people with a temporary problem, rather than as addicts. Just as a culture can be influenced by a widespread belief in the existence of addiction, an individual who thinks of himself as an addict will more readily feel the addictive effects of a drug. Unlike the street addict, whose life-style they probably despise, medical patients and G.I.'s naturally assume that they are stronger than the drug. This belief enables them, in fact, to resist addiction. Reverse this, and we have the orientation of someone who *is* susceptible to addiction: he believes the drug is stronger than he is. In both cases, people's estimate of a drug's power over them reflects their estimate of their own essential strengths and weaknesses. Thus an addict believes that he can be overwhelmed by an experience at the same time he is driven to seek it out.

Who, then, is the addict? We can say that he or she is someone who lacks the desire—or confidence in his or her capacity—to come to grips with life independently. His view of life is not a positive one which anticipates chances for pleasure and fulfillment, but a negative one which fears the world and people as threats to himself. When this person is confronted with demands or problems, he seeks support from an external source which, since he feels it is stronger than he is, he believes can protect him. The addict is not a genuinely rebellious person. Rather, he is a fearful one. He is eager to rely on drugs (or medicines), on people, on institutions (like prisons and hospitals). In giving himself up to these larger forces, he is a perpetual invalid. Richard Blum has found that drug users have been trained at home, as children, to accept and exploit the sick role. This readiness for submission is the keynote of addiction. Disbelieving his own adequacy, recoiling from challenge, the addict welcomes control from outside himself as the ideal state of affairs.

A SOCIAL-PSYCHOLOGICAL APPROACH TO ADDICTION

Working from this emphasis on subjective, personal experience, we can now attempt to define addiction. The definition we have been moving toward is a social-psychological one in that it focuses on a person's emotional states and his relationship to his surroundings. These must in turn be understood in terms of the impact which social institutions have had on the person's outlook. Instead of working with biological or even psychological absolutes, a social-psychological approach tries to make sense out of people's experience by asking what people are like, what in their thinking and feeling underlies their behavior, how they come to be as they are, and what pressures from their environment they currently face.

In these terms, then, *an addiction exists when a person's attachment to a sensation, an object, or another person is such as to lessen his appreciation of and ability to deal with other things in his environment, or in himself, so that he has become increasingly dependent on that experience as his only source of gratification.* A person will be predisposed to addiction to the extent that he cannot establish a meaningful relationship to his environment as a whole, and thus cannot develop a fully elaborated life. In this case, he will be susceptible to a mindless absorption in something external to himself, his susceptibility growing with each new exposure to the addictive object.

Our analysis of addiction starts with the addict's low opinion of himself and his lack of genuine involvement in life, and examines how this malaise progresses into the deepening spiral which is at the center of the psychology of addiction. The person who becomes an addict has not learned to accomplish things he can regard as worthwhile, or even simply to enjoy life. Feeling incapable of engaging himself in an activity that he finds meaningful, he naturally turns away from any opportunities to do so. His lack of self-respect causes this pessimism. A result, too, of the addict's low self-esteem is his belief that he cannot stand alone, that he must have outside support to survive. Thus his life assumes the shape of a series of dependencies, whether approved (such as family, school, or work) or disapproved (such as drugs, prisons, or mental institutions).

His is not a pleasant state of affairs. He is anxious in the face of a world he fears, and his feelings about himself are likewise unhappy. Yearning to escape from a distasteful consciousness of his life, and having no abiding purpose to check his desire for unconsciousness, the addict welcomes oblivion. He finds it in any experience that can temporarily erase his painful awareness of himself and his situation. The opiates and other strong depressant drugs accomplish this function directly by inducing an all-encompassing soothing sensation. Their pain-killing effect, the feeling they create that the user need do nothing more to set his life straight, makes the opiates prominent as objects of addiction. Chein quotes the addict who, after his first shot of heroin, became a regular user: "I got real sleepy. I went in to lay on the bed. . . . I thought, this is for me! And I never missed a day since, until now." Any experience in which a person can lose himself—if that is what he desires—can serve the same addictive function.

There is a paradoxical cost extracted, however, as fee for this relief from consciousness. In turning away from his world to the addictive object, which he values increasingly for its safe, predictable effects, the addict ceases to cope with that world. As he becomes more involved with the drug or other addictive experience, he becomes progressively less able to deal with the anxieties and uncertainties that drove him to it in the first place. He realizes this, and his having resorted to escape and intoxication only exacerbates his self-doubt. When a person does something in response to his anxiety that he doesn't respect (like getting drunk or overeating), his disgust with himself causes his anxiety to increase. As a result, and now also faced by a bleaker objective situation, he is even more needful of the reassurance the addictive experience offers him. This is the cycle of addiction. Eventually, the addict depends totally on the addiction for his gratifications in life, and nothing else can interest him. He has given up hope of managing his existence; forgetfulness is the one aim he is capable of pursuing wholeheartedly.

Withdrawal symptoms occur because a person cannot be deprived of his sole source of reassurance in the world—a world from which he has grown increasingly alienated—without considerable trauma. The problems he originally encountered are now magnified, and he has gotten used to the constant lulling of his awareness. At this point, dreading reexposure to the world above all else, he will do whatever he can to maintain his protected state. Here is the completion of the addiction process. Once again the addict's low self-esteem has come into play. It has made him feel helpless not only against the rest of the world, but against the addictive object as well, so that he now believes he can neither live without it nor free himself from its grasp. It is a natural end for a person who has been trained to be helpless all his life.

Interestingly, an argument which is used against psychological explanations for addiction can actually help us understand the psychology of addiction. It is often contended that because animals get addicted to morphine in laboratories, and because infants are born drug-dependent when their mothers have taken heroin regularly during pregnancy, there is no possibility that psychological factors can play a part in the process. But it is the very fact that infants and animals do not have the subtlety of interests or the full life that an adult human being ideally possesses which makes them so uniformly susceptible to addiction. When we think of the conditions under which animals and infants become addicted, we can better appreciate the situation of the addict. Aside from their relatively simple motivations, monkeys kept in a small cage with an injection apparatus strapped to their backs are deprived of the variety of stimulation their natural environment provides. All they can do is push the lever. Obviously, an infant is also not capable of sampling life's full complexity. Yet these physically or biologically limiting factors are not unlike the psychological constraints the addict lives with. Then, too, the "addicted" infant is separated at birth both from the womb and from a sensation—that of heroin in its bloodstream—which it associates with the womb and which in itself simulates womb-like comfort. The normal trauma of birth is made worse, and the infant recoils from its harsh exposure to the world. This infantile feeling of being deprived of some necessary sense of security is again something which has startling parallels in the adult addict.

CRITERIA FOR ADDICTION AND NONADDICTION

Just as a person can be a compulsive or a controlled drug user, so there are addictive and nonaddictive ways of doing anything. When a person is strongly predisposed to be addicted, whatever he does can fit the psychological pattern of addiction. Unless he deals with his weaknesses, his major emotional involvements will be addictive, and his life will consist of a series of addictions. A passage from Lawrence Kubie's *Neurotic Distortion of the Creative Process* dramatically focuses on the way personality determines the quality of any kind of feeling or activity:

> There is not a single thing which a human being can do or feel, or think, whether it is eating or sleeping or drinking or fighting or killing or hating or loving or grieving or exulting or working or playing or painting or inventing, which cannot be either sick or well. . . . The measure of health is flexibility, the freedom to learn through experience,

the freedom to change with changing internal and external circumstances . . . the freedom to respond appropriately to the stimulus of reward and punishment, and especially the freedom to cease when sated.

If a person cannot cease after being sated, if he cannot be sated, he is addicted. Fear, and feelings of inadequacy, cause an addict to seek constancy of stimulation and setting rather than to chance the dangers of novel or unpredictable experience. Psychological security is what he wants above all. He searches for it outside himself, until he finds that the experience of addiction is completely predictable. At this point, satiation is impossible—because it is the sameness of sensation that he craves. As the addiction proceeds, novelty and change become things he is even less able to tolerate.

What are the key psychological dimensions of addiction, and of the freedom and growth which are the antitheses of addiction? A major theory in psychology is that of achievement motivation, as summarized by John Atkinson in *An Introduction to Motivation*. The motive to achieve refers to a person's positive desire to pursue a task, and to the satisfaction he gets from successfully completing it. Opposed to achievement motivation is what is called "fear of failure," an outlook which causes a person to react to challenges with anxiety rather than positive anticipation. This happens because the person does not see a new situation as an opportunity for exploration, satisfaction, or accomplishment. For him, it only holds out the threat of disgrace through the failure he believes is likely. A person with a high fear of failure avoids new things, is conservative, and seeks to reduce life to safe routines and rituals.

The fundamental distinction involved here—and in addiction—is the distinction between a desire to grow and experience and a desire to stagnate and remain untouched. Jozef Cohen quotes the addict who says, "The best high . . . is death." Where life is seen as a burden, full of unpleasant and useless struggles, addiction is a way to surrender. The difference between not being addicted and being addicted is the difference between seeing the world as your arena and seeing the world as your prison. These contrasting orientations suggest a standard for assessing whether a substance or activity is addictive for a particular person. If what a person is engaged in enhances his ability to live—if it enables him to work more effectively, to love more beautifully, to appreciate the things around him more, and finally, if it allows him to grow, to change, and expand—then it is not addictive. If, on the other hand, it diminishes him—if it makes him less attractive, less capable, less sensitive, and if it limits him, stifles him, harms him—then it is addictive.

These criteria do not mean that an involvement is necessarily addictive because it is intensely absorbing. When someone can truly engage himself in something, as opposed to seeking out its most general, superficial features, he is not addicted. Addiction is marked by an intensity of need, which only motivates a person to expose himself repeatedly to the grossest aspects of a sensation, primarily its intoxicating effects. Heroin addicts are most attached to the ritualistic elements in their use of the drug, such as the act of injecting heroin and the stereotyped relationships and hustling that go along with getting it, not to mention the deadening predictability of the action that narcotics have.

When someone enjoys or is energized by an experience, he wishes to pursue it further, master it more, understand it better. The addict, on the other hand, wishes only to stay with a clearly defined routine. This obviously does not have to be true for heroin addicts alone. When a man or woman works purely for the reassurance of knowing that he or she is working, rather than positively desiring to do something, then that person's involvement with work is compulsive, the so-called "workaholic" syndrome. Such a person is not concerned that the products of his labors, that all other concomitants and results of what he does, may be meaningless, or worse, harmful. In the same way, the heroin addict's life does include the discipline and challenge entailed in obtaining the drug. But he cannot maintain respect for these efforts in the face of society's judgment that they are nonconstructive and, worse, vicious. It is difficult for the addict to feel that he has done something of lasting value when he works feverishly to get high four times a day.

From this perspective, while we might be tempted to refer to the dedicated artist or scientist as being addicted to his or her work, the description doesn't fit. There may be elements of addiction in a person's throwing himself into solitary creative work when it is done out of an incapacity to have normal relationships with people, but great achievements often require a narrowing of focus. What distinguishes such concentration from addiction is that the artist or scientist is not escaping from novelty and uncertainty into a predictable, comforting state of affairs. He receives the pleasure of creation and discovery from his activity, a pleasure that is sometimes long deferred. He moves on to new problems, sharpens his skills, takes risks, meets resistance and frustration, and always challenges himself. To do otherwise means the end of his productive career. Whatever his personal incompleteness, his involvement in his work does not diminish his integrity and his capacity to live, and thus does not cause him to want to escape from himself. He is in touch with a difficult and demanding reality, and his accomplishments are open to the judgment of those who are similarly engaged, those who will decide his place in the history of his discipline. Finally, his work can be evaluated by the benefits or pleasures it brings to humanity as a whole.

Working, socializing, eating, drinking, praying—any regular part of a person's life can be evaluated in terms of how it contributes to, or detracts from, the quality of his experience. Or, looked at from the other direction, the nature of a person's general feelings about living will determine the character of any of his habitual involvements. As Marx noted, it is the attempt to separate a single involvement from the rest of one's life which allows for addiction:

> It is nonsense to believe . . . one could satisfy one passion separated from all others without satisfying *oneself*, the whole living individual. If this passion assumes an abstract, separate character, if it confronts him as an alien power . . . the result is that this individual achieves only a one-sided, crippled development.
>
> (quoted in Erich Fromm,
> "Marx's Contribution to the Knowledge of Man")

Yardsticks like this can be applied to any thing or any act; that is why many involvements besides those with drugs meet the criteria for addiction. Drugs, on the other hand, are *not* addictive when they serve to fulfill a larger purpose in life, even if the purpose is to increase self-awareness, to expand consciousness, or simply to enjoy oneself.

The ability to derive a positive pleasure from something, to do something because it brings joy to oneself, is, in fact, a principal criterion of nonaddiction. It might seem a foregone conclusion that people take drugs for enjoyment, yet this is not true of addicts. An addict does not find heroin pleasurable in itself. Rather, he uses it to obliterate other aspects of his environment which he dreads. A cigarette addict or an alcoholic may once have enjoyed a smoke or a drink, but by the time he has become addicted, he is driven to use the substance merely to maintain himself at a bearable level of existence. This is the tolerance process, through which the addict comes to rely on the addictive object as something necessary to his psychological survival. What might have been a positive motivation turns out to be a negative one. It is a matter of need rather than of desire.

A further, and related, sign of addiction is that an exclusive craving for something is accompanied by a loss of discrimination toward the object which satisfies the craving. In the early stages of an addict's relationship to a substance, he may desire a specific quality in the experience it gives him. He hopes for a certain reaction and, if it is not forthcoming, he is dissatisfied. But after a certain point, the addict cannot distinguish between a good or a bad version of that experience. All he cares about is that he wants it and that he gets it. The alcoholic is not interested in the taste of the liquor that is available; likewise, the compulsive eater is not particular about what he eats when there is food around. The difference between the heroin addict and the controlled user is the ability to discriminate among conditions for taking the drug. Zinberg and Jacobson found that the controlled drug user weighs a number of pragmatic considerations—how much the drug costs, how good the supply is, whether the assembled company is appealing, what else he might do with his time—before indulging on any given occasion. Such choices are not open to an addict.

Since it is only the repetition of the basic experience for which the addict yearns, he is unaware of variations in his environment—even in the addictive sensation itself—as long as certain key stimuli are always present. This phenomenon is observable in those who use heroin, LSD, marijuana, speed, or cocaine. While light, irregular, or novice users are very dependent on situational cues to set the mood for the enjoyment of their trips, the heavy user or the addict disregards these variables almost entirely. This, and all our criteria, are applicable to addicts in other areas of life, including love addicts.

GROUPS AND THE PRIVATE WORLD

Addiction, since it avoids reality, amounts to the substitution of a private standard of meaning and value for publicly accepted standards. It is natural to bolster this alienated worldview by sharing it with others; in fact, it is often learned from others in the first place. Understanding the process by which groups coalesce around obsessive, exclusive activities and systems of belief is an important step in exploring how groups, including couples, can themselves comprise an addiction. By looking at the ways in which groups of addicts construct their own worlds, we gain essential insights into the social aspects of addiction, and—what directly follows from this—social addictions.

Howard Becker observed groups of marijuana users in the fifties showing new members how to smoke marijuana and how to interpret its effect. What they were also showing them was how to be part of the group. The initiates were teaching the experience which made the group distinctive—the marijuana high—and why this distinctive experience was pleasurable, and therefore good. The group was engaged in the process of defining itself, and of creating an internal set of values separate from those of the world at large. In this way, miniature societies are formed by people who share a set of values relating to something which they have in common, but which people generally do not accept. That something can be the use of a particular drug, a fanatical religious or political belief, or the pursuit of esoteric knowledge. The same thing happens when a discipline becomes so abstract that its human relevance is lost in the interchange of secrets among experts. There is no desire to influence the course of events outside of the group setting, except to draw new devotees into its boundaries. This happens regularly with such self-contained mental systems as chess, bridge, and horse-race handicapping. Activities like bridge are addictions for so many people because in them the elements of group ritual and private language, the bases of group addictions, are so strong.

To understand these separate worlds, consider a group organized around its members' involvement with a drug, such as heroin, or marijuana when it was a disapproved and deviant activity. The members agree that it is right to use the drug, both because of the way it makes one feel and because of the difficulty or unattractiveness of being a total participant in the regular world, i.e., of being a "straight." In the "hip" subculture of the drug user, this attitude constitutes a conscious ideology of superiority to the straight world. Such groups, like the hipsters Norman Mailer wrote about in "The White Negro," or the delinquent addicts that Chein studied, feel both disdain and fear toward the mainstream of society. When someone becomes a part of that group, accepting its distinct values and associating exclusively with the people in it, he becomes "in"—a part of that subculture—and cuts himself off from those outside it.

Addicts need to evolve their own societies because, having devoted themselves entirely to their shared addictions, they must turn to each other to gain approval for behavior that the larger society despises. Always fearful of and alienated by broader standards, these individuals can now be accepted in terms of internal group standards that they find easier to meet. At the same time, their alienation increases, so that they become more insecure in the face of the outside world's values. When they are exposed to these attitudes, they reject them as irrelevant, and return to their circumscribed existence with a strengthened allegiance. Thus, with the group as well as with the drug, the addict goes through a spiral of growing dependency.

The behavior of people who are under the influence of a drug is explicable only to those who are likewise intoxicated. Even in their own eyes, their behavior only makes sense when they are in that condition. After a person has been drunk, he may say, "I can't believe I did all that." In order to be able to accept his behavior, or to forget that he had appeared so foolish, he feels that he has to reenter the intoxicated state. This discontinuity between ordinary reality and the addicts' reality makes each the negation of the other. To participate in one is to reject the other. Thus, when someone quits a private world, the break is likely to be a sharp one, as when an alcoholic swears off drinking or seeing his old drinking friends ever again, or when political or religious extremists turn into violent opponents of the ideologies they once held.

Given this tension between the private world and what lies outside, the task which the group performs for its members is to bring about self-acceptance through the maintenance of a distorted but shared outlook. The other people who also participate in the group's peculiar vision, or in the intoxication it favors, can understand the addict's perspective where outsiders cannot. Someone else who is drunk is not critical of a drunk's behavior. Someone who begs or steals money to obtain heroin is not likely to criticize someone similarly occupied. Such groupings of addicts are not predicated on genuine human feelings and appreciation; the other group members in themselves are not the object of the addict's concern. Rather, his own addiction is his concern, and those other people who can tolerate it and even help him pursue it are simply adjuncts to his one preoccupation in life.

The same expediency in forming connections is there with the person addicted to a lover. It is there in the use of another person to shore up a beleaguered sense of self and to obtain acceptance when the rest of the world seems frightening and forbidding. The lovers gladly lose track of how insular their behavior becomes in the creation of their separate world, until such time as they may be forced to return to reality. But there is one respect in which the isolation of addicted lovers from the world is even more stark than that of other alienated groups of addicts. While drug users and ideologues support each other in maintaining some belief or behavior, the relationship is the sole value around which the private society of the interpersonal addict is organized. While drugs are the theme for groups of heroin addicts, the relationship is the theme for the lovers' group; the group itself is the object of the members' addiction. And thus the addicted love relationship is the tightest group of all. You are "in" with only one person at a time—or one person forever.

"I never saw a more promising inclination. He was growing quite inattentive to other people, and wholly engrossed by her. Every time they met, it was more decided and remarkable. At his own ball he offended two or three young ladies, by not asking them to dance, and I spoke to him twice myself, without receiving an answer. Could there be finer symptoms? Is not general incivility the very essence of love?"

—JANE AUSTEN, *Pride and Prejudice*

4

"Love" as an Addiction

There is an understandable resistance to the idea that a human relationship can be equivalent psychologically to a drug addiction. Yet it is not unreasonable to look for addiction between lovers when psychologists find the roots of drug addiction in childhood dependency needs and stunted family relationships. Chein, Winick, and other observers interpret drugs to be a kind of substitute for human ties. In this sense, addictive love is even more directly linked to what are recognized to be the sources of addiction than is drug dependency.

Almost everyone knows of people who replace romantic relationships with other kinds of escapes, including drug escapes, at least until the next relationship comes along. Immediately after or immediately before an affair, such individuals are deeply immersed in psychiatry, religion, alcohol, marijuana, and the like. Just as some addicts shift between opiate, alcohol, and barbiturate addictions, so we find others using drugs interchangeably with all-consuming systems of belief or social involvements. Consider this testimony by a member of a fanatical religious commune: "I used to do acid, chug wine. I thought it was the answer. But it didn't satisfy, just like everything else. I went to a head shrink. . . . Nothing ever did satisfy till I came to Jesus." He might have added, "I used to make it with chicks," for other converts are the spurned lovers who in an earlier era would have entered a convent or monastery.

I know of a man who started drinking heavily after a long-time woman friend left him. He wrote about his reactions at the time of the breakup:

> Since Linda left I mainly just lie in bed. I'm just too weak to move, and I have the chills all the time. . . . I've been crying a lot. . . . I try to calm myself by drinking the scotch my sister left here. . . . I feel so horrible, so dispossessed—like the real me doesn't exist anymore.

He couldn't sleep, and his heartbeat sometimes sped up frighteningly when he wasn't doing anything. These are symptoms of acute withdrawal. We know they can occur—perhaps quite often in certain groups and at certain ages—when one is deprived of a lover. Popular music sings paeans to the experience as a hallmark of true love: "When I lost my baby, I almost lost my mind . . . Since you left me baby, my whole life is through." What is there about love that produces withdrawal in people we have all known, maybe even in ourselves? Can we envision a kind of love that does *not* bring such devastation in its wake? Let us look closely at how "love" can be an addiction, and how addictive love differs from genuine love.

In a monograph entitled "Being in Love and Hypnosis," Freud noted important parallels between love and another psychologically compelling process—hypnotism. According to Freud, a person's self-love can be transferred from the person's own ego to a loved object. When this occurs, the other person more and more gains "possession of the entire self-love of the ego, whose self-sacrifice thus follows as a natural consequence. The object has, so to speak, consumed the ego." The ultimate development of this sort of love is a state where the lover's ego "is impoverished, it has surrendered itself to the object, it has substituted the object for its own most important constituent." Freud goes on to say:

> From being in love to hypnosis is evidently only a short step. The respects in which the two agree are obvious. There is the same humble subjection, the same compliance, the same absence of criticism, toward

the hypnotist as toward the loved object. There is the same sapping of the subject's own initiative. . . . The hypnotist [as a model of a loved other] is the sole object, and no attention is paid to any but him.

Love is an ideal vehicle for addiction because it can so exclusively claim a person's consciousness. If, to serve as an addiction, something must be both reassuring and consuming, then a sexual or love relationship is perfectly suited for the task. If it must also be patterned, predictable, and isolated, then in these respects, too, a relationship can be ideally tailored to the addictive purpose. Someone who is dissatisfied with himself or his situation can discover in such a relationship the most encompassing substitute for self-contentment and the effort required to attain it.

When a person goes to another with the aim of filling a void in himself, the relationship quickly becomes the center of his or her life. It offers him a solace that contrasts sharply with what he finds everywhere else, so he returns to it more and more, until he needs it to get through each day of his otherwise stressful and unpleasant existence. When a constant exposure to something is necessary in order to make life bearable, an addiction has been brought about, however romantic the trappings. The ever-present danger of withdrawal creates an ever-present craving.

WHO IS THE INTERPERSONAL ADDICT?

Since the person who addicts himself to a lover has essentially the same feelings of inadequacy as the drug addict, why should such an individual choose another person, rather than a drug, for the object of his addiction? One characteristic which distinguishes the two groups of addicts is their social class. Opiate use is found primarily in people in lower social and economic positions, especially racial minorities. Lower-class whites more normally take to alcohol as their escape. Middle-class Americans, on the other hand, while not quite as prone to alcoholism and while certainly not interested in heroin, are no less subject to addictive tendencies; they just express them differently.

As a rule, other human beings play a role in the middle-class person's lifestyle that they do not for the lower-class person. Lee Rainwater, who reports such social class differences in *Family Design,* found that sexual relationships in the lower class tend not to involve as great a degree of life-sharing. To take an extreme case, Chein's analysis of New York City heroin addicts shows that they are distrustful of people; drugs are the only things in their lives they feel they can rely on. Even the middle-class English opiate addicts whom Edwin Schur studied in *Narcotic Addiction in Britain and America* are generally alienated from other people. And perhaps an explanation for widespread drug abuse among young dropouts from the middle class is that the disruptive nature of their living habits leaves them with only fragmental and temporary relationships. But though this inability to form strong interpersonal ties characterizes drug and alcohol addicts no matter what their social class, weakened and unstable social networks are more common among economically and otherwise deprived groups. Hence individuals in these settings more frequently succumb to heroin addiction and debilitating alcoholism, while people (mainly lovers) serve the same purpose for those who are better off. In either case, the combination of dependency and manipulativeness that Chein observed in heroin addicts lies behind the addict's exploitativeness. Unsure of his own identity, the addict sees other people as objects to serve his needs. But for the drug addict, using people is only a means to other ends; for the middle-class addict, possessing people is the end.

Rainwater makes these differences clear in an article entitled, "A Study of Personality Differences Between Middle and Lower Class Adolescents." There he states that "The lower class person . . . is less dependent on people, and more oriented toward those gratifications which can be achieved without complicated cooperation of other human beings." Among the middle-class children in the study, a distinct pattern emerged which explains how people can be the drugs of middle-class addiction. Two-thirds of the middle-class children (as compared to only one-fifth of the children from lower-class families) showed evidence of a "social dependency constellation." The latter can be defined as the need to cling to one human object for love and support. That object may not even be a true person, but only a conception of a person.

When people are economically comfortable but still sense a large deficiency in their lives, their yearnings are bound to be more existential than material. That is, these yearnings are tied into their basic conception of and feelings about themselves. D. H. Lawrence describes such a case in his novel *Women in Love*. The character is Gerald Crich, the well-to-do son of an industrial magnate. When his father dies, Gerald's world begins to fall around him, and he experiences the spiritual catastrophe which leads him to a relationship of desperation with Gudrun Brangwen.

> But as the fight went on, and all that he had been and was continued to be destroyed, so that life was a hollow shell all around him, roaring and clattering like the sound of the sea, a noise in which he participated externally, and inside this hollow shell was all the darkness and fearful space of death, he knew he would have to find reinforcements, otherwise he would collapse inwards upon the great dark void which circled at the centre of his soul. His will held his outer life, his outer mind, his outer being, unbroken and unchanged. But the pressure was too great. . . . For day by day he felt more and more like a bubble filled with darkness. . . .

The emotional state Lawrence depicts is very much like what R. D. Laing calls schizoid alienation, in which an individual is so detached from his or her experience that he cannot get from it a sense of himself as an integrated being. The schizoid person doesn't feel that he is the person living his life, the personality occupying his own skin. In *The Divided Self*, Laing suggests that schizoid alienation is not only a common contemporary form of madness, but also a prevalent feature of life in modern society. The "ontological anxiety"—uncertainty about our very existence—that Laing speaks of is what makes some of us compulsively seek relationships.

Gerald Crich is a fictional example of someone who lacks a well-developed core being, a secure sense of himself. A person feeling this inner emptiness must strive to fill it. In relationships, this can only be done by subsuming someone else's being inside yourself, or by allowing someone else to subsume you. Often, two people simultaneously engulf and are engulfed by each other. The result is a full-fledged addiction, where each partner draws the other back at any sign of a loosening of the bonds that hold them together.

F. SCOTT FITZGERALD AND SHEILAH GRAHAM

To show concretely what it means to be hooked on a lover, we can take a well-known example—F. Scott Fitzgerald's love affair with Sheilah Graham. In the period following his wife Zelda's final emotional breakdown, Fitzgerald felt that his life's promise had in large part gone unfulfilled, and that he had exhausted his spiritual and emotional energy. All his life he had tried and failed to achieve a firm sense of his place in the world. He aspired to a social standing he never had possessed, a financial standing he could never gain, and a literary standing that was often questioned in his lifetime. In *The Far Side of Paradise* Arthur Mizener shows that all things seemed to conspire to deny psychological peace and security to Fitzgerald, who had written of himself, "Generally—I knew that at the bottom I lacked the essentials. At the last crisis, I knew I had no real courage, perseverance or self respect."

After his initial success as a writer, Fitzgerald and Zelda entered a downward spiral that was relieved only a few times before his death in 1940. During this period he had difficulty sustaining his work, which he and Zelda frequently interrupted with their drinking and moving around, and with their generally taxing pursuit of pleasure. In the aftermath of such periods of abandon, Fitzgerald would be stricken with remorse. To allay this guilt and consciousness of failure, he would then often embark on another bout of drinking and abandonment. By the end of the twenties, the frantic emptiness of his existence had begun to claim a horrible toll. Zelda suffered a breakdown which finally led to institutional confinement. Fitzgerald himself began to have physical and mental collapses and many more uncontrolled alcoholic binges. His finances, with which he was always preoccupied, became an even bigger problem. When he was finally able to complete his last novel, *Tender Is the Night*, it was not well received at its publication in 1934. The period following this shock to his confidence, during which his personal tragedies also increased unbearably, was more painful than any that had come before. His alcoholism reached unmanageable bounds.

In 1937, Fitzgerald moved to Hollywood to write movie scripts, leaving, but not deserting, Zelda in a sanitarium in North Carolina. In July of that year, he met Sheilah Graham, a movie columnist. She became his mainstay for the rest of his short life, helping him to stay on the wagon for the most part and to remain relatively content while he did a creditable stint as a screenwriter and was at work on a novel. Though it was some salvation for a tormented soul, their relationship, as described in Sheilah Graham's book *Beloved Infidel,* portrays the distorted, addicted form human intimacy can take when it is wrapped around a misshapen life.

In the first place, Fitzgerald did not entirely relinquish chemical help in the absence of his drinking. Sheilah Graham relates that ". . . he was once more on his Coca-Cola and coffee regimen," and that he relied on "sleeping pills and, to wake him in the morning, benzedrine." But his main stimulant and sedative was his love. Although he had been dramatically attached to Zelda (as one of the faults of Dick Diver, a character who embodies his own downfall, Fitzgerald listed "the desperate clinging to one woman"), it was now—when his original enthusiasm for life had been so thoroughly extinguished—that he shed all of life for one woman and demanded the same sacrifices from her. Graham writes:

> By early 1938 we were virtual recluses in Hollywood. I attended few evening events or industry parties. So that I could be with Scott [and still write her column], Jonah Ruddy for a weekly fee covered these occasions for me. We rarely went out: it was enough for us to be together, and when we were not together hardly an hour went by that Scott did not make me aware of his presence. He telephoned me five and six times during the day.

Once, when she wanted to make a trip to New York, Fitzgerald remonstrated:

> "But who are the people you see . . . ? They're not real. I have been there. I have given all that up. What can you get from such people? What can you get from New York?"
>
> "Oh . . ." I could not find the words. "New York excites me. It thrills me."
>
> "Sheilah, what you are looking for, you have found. You are looking for love, for someone to understand you. You have me. I love you and understand you. There's no need for you to go to New York."

Moreover, when her best friend was coming to Hollywood from New York, Fitzgerald insisted that they go away the weekend she was to arrive, and that the friend move into her own apartment immediately. He even went to the point of picking an apartment out for her and putting down the deposit. When the friend arrived at Sheilah's residence, she found an apologetic note and a key. Graham comments: "This Scott made me do to my best friend. He was jealous of her. He was so obviously unhappy, I could not refuse him." Perhaps even more extreme was the way Fitzgerald and his lover reacted to a prospective visit by her boss, John Wheeler:

> As the day of Wheeler's arrival approached, Scott grew more and more glum. He would not be reassured. And as had happened many times before when I found myself in difficulty, inspiration came. The night before Wheeler arrived, I went into the Good Samaritan Hospital for a minor operation, something my doctor had said could be done "any time—no hurry about it." I chose this time so that I would be too ill to see John Wheeler. Scott took me to the hospital, reassured at last.

While she found Fitzgerald's grasping behavior peculiar at times, Graham did not find it unattractive. She regarded these last two stories as examples of "Scott's unceasing tenderness." Her own attitude was characterized by her feeling that "my living began when he arrived." She relates her desire for enclosure by her lover:

> I looked into his face, searching it, trying to find its mystery, its wonder for me, and I said, almost prayerfully, "If only I could walk into your eyes and close the lids behind me, and leave all the world outside—"
> He held me close and I clung to him. . . .

The relationship was an addiction. F. Scott Fitzgerald and Sheilah Graham sealed themselves off from the outside world by neglecting their work and by dropping all their other personal relationships in Hollywood. Each seemed to feel that all experience was only valuable, or allowable, if it was mediated by the other. The belief which underlay this feeling—and all of the relationship—was expressed by Graham when she said that "my living began when he arrived." If there is a need to participate in every aspect of another's life, its conclusive form is the complete control of or reliance on another, so that one person does not exist without the other's being there, too. This is the essential similarity to drug addiction, where a person feels he is living only when he is on the drug. The ultimate statement of the desire to be consumed by love is in the last passage quoted from Graham, where she wanted to crawl into Scott's mind, lose her consciousness in his, and form one human entity out of two incomplete beings.

In their interactions, Fitzgerald claimed most of the prerogatives. He retained the right to return East to visit Zelda, and to have his daughter visit him, at the same time that he denied these things to Sheilah. He also generally insisted on keeping up his work schedule (when he wished) while disrupting hers. Fitzgerald's personal domination was characteristic of the relationship even where he helped his lover, as when he tutored her in history and literature. Such male domination, while hardly constituting the only form an addictive relationship can take, is not uncommon in these relationships. But it shouldn't be interpreted as an indication that the one partner is more in control of himself, or of the situation, than the other. Fitzgerald's need for Graham was every bit as strong as hers for him. Consider Erich Fromm's description, in *The Art of Loving,* of mutual need within an unequal relationship:

> The sadistic person is as dependent on the submissive person as the latter is on the former; neither can live without the other. The difference is only that the sadistic person commands, exploits, hurts, humiliates, and that the masochistic person is commanded, exploited, hurt, humiliated. This is a considerable difference in a realistic sense; in a deeper emotional sense, the difference is not so great as that which they both have in common: fusion without integrity.

The intensity of Fitzgerald's need is shown by his behavior when Graham finally broke up with him during one of his alcoholic binges. Eventually he succeeded in getting her back by vowing to give up drinking, but first he attempted a number of futile ploys that clearly revealed his desperation. For example, he phoned her all night, and he threatened to kill her. His most hateful act was to send a telegram to her boss with the intention of destroying her career. SHEILAH GRAHAM TODAY BANNED BY EVERY STUDIO . . . SUGGEST YOU SEND HER BACK TO ENGLAND WHERE SHE BELONGS STOP DO YOU KNOW HER REAL NAME IS LILY SHEIL? Deeply insecure about her origins, Graham had imparted her real name to Fitzgerald alone of all the people she knew in Hollywood.

There is no way to discount the malice behind this attack on her livelihood and personal identity. Fitzgerald may have been insanely drunk, but his behavior reflects an antagonism that could only be directed toward someone whom he hated. Could this be the way he felt toward the woman to whom he was totally devoted a few days before? The process on the other side, in Sheilah Graham's thoughts, was the same:

> I was not sorry for Scott's predicament . . . *Let Scott suffer.* The more I thought about it the angrier I became. *I'll fix him.* I took the first editions he had given me of his books—each with an inscription in it—and deliberately tore them from cover to cover . . . *I don't want to see his name again, I don't want to hear his name again, I don't want to be reminded of him.* I hated this man. He had betrayed me.

Naturally, she had good cause to act this way, and perhaps her attitude was momentary, a fit of pique. Yet it still represents complete alienation from that with which she formerly felt as one.

Above all else, these extreme emotional reactions conclusively establish that the relationship was an addiction. All along, the lovers' actions toward each other were dictated by their own needs. Therefore, when their connection was severed—even temporarily—they had no basis on which to relate. Each was incapable of respecting, or even conceiving of, the other in his or her own terms, as continuing to live his or her own life. It was impossible for either to be concerned about the other's well-being; if the one lover wasn't there to satisfy the other's needs, then he or she ceased to exist. In addition to this, when viewed in isolation from the ongoing relationship, the weird behavior which the two of them had participated in together now appeared grotesque. These love addicts were like the person who cannot use moderately a drug to which he was addicted. An addict, when he stops, must stop altogether. Because an addiction is sought only for the total experience it provides, it can only be accepted emotionally in that form. The ex-addict cannot conceive of relating to what was formerly the addictive object in anything less than a total way.

ERICH FROMM: A POSITIVE CONCEPT OF LOVE

Love is the opposite of interpersonal addiction. A love relationship is based on a desire to grow and to expand oneself through living, and a desire for one's partner to do the same. Anything which contributes positively to a loved one's experience is welcomed, partly because it enriches the loved one for his own sake, and partly because it makes him a more stimulating companion in life. If a person is self-completed, he can even accept experiences which cause a lover to grow away from him, if that is the direction in which the lover's fulfillment must take her. If two people hope to realize fully their potential as human beings—both together and apart—then they create an intimacy which includes, along with trust and sharing, hope, independence, openness, adventurousness, and love.

When we speak of a desire for intimacy that respects the loved one's integrity, we naturally think of Erich Fromm's classic work *The Art of Loving.* Fromm's theme is that man or woman can only achieve love when he has realized himself to the point where he can stand as a whole and secure person. "Mature *love*," Fromm states, "is *union under the condition of preserving one's integrity,* one's individuality." It requires "a state of intensity, awakeness, enhanced vitality, which can only be the result of a productive and active orientation in many other spheres of life." This permits us, as lovers, to manifest an *"active concern for the life and the growth of that which we love."*

Unless we have reached this state, and "unless we have faith in the persistence of our self, our feeling of identity is threatened and we become dependent on other people whose approval then becomes the basis for our feeling of identity." In that case, we are in danger of experiencing union *without* integrity. Such a union is a "full commitment in all aspects of life," but one which lacks an essential ingredient, a regard for the rest of the world:

> If a person loves only one other person and is indifferent to the rest of his fellow men, his love is not love but a symbiotic attachment, or an enlarged egotism.

These comments, and much else that Fromm writes, reveal a sharp awareness of the potential for addiction inherent in the "powerful striving" man feels for "interpersonal fusion." * Fromm notes that

---

* In fact, one way in which Fromm sees man trying to overcome his feeling of separateness is through orgiastic states, including drugs. In a culture like ours where this behavior is disapproved of, "while they [drug users] try to escape from separateness by taking refuge in alcohol or drugs, they feel all the more separate after the orgiastic experience is over, and thus are driven to take recourse to it with increasing frequency and intensity."

two passionately attracted people "take the intensity of the infatuation, this being 'crazy' about each other, for proof of the intensity of their love, while it may only prove the degree of their preceding loneliness."

Fromm is a social critic who wants to alert his readers to the harmful effect which society, particularly modern capitalist society, can have on the individual and on personal relationships. Thus he emphasizes the materialism in self-seeking behavior toward others, especially lovers—that is, the tendency to regard social partners as commodities. People who show this orientation "fall in love when they feel they have found the best object available on the market, considering the limitations of their own exchange values." Fromm feels that any such person is seriously disabled in going about the business of making love, for "the marketing character is willing to give, but only in exchange for receiving; giving without receiving for him is being cheated." Seeking lovers in this way is like "buying real estate, [where] the hidden potentialities which can be developed play a considerable role in this bargain." Fromm therefore stresses that the respect inherent in all love requires a lover to think, "I want the loved person to grow and unfold for his own sake, and in his own ways, and not for the purpose of serving me."

As Fromm rightly insists, this altruism encourages the loved one's growth. But we have to ask also whether it allows for an uncritical attitude toward the lover that is reminiscent of the mindless romanticism Fromm criticizes. Fromm sees any evaluation of what another can contribute to one's own successful dealing with life as an illegitimate consideration in love. What misleads him, and many others, is the habit of conceiving of love exclusively in terms of the lovers' relation to each other—as if this could be separated from the contexts of the lovers' individual lives. This is actually a romantic perspective, and within it judgments of another's worth can only be viewed as self-serving. Yet a different order of judgment is implied by Fromm's rejection of sterile, solely self-gratifying interdependency. For if you aren't just going to use someone else as a dehumanized substitute for—or extension of—yourself (just like any other addictive object), then you will want to ask whether that person is himself mature and strong. Mature people, concerned with the quality of their lives, engage naturally in a continuing evaluation of their relationships, testing alternatives and questioning their commitments. An independent, open person exploring life seriously will instinctively (if not consciously) consider whether someone has anything of substance to add to his or her existence.

Germaine Greer makes a similar point in her book *The Female Eunuch*. While sharing Fromm's dislike of superficial, commercial standards for assessing potential mates, she accepts the need for some external means of validation in a relationship: "A woman shows her own value to her sisters by choosing a successful and personable man. It is probably a part of the process of natural selection, operating at the very outset of the courting game, and a healthy egotism at that, if only the criteria involved in such judgments were not so ersatz and commercial, and so trivial."

CRITERIA FOR LOVE VS. ADDICTION

In Fromm's notion of integrity in love and Greer's emphasis on self-actualization and personal pride, we have the elements of a positive concept of love. By contrasting this model with that of addictive love, we can develop specific criteria for assessing the character of our relationships. These criteria follow from our more general standards for distinguishing between the addictive and the nonaddictive approach to life. They are points at which a relationship either expresses health and the promise of growth, or leans toward addiction:

1. Does each lover have a secure belief in his or her own value?
2. Are the lovers improved by the relationship? By some measure outside of the relationship are they better, stronger, more attractive, more accomplished, or more sensitive individuals? Do they value the relationship for this very reason?
3. Do the lovers maintain serious interests outside the relationship, including other meaningful personal relationships?
4. Is the relationship integrated into, rather than being set off from, the totality of the lovers' lives?
5. Are the lovers beyond being possessive or jealous of each other's growth and expansion of interests?
6. Are the lovers also friends? Would they seek each other out if they should cease to be primary partners?

These standards represent an ideal, and as such they cannot be fulfilled completely even by the healthiest relationships. But given that every relationship is bound to contain some elements of addiction, we can still tell what makes one predominantly addictive. This occurs, as in drug addiction, when a single overwhelming involvement with one thing serves to cut a person off from life, to close him or her off to experience, to debilitate him, to make him less open, free, and positive in dealing with the world.

Interpersonal addiction need not be a one-to-one affair. An addict may form successive or simultaneous relationships, either because he or she never allows himself to become seriously involved, or because he can't find a partner who completely accepts him. In all cases, however, addiction has at its center a diminished sense of self. The addict uses relationships to seal off his inner self from a frightening environment. In the process, the already weakened self ceases to develop, and the addict's life contracts further.

D. H. Lawrence used the term *égoisme à deux* to describe the overgrown, quasi-permanent connection between two lovers. Like any form of addiction, an *égoisme à deux* involves people who have not received from life a self-completeness that would enable them to come to an experience whole in themselves. The result is that they are drawn to an object—the lover—which can secure their shallow or fragmented selves. But they become trapped by this object, because even as it stabilizes them, it prevents them from extending themselves outward to meet other people or events that they encounter. As their inadequacy and rigidity worsen, each must lean more heavily on the other. Thus they draw each other into an increasingly closed, isolated, and mutually protective relationship.

Because the partners in an addictive relationship are motivated more by their own needs for security than by an appreciation of each other's personal qualities, what they want most from each other is the reassurance of constancy. Thus they are likely to demand unchallenged acceptance of themselves as they are, including their blemishes and peculiarities. In exchange, they are willing to tolerate passively all similar quirks in each other's makeup. In fact, to justify their total involvement, the lovers may identify each other's idiosyncrasies as their standards for attractiveness. In this way they create a private world which others can't enter and would not want to enter.

Such lovers do, of course, require each other to change in certain
ways. But the adaptations expected or demanded are entirely toward each other and do not entail an improved ability to deal with
other people or the environment. On the contrary, the changes one
partner requests of the other to better satisfy his own needs are almost always harmful to the other's general development as a person.
The lovers are not concerned if an "inward" adjustment is a debilitating one overall. In fact, a lessened ability to cope with anything or
anyone else is welcomed in the other as a stronger guarantee of
allegiance to the relationship. This is why jealousy and posses-
siveness are so much a part of addictive love. It is why an addict actually hopes that his lover will not meet new people and enjoy the
world, since this suggests competing ties and interests that would
make her less dependent on him. As Germaine Greer's penetrating
analysis puts it:

> The hallmark of egotistical love, even when it masquerades as altruis-
> tic love, is the negative answer to the question "Do I want my love to be
> happy more than I want him to be with me?" As soon as we find our-
> selves working at being indispensable, rigging up a pattern of vulnera-
> bility in our loved ones, we ought to know that our love has taken the
> socially sanctioned form of egotism. Every wife who slaves to keep her-
> self pretty, to cook her husband's favorite meals, to build up his pride
> and confidence in himself at the expense of his sense of reality, to be his
> closest and effectively his only friend, to encourage him to reject the
> consensus of opinion and find reassurance only in her arms is binding
> her mate to her with hoops of steel that will strangle them both. Every
> time a woman makes herself laugh at her husband's often-told jokes she
> betrays him. The man who looks at his woman and says, "What would I
> do without you?" is already destroyed. His woman's victory is complete,
> but it is Pyrrhic. Both of them have sacrificed so much of what initially
> made them lovable to promote the symbiosis of mutual dependence that
> they scarcely make up one human being between them.

Paradoxically, at the stage where they have rejected the rest of
the world—when they need each other most—the lovers have become least critical and aware of each other as unique individuals.
The partner is just *there,* a completely necessary point of certainty in
a bewildering and dangerous world. Under these conditions, acceptance of another is not a recognition of that person's integrity.

Where need is so intense, there is no room in the lovers' minds for such a concept of dignity, either the other person's or one's own. Their lack of feeling for themselves makes them want to be absorbed by each other, and their lack of self-development and ability to express themselves individually makes it possible for them to be so engulfed.

Then, too, the lovers' ultimate lack of interest in each other gives the lie to the romantic notion of addicted love as a kind of intense passion. The intensity that we see is that of desperation, not of a desire to know each other better. In healthy relationships the growing attachment to another person goes with a growing appreciation of that person; among these relationships are those inspiring love affairs where two people continually find new facets of each other to admire and delight in. In addiction what is apparent is not the intensity of passion, but its shallowness. There is no emotional risk in this sort of relationship, or, at least, the addict tries to eliminate that risk as much as possible. Because he is so vulnerable, what the addict is ideally striving for is perfect invulnerability. He only gives of himself in exchange for the promise of safety.

From this perspective, love at first sight becomes understandable in the sense that addiction to heroin on the first injection is understandable. A description by an addict in *The Road to H* of his first shot of heroin can apply equally well to the addicted lover's experience: "I felt I always wanted to feel the same way as I felt then." Both addicts have discovered something reassuring that they hope will never change. From the turmoil of their inner worlds, they recognize and latch onto the one sensation they have encountered which they feel can bring them peace.

Addicted lovers see each other more and more in order to maintain this secure state. They settle into each other, requiring ever more frequent interactions, until they find themselves consistently together, unable to endure significant separations. When they are apart, they long for each other. The two people have grown together to such an extent that, as in our example of Vicky and Bruce in Chapter 1, neither feels like a whole person when alone. This is the development of tolerance in a relationship. The excitement that originally brought the lovers together has dissipated, yet the lovers are less able than before to be critical of their arrangement. Even if their contact degenerates into constant conflict, they cannot part.

As with heroin and its irrecoverable euphoria, or cigarettes smoked in routine excess, something initially sought for pleasure is held more tightly *after* it ceases to provide enjoyment. Now it is being maintained for negative rather than positive reasons. The love partner must be there in order to satisfy a deep, aching need, or else the addict begins to feel withdrawal pain. His emotional security is so dependent on this other individual around whom he has organized his life, that to be deprived of the lover would be an utter shock to the system of his existence. If the world he has built with the lover is destroyed, he desperately tries to find some other partner so as to reestablish his artificial equilibrium. For as with heroin and other addictions, it is traumatic for addict lovers to reenter the broader world with which they have lost touch. "It was as though I was lost in a dream world," they say, "I thought everything we did was so cool, and now I see it was all so sick."

The addictive foundations of such a relationship are revealed when it ends in an abrupt, total, and vindictive breakup. Since the relationship has been the person's one essential contact point with life, its removal necessarily leaves him in a disoriented agony. Because the involvement has been so total, its ending must be violent. Thus it is possible for two people who have been the most intimate of friends suddenly to turn around and hate each other, because they have been thinking more of themselves than each other all along. The exploitation that has been going on throughout the relationship simply becomes more overt when the breakup occurs; then the two ex-lovers withdraw emotionally, perhaps to the point of trying to hurt each other. Such betrayals are most striking when a lover breaks off from an established relationship in favor of a new partner who better satisfies his or her needs. Only where "love" is a self-serving device can an external accident destroy the feelings that two people supposedly have for each other. The addict's haphazard, seemingly innocent couplings are more volatile and more destructive than those formed by people who maintain a questioning attitude toward their lives and relationships.

When there is a willingness to examine one's motivations and behavior toward others, the idea of addiction can be treated not as a threatening diagnosis, but as a means for heightening the awareness of some dangers which are very common in relationships. By establishing the antithesis of addiction, we can delineate an ideal with which to oppose the tendencies toward self-suppression and suppression of others that can appear in love. Just as it is important to keep the addictive elements that are somewhere present in all human contact from becoming full-blown addictions, it is at least equally valuable to expand the positive, life-seeking potential that also exists within any relationship.

A loving relationship, as Erich Fromm makes clear, is predicated on the psychological wholeness and security of the individuals who come to it. Out of their own integrity, the lovers seek a constant, nondisruptive growth for each other and for the relationship. Respecting the people they are and have been, and the lives they have formed, they try to maintain the prior interests and affections they have known. Where possible, they want to incorporate these things into the relationship, in order to broaden the world they share. They also reserve the time—and the feeling—to keep up those activities or friendships which it would be impossible or inappropriate to offer each other.

Because they are well-composed individuals before the relationship is conceived, their approach to that relationship is not frantic. They may be passionately attracted and want very much to become better friends, but they also recognize there are points at which pressure and intensity are hurtful to what they desire. They accept the need for privacy and for different viewpoints and tastes, they realize that forcing certain commitments or declarations is unwise and ultimately self-defeating, and they appreciate that it takes time for two people to know each other and to discover the extent and depth of their compatibility. They can now carry over to their relationship together the same good feelings that they have about themselves as whole, secure, and reasonable people.

What makes this relationship fulfilling to them, what convinces them that it is love, is their seeing that what they have together is particularly rewarding among the alternatives that each of them has. Rather than making the relationship dry or emotionless, this perspective enables them to give without reserve as mature people who know why they love and sacrifice, and why they can inspire these feelings in someone else. The fact that they are discriminating makes clear that their choice of each other has been made on both sides out of something other than desperation, and thus cannot be blown away by a chance wind. There is no reason for them to doubt that their feeling for each other is genuine, substantial, and long-lived, and hence there is no reluctance to explore life both within the relationship and outside it.

The impetus for this exploration is the life instinct of the individuals involved: they were growing beings before they met, and they entered upon their union as a positive choice for continued growth, only this time to be carried out in conjunction with—though not exclusively with—another person. The lovers approach the relationship itself as an opportunity for growth. They want to understand more about it, about themselves, and about each other. For this reason, a love relationship necessarily becomes deeper, out of the experience the lovers share, and out of their constant desire to uncover new facets of their connection and to better understand its old facets. Each of the lovers wants to become a better person and wants the other to become a better person, both out of a love for that person and a desire to see the best things happen to him or her, and out of the knowledge that this will make him or her—and oneself—a more stimulating, accomplished, happy person to love and be with.

For these things to come about, a loving relationship must be a helping relationship. The lovers have to support each other in their areas of weakness and their areas of strength, though with a different attitude toward each. The first is understood as something undesirable which it may be hard to change. The second is welcomed, admired, utilized, and expanded. In both cases, there is a loving attention, an appreciation of each other's individuality, and a striving to bring out what is best in each other. To do this may require gentle but persistent reminders, on the one hand, or encouragement and congratulations on the other. But the aim of both is the same: support for one's partner to become the best human being he or she is reasonably capable of being.

While it is impossible to overstate the role of nurturance and reassurance in love, it is also true that love itself is demanding and sometimes exhausting. The issue between addiction and love is whether the demands will be preordained and immediately self-serving, or whether they will be in the service of some larger sense of individual and mutual progress. The exhaustion that sometimes results from intense contact between two people can be due either to the self-disgust and despair of addiction, or to an impatience and dismay at seeing challenges go unmet. Human emotion necessarily involves risk. The risk may stem from the possibility that a rigid coupling will be cataclysmically disrupted by some new, unanticipated experience, or from the chance that two people who do not allow their lives to be totally defined will evolve in different directions. There is always this danger in love; to deny it is to deny love. But where the people involved are genuine and self-sustaining, and where they have been in love, the parting—made with whatever pain and regret—will not be the end of them as individuals or as loving friends.

This feeling of existential confidence in oneself and one's relationships is hard to achieve, and may only very rarely be encountered. A host of social forces work against it, and, as a result, it is unfortunately easier to find examples of addiction than of self-fulfillment in love.

5

Addicted Lovers Together

The vignettes that follow, like that of Vicky and Bruce in Chapter 1, are in a way unusual for a book of this kind. We think of a psychological study as depicting some obvious abnormality. This is not true of the psychological studies presented here. People like the ones portrayed in these narratives do not think of themselves, and are not generally thought of, as pathological cases. On the contrary, they are reckoned as healthy, contributing members of society. Some of our characters, in fact, are cast as highly accomplished professionals. Their attitudes toward their own lives range from complacency to bearable dissatisfaction, from total unawareness to fatalistic self-knowledge. Such individuals lead lives that most would deem acceptable, but they could fulfill themselves at a wholly different level were it not for the fact that they are addicted.

Addiction is not always an all-or-none proposition. Although there are differences in personality that tip an individual's balance toward an addictive or a nonaddictive orientation, we all are susceptible to addiction in greater or lesser degree. Habit and repetition are necessary parts of any life, and none of us is altogether free

...the univers...

...scontent and paralysis can exist in people who he... ...n of normality, then society is accepting, and even ...ind of spiritual disability.

...d union of our prototype couple, Vicky and Bruce, il- ...what an addictive relationship ideally aims to be, that is, un- ...ed by time and place. What happens to such a couple ten, ...wenty, thirty years later? Can an unsound relationship survive indefinitely? With Vicky and Bruce, it is likely they can persist in their feeling that their marriage is a success, as long as they continue to isolate themselves from the world. This isolation is not physical so much as it comes from a way of looking at interactions with all other people as external and perfunctory. By dealing seriously only with each other and their families, such couples don't face the tensions that would arise from exposure to a more fluid environment.

The stories that follow are both more complex and more typical. In them, addictive needs are in conflict with other personal motivations and with cultural forces which endanger the stability of fragile relationships. These cases show that the character of an addictive relationship is most clearly revealed when the relationship is under stress. They also show why there is probably no such thing as a one-sided addiction, and how different but complementary needs, in combination with certain social pressures, can temporarily bring ill-matched couples together.

A MARRIAGE UNDER ATTACK

Like Vicky and Bruce, Gail and Allen were originally motivated to create an *égoisme à deux*. But because they chose to maintain contact with the rest of the world, they failed to seal themselves off so effectively as did Vicky and Bruce. Their story provides an example of what happens to an addictive marriage when its weaknesses are played upon by a changing cultural climate.

Allen and Gail were students together at Ohio State University. At the time they met, he was a junior and she a freshman. The two young people had traveled quite different routes on their way to meeting at college. Gail's parents had been killed in a car accident when she was five. Fortunately, however, an aunt and uncle who were close to her family had immediately taken Gail (and her eight-year-old brother) into their home in Akron. Gail's new parents were kind and attentive to her, as they were to their own children—two boys and a girl a year and a half younger than Gail. But the new household also had its unsettling aspects. Gail's uncle had been a chemical engineer with a promising future in a large rubber manufacturing company until, claiming that an invention of his had been taken over without acknowledgment, he ran afoul of his employers. He eventually left this position and went into business on his own while he pursued litigation to gain redress. He subsequently had some good years financially and some bad ones. Perhaps because he never secured his place in the community, his wife was especially concerned that all her children act properly, and that they be accepted socially.

Allen had come from a much more staid and conventional home, one managed tightly by a father who had attended medical school, but who had been forced to drop out and become a science teacher instead. Now a school superintendent, he made sure that his two sons were outstanding students. While still in high school Allen had to contend with the image of an older brother who was popular, brilliant, and already an acknowledged personal and professional success. But Allen, too, had a great deal of natural ability, and at Ohio State he gravitated to the science courses which showed his technical aptitude in its best light. There was another side to his mind, though, one which poked fun at things and led him to associate with people who questioned façades and hypocrisies. He became one of a group of male friends who criticized the rules and unspoken social forms that governed life for most students at Ohio State. He and his friends wore their hair a little longer than average, prided themselves on reading more widely, and in other ways set themselves off from their classmates.

But when Allen found Gail, he showed little interest in continuing his association with these men. At one time his closest friends, they became superfluous to him. As he put it, he no longer "needed" to be with them now that he was in love with Gail. In fact, the role of mentor to this young woman appealed greatly to a man who felt he had never been granted his due by other men. Allen's old pals in some ways accepted his separation from them, because they, too, believed in the ideal of a close, sharing relationship with a woman— one that meant leaving many other things behind. In other ways, however, they resented the change in Allen. His roommates, for example, regarded his bringing Gail into the dormitory at times when they were trying to study as selfish and inconsiderate. Once a classmate came to Allen's room to get some help for a test the next day. Instead, he was forced to wait an hour (after which he left) while Allen talked on the phone to Gail in an effort to calm her down about a traumatic mishap in one of her classes.

Many upsetting things happened to Gail at college. With warmth and affection from her stepparents, she had come through adolescence an outwardly happy and well-adjusted girl, with insecurities that seemed not to be outside the normal range for a person of her age. Yet although attractive and energetic, she was also skittish and temperamental, and still relied on regular calls from her aunt for a sense of security. At the same time, she wanted deeper answers to life than her aunt and Akron society could offer. Having met with tragedy early on and later having identified with her uncle's maverick stance, she felt as though she had been singled out by fate for a depth of experience that passed most of her acquaintances by. While not a particularly good student in high school, she wrote poems and wanted better to understand herself and life. But she had no intellectual forms in which to cast her thoughts and observations. These Allen provided in the long talks they had while they walked around the campus in the evenings.

As Gail grew closer to Allen that first year away from home, her aunt's phone calls took on a new air. She seemed to be checking up on Gail. In particular, she got in the habit of calling early on both Saturday and Sunday mornings, as if to make sure that Gail had not slept away from her room. In addition, the aunt began to take up Gail's time on the phone with paeans about her cousin, who was a cheerleader and social luminary in high school, dating a different boy each Friday and Saturday night. The cousin had always been better able to live out the role her mother had in mind for the girls.

Now, with Gail having an intimate relationship with a man, it seemed that a rift was developing within the family. The person to whom Gail had most consistently looked for love and emotional support was disapproving of her.

In the place of her aunt's devotion, Gail looked more and more toward Allen for guidance. Allen gave her advice on how to think and how to live. He encouraged her and gave her confidence in herself, but the implication was that what he gave he could take away. In return, Allen called upon Gail to side with him in the various conflicts of egos that were a normal part of college life among men, even those who criticized collegiate society and stayed on its fringes. While Allen himself was not aggressive, challenges from others elicited in him a privatism that led him to retreat to home ground. He generally preferred a retiring life, contentedly working late into the night on his studies, and Gail was all he felt he needed to fulfill himself personally. As long as he had Gail's respect and loyalty, and her unquestioning acceptance of his versions of the daily events he was involved in, he sought no more.

Allen's excessive reliance on Gail was a complex matter. Although his tendency toward isolation could be called defensive, it did not completely obscure his considerable personal appeal and intellectual capacities. The use of his mind was not limited to schoolwork, and when he was with people he had a lot to offer. Both witty and insightful, he was an engaging person to be around. For his own part, he enjoyed the company of serious and rounded people more than that of his narrow, technically oriented scientist colleagues. Yet the constricted lifestyle and personal inertia that made him so willing to shut himself off with one person reflected a deep fatalism. He was pessimistic about his ability to give direction to his life or to have any impact on his world. This inertia characteristically overcame his energetic side and resulted in the care he took to build into his life a number of devices for ensuring his comfort. A doting girlfriend was one more of these devices.

Altogether, this relationship was not much different from other involvements formed by college students newly awakened to the possibilities for life-sharing that being away from home afforded. A man who can protect his woman and a woman who sides with her man in any dispute are ever-present ideals in our culture. But Allen and Gail forged a permanent connection out of what was a very immature tie, as they created a relationship almost solely for the sake of alleviating their respective insecurities.

One day, after a weekend at home, Gail returned to school terrifically depressed. She had been forced to endure one critical lecture after another, culminating in a hushed conversation in which her cousin told her how unhappy her behavior was making her aunt. As she sat with Allen, discussing how they could circumvent the dormitory regulations which prevented them from spending as much time together as they wanted, Gail began to wonder if it was all worth it. Then Allen made a startling proposition: "Why don't we just get married, and stop all this sneaking around?" For Gail, it suddenly seemed the obvious solution. She could leave behind her untidy family situation and join up with the boy she loved. Besides being knowledgeable in the areas that mattered to her, Allen was kind, and she saw in him a chance to realize all the things she wanted but could not get for herself. She especially admired Allen's intellectual attainments and his association with a group of offbeat, critically minded students. Although she felt intimidated by this group, she envied their clear and certain vision of things. This is not to say that she anticipated specific advantages from marrying Allen. She actually went into the marriage with a genuine enthusiasm and hopefulness, rather than a calculated opportunism. But never having dealt with her lack of personal definition, she also went into the marriage as a child, looking for a way of maintaining her childlike role. For his part, Allen was delighted to have an attractive wife who would keep him company and share his perspective in life. Never before having held so securely the affection of another person, he would do whatever was necessary to guarantee the continuation of this relationship.

By the time they got married, in the summer after Gail's freshman year, the two had had a smoothly functioning relationship for almost a year. Thus, their friends and acquaintances readily accepted the move as a reasonable step. Since even the more iconoclastic students at this time and place favored permanent, monogamous attachments, there was no reason to question this one, even if it seemed somewhat premature. With the families, it was a different story. Allen's parents were suspicious of this young woman who wanted to avail herself of their son's background and promising future, while Gail's aunt protested vehemently that a coed should get around more and should only marry when she was in a position to choose from among many men. The aunt was not impressed with Allen's academic record when she knew that he had years of schooling to go through before he could support a wife. But as Allen and Gail persisted in their intentions, their parents gradually accepted the fact that they were serious about each other. Finally, the two families met and agreed that as long as the young people were going to be so deeply involved with each other anyway, their intimacy might as well be acknowledged and brought into the family. So Allen and Gail married with Allen not yet out of college, and Gail barely into it. Neither had had any serious boyfriends or girlfriends, and Gail had not dated, not kissed, another boy since before her eighteenth birthday.

As a married couple ensconced in an apartment away from the main campus, they occasionally saw their old friends, but mainly they spent their time alone together. They no longer had to relate so intensely as when they had desperately sought reassurance from each other in the face of outside threats. Instead, they settled into a quiet domestic existence—one very much in keeping with the staid atmosphere that prevailed on this Ohio campus. But it all came to an end when Allen went on to graduate school the next year. Sensing that the limited purview of the science courses he had taken didn't reflect his own broader interests and concerns, Allen decided to study environmental sciences. He hoped in this way to turn his abilities to applied research that was both more useful and more stimulating.

As he turned away from abstract scientific work, Allen also rejected the option of staying at Ohio State. Instead, he chose to go to the West Coast, to the University of Oregon, where there was a well-developed awareness of environmental issues and a clear mandate for doing something about them. Gail, too, welcomed this chance to enter a fresh, exciting world. She felt that unlike Ohio State, Eugene would be a real intellectual community. Gail was a vibrant person—after all, choosing to side with Allen against her family was not something a completely timid and yielding person would have been able to do—and it was her and Allen's vital, inquisitive side that moved them toward a more fluid environment. In taking this chance to grow as individuals, however, they unwittingly placed themselves in a setting that would be fatal to their life together.

When Gail arrived in Eugene, she found a world even more invigorating than she had imagined it would be. Just entering her junior year in college, she embarked on a program that the university had recently created. It was called "Human Development," and it drew on the range of social, psychological, and biological sciences for an understanding of human behavior. Many of her fellow students in the program were seeking, as she was, to make themselves into more contented human beings by overcoming past hangups, and thus the courses showed an emphasis on contemporary psychological movements such as primal, gestalt, and Reichian therapies. Gail was attracted by a group of Reichian devotees, and in their teachings and practices she found a way to release what she felt was her real self.

As she was drawn into these explorations, Gail tried to bring Allen with her. But he was reluctant to follow. Perhaps he was just not used to seeing Gail take the lead. In any case, his life in Oregon was very different from hers. As a serious graduate student, he busied himself with secluded research, conducted alone or in conjunction with a few colleagues. Allen was content to transplant the privacy and self-containment of his life in the Midwest to this new milieu, seeking from his surroundings only some faint diversion in the form of observing the various West Coast movements taking place around him. Gail was not satisfied with indirect involvement. Initially looking toward Allen to continue to provide the stability and competence that she relied on to obtain the things she wanted, she now began to see him as irrelevant to her needs. She had always thought of him as a more experienced person than herself, but now she saw him as living in a limited world. After a while, as she came home from the campus each evening to find Allen engrossed in his research, her resentment flared. She felt that she was living on the margins of life.

As for Allen, his increasing indifference to Gail's constant demands may have signaled *his* disenchantment. He certainly was dubious about Gail's new enthusiasms, although he didn't reveal to anyone the way he actually felt. He seemed to carry on in the old groove more out of reflex than present desire, more because he dreaded the consequences of a split than because he was still getting the satisfactions from the relationship that he once had. Just as Gail needed him less now that she had her own set of intellectual peers, maybe he needed her less, too, now that he was safely away from the undergraduate friends with whom he had been emotionally involved in such an uncomfortable way. With personal relationships in graduate school so much less complicated, he felt less need for the constant support of a woman who still demanded quite a bit of him.

Allen, however, would have done nothing on his own. He just tried to keep things as they were, as when he rebuffed Gail's proposal that they move into a commune of Reichian therapy adherents that she had been invited to join. Whenever he turned his back on her like that, she felt on the verge of doing something final. Then, with a noisy announcement, her young cousin showed up in Los Angeles. In a radical turnabout, the cousin came to live the West Coast life with a vengeance, becoming one of the followers of a powerful guru who reportedly used his spiritual teachings as a cover for his sexual gratifications. When Gail heard of this, she had a perplexed reaction of envy and frustration, of having been upstaged in some odd way by a person whom she had left behind. It was the last straw.

One morning, while Allen was at the lab, Gail took their tape recorder and spoke about her feelings of being stifled, her desire to branch out more, and her intention to start a new life on her own. A few minutes of taped conversation, after which she left their apartment for good, and their life together was ended. Allen came home, read a note directing him to turn on the recorder, and there found his life broken asunder. Their love had turned to resentment—Gail's resentment as the child whose potential for an independent life was being suppressed, Allen's resulting feelings of having been betrayed by an ungrateful child. She rejected what he was, and he resented what she was becoming. Ideally, they could have tried to approach each other in an entirely new way, with an appreciation of each other as independent beings. In reality, they didn't have enough in common to make the effort worthwhile. As often happens in addiction, the choice of partners had been almost accidental.

These things are very clear in retrospect. But at the time, Allen and Gail's old college acquaintances were shocked by the suddenness and totality of the breakup. Until then, everyone had been compelled to conceive of the relationship in its own stated terms. How else was it possible to make sense of both partners' enormous sacrifices of other friendships and interests—past, present, and future—except by assuming that a great love existed between them? Yet when Gail withdrew from the union, it was done precipitously and unilaterally—in response, we might say, to a series of smaller unilateral disengagements on Allen's part. Neither tried very hard to work things out with the other. Could this have been love? The unexpected denouement should cause us, as it did them, to reevaluate the whole relationship from its beginnings, and to see that what all had called love was more like addiction. The couple's closeness was an artificial creation, based on their having been available to each other at a time when they shared a special need. Once their needs changed, or they found better ways to satisfy their needs, they knew they had no further use for each other. Their relationship could not allow for growth in either of the two lovers. And they were both ready to grow.

After the initial disruption stemming from their separation, Gail and Allen threw themselves into the West Coast culture that lay in wait for them outside their marriage. Today they can hardly imagine themselves to be the same people who were once married to each other. They have put themselves through a lot of experience, and they both date their growth into "real" life from their splitting off to go into the world independently. They have now gone off, for the most part, in different directions. Gail feels that her emulation of Allen and his college friends' intellectuality was misguided, especially since she now sees their "rational" approach as wrongheaded, and itself a product of middle-class hangups. But relatively soon after she became immersed in Reichian therapy, she decided that the particular commune she had joined was not for her. What's more, she suspected that her whole frenetic involvement in West Coast life was superficial and did not really allow her to deal with her psychological conflicts. As a result, she has returned to Akron and to a way of life which does not subject her high-strung nature to such strains. She has continued her Reichian analysis in an effort to sort out her motives and desires, and to free more of what she still regards as her blocked energy. She has chosen to do this by living close to her aunt and uncle and by sorting out her family situation through the use of her new psychological tools.

It is Allen, surprisingly, who has made the West Coast his home. At the time of the sudden dissolution of the marriage, he faced a situation which appeared bleaker than Gail's. Moving immediately into her commune, Gail had ready-made emotional resources to draw upon, while Allen, with no one he felt close to in Eugene, had nothing comparable to rely on. That he found himself so desperate was probably fortunate in the long run. After a miserable six months in which he did little but go to the lab every day, he began to get into campus and community activities. Among other things, he joined a commune dedicated to action on ecological issues, where he could bring to bear his academic training in concrete ways. His participation in this group has placed him in close contact with a number of people and has brought him many good friendships and working relationships. It has also led to his putting less of himself into his academic work, and he has now begun to doubt whether an academic career holds much meaning for him anymore. On the other hand, he was unwilling to apply for a position he might easily have obtained in a state office created to preserve Oregon's natural resources and beauty. He seems not to be sure of what he wants to do professionally.

Both Allen and Gail have now been allowed to follow out the courses their lives almost seemed destined to travel. Gail's inward movement and Allen's outward movement have made them more complete individuals, correcting somewhat their past imbalances. In this sense, they have broken out of the barriers their relationship built around them. Neither is very self-critical about their marriage, however, which they seem to regard as just another experience that contributed to making them what they are today. They feel that given what they were when they met, it was something they had to get into; given what they later became, it was something they had to get out of. While it is probably healthy for them to adopt this attitude—it would certainly be foolish for them to weigh themselves down with guilt at this time—it may still be that Allen and Gail are not ready to confront what it is in themselves which threw them off by so much when they felt they were forming a lasting love relationship.

Neither of them has yet found a single, stable relationship with another person, which they both say they want, even though they now know a great deal more about who they are when they enter into an involvement. Gail has shied away from serious, long-term entanglements altogether. Allen has striven to achieve more honest, mature relationships with women, but he, too, has not been able to find what he wants in these, and his affairs have drifted into disinterest or disillusionment on either his or the woman's part. With both Allen and Gail, the realization of where their marriage failed has not been such as to enable them to understand where they go wrong when they enter into a new relationship. Perhaps they have not identified their insecurities sufficiently well. Perhaps they misconceive their goals, and while they think they want another permanent lover, they should really be thinking of personal satisfaction in other, less grand terms. Finally, since neither has found a basic career interest—they have subordinated this consideration to more personal concerns—their lives show an overall lack of direction that may make secure personal resolutions almost impossible for them.

Allen and Gail seem not to have overcome the childhood training which left them passive when it came to giving their lives a larger momentum. It is not an accident that Allen is still a student as he nears thirty, and that Gail's deepest emotional ties are still within her family. Apparently, the culture into which they were born produced individuals who could not act effectively outside the structures of family and school. This is why they turned to an addictive panacea in the first place. As Allen and Gail conceive of it, what they have been going through both in their marriage and in the years since is a kind of retooling that is required of many people because they were inadequately prepared for the new demands society has placed on them.

After Gail and Allen got married, Gail's aunt came to accept and even to endorse the relationship. How stricken she was, then, when Gail confessed her desertion several weeks after the fact. The aunt now disapproved of Gail's having given up so quickly. "I don't see why two adults can't sit down and work these things out," she insisted. "Things have not always been easy between me and Dad." To Gail and Allen this made no sense, since they wanted more from life than the security of a makeshift partnership. If anything can be learned from this story, it is that to "fall in love" and take on the pseudo-adult roles of a married pair is, as a substitute for personal growth, becoming easier to do, but harder to get away with.

AN ODDLY MATCHED COUPLE

Carl and Shelley, a couple in their late twenties, also were involved in an addictive relationship that broke down under stress. But their story has a different flavor from that of Allen and Gail. There was no idealized marriage, no parental guidance; the relationship ran its course inside the complex and sometimes brutal world of young, single professionals. This case also has an extra wrinkle, for in it one partner appeared to be addicted while the other did not. It is actually a case where two contrasting and conflicting personal styles interacted so as to produce a surprisingly tenacious mutual dependency.

We get a glimpse of this relationship in a story told by another couple about a trip they took with Carl and Shelley and a fifth person. "It had been snowing between here and Montreal, so we took our jeep, which has two seats in front and a bench seat in back. You can squeeze three people into that rear seat, but it's very uncomfortable. We were the only two who could drive the jeep, so we worked the seating like this: Whichever one of the two of us wasn't driving sat in back. The other three passengers took turns sitting beside the driver where they could spread out a bit. Except for Shelley, that is. She always gave up her turn in front so she could stay with Carl in back. She did this throughout the 800-mile round trip, even though Carl took every chance *he* could get to sit up front, and she never said anything to him about it."

Who were this couple, and why did they act that way? Carl was a young doctor who came to New York to do his internship. When he arrived he called all the women he knew around New York, as was his custom upon reaching any new locale. Among these women was Shelley, whom Carl had met briefly on a previous visit to the city. He didn't feel a special attraction to her, but when some of his other contacts didn't turn out, he arranged to see Shelley again. She was living outside the city in a semirural house with several other women. Carl had a pleasant time there and so he continued to get together with Shelley, either by driving up to her house or having her take the train down to the city.

Carl welcomed these relaxing interludes very much. As an intern, he was immersed in hospital work for days—and even weeks—at a time. After such a stretch, he found it irresistible to drive up to Shelley's place and unwind. He enjoyed the countryside, Shelley's home, the meals she made for him, and the pleasures of sex and company that she provided. Although Carl considered himself something of a swinger, in the period since he had come to New York he had had difficulty meeting other women, given the demands of his schedule. So he naturally fell more deeply into this relationship. Shelley, meanwhile, could see Carl whenever and for however long he was free, because her job as a commercial artist allowed her to make her own hours. Carl could count on her always being glad to see him, and he could make plans with her at a moment's notice. She didn't seem to have much else on tap. She certainly didn't seem to be very interested in the other women with whom she lived; in fact, she usually complained about them to Carl during his visits, and kept her distance from them while he was there.

If Carl had thought about it, he might have been surprised that he could have such complete access to an established professional of Shelley's age. But Shelley's background was unusual for a woman in her position. Starting as a young bride, she quickly became a mother and then a widow—all before she was twenty-five. At that age she suffered a breakdown. After her parents took her child in, Shelley began to build a career. Socially, though, she repeatedly sought out men she could cling to. One such attachment had just ended when she met Carl.

After a while, Carl became uneasy about the amount of time he was spending with Shelley, what with his grand designs on the female population of New York. He prepared Shelley for the lessened contact he foresaw by telling her that he didn't feel he could take as much time off to come up to see her, and that, anyway, he was a little uncomfortable in the strained atmosphere created by her housemates. On his next visit, Carl noticed that Shelley had packed all her belongings into boxes. When he asked her about this, he discovered that she had interpreted his comments as a request that she move into his apartment with him. Carl was shocked, but he didn't see any easy way out of his predicament. What's more, he reflected that it might be fun to have a companion in the city, and someone to provide him with the domestic comforts. So he dutifully took Shelley and her things back with him.

As Carl told everyone he knew—but mostly himself—this was not meant to be a permanent arrangement. He attempted to justify that claim by treating Shelley in an increasingly detached way. But he never made a move to end things. When his internship was completed and he entered his residency, his working hours became more nearly normal, so that he no longer had external constraints to blame for his plight. Whatever his long-range goals, he could not bring himself to take an action whose immediate impact would be to deprive him of something comfortable. Instead, he began to have secret affairs, principally with women he had known elsewhere who were stopping by in New York. These were compromised, though, by Carl's tendency to take up the women's time with complaints about Shelley. Given the trouble a woman had to go through to contact Carl—either calling when Shelley was away, or else pretending she was a cousin of his—the affairs amounted to little more than silly escapades. Shelley was suspicious of Carl's shenanigans over the phone and his late nights at the hospital, and at times she would become extremely angry. She couldn't muster a serious threat to walk out of this demeaning situation, however, because her discontent was so totally and patently that she wanted more of Carl, not less.

Each time Carl tried to make his position clear to Shelley, she insisted that he could not possibly feel as he said he did, and that his uninvolved stance was merely a pose. He, by not taking any action, and by (in effect) acknowledging the status of the relationship when he lied about his affairs, made her retorts sound reasonable. The relationship that existed in Carl's mind was entirely different from the one in Shelley's mind. Both partners stated their wishes in no uncertain terms, and both allowed themselves to believe that the other's acquiescence implied an acceptance of those terms, or at least a hope of eventual acceptance. Neither had much concern for how the other actually felt; they existed for each other mainly as objects to be manipulated (or imagined) into playing a desired role.

The frequent arguments between the two served no purpose, for no changes in behavior were ever made on either side. A remark of Shelley's during one of these confrontations nakedly revealed her addiction. "If you leave me now," she said, "then what was it all for?" She valued their time together not for the pleasures it had brought her, not for whatever intangible contribution it had made to her experience, but only insofar as it guaranteed her lover's continuing presence. In this respect, she was just like a heroin addict obsessed with making sure her next fix will be available when she wants it. The question we have to ask is whether—or how—Carl was really any different.

After two years, realizing that he would never be able to leave Shelley except by leaving New York (but not realizing what this implied about himself), Carl decided to finish his residency elsewhere, namely in Newport News, Virginia. He told friends that by going to the South he would be able to get away from Shelley. But Shelley—asserting herself in a way Carl had never seen before—pestered one of her business clients who had offices in Washington, D.C. until she finally got a job there. The couple drove South together. Shelley had made arrangements to move in with a friend in Washington, but as long as Carl remained there before continuing on to Virginia, she stayed with him in his hotel room.

When Carl finally left, Shelley's first reaction was to fall apart. Then she began to come across as sane and reasonable in her letters and phone calls to him, disarming any apprehensions he might have about her. She spoke about a new lover she was seeing in Washington—not to make Carl jealous, but to reassure him that she would no longer be an unpleasantness to him. Eventually he invited her to Virginia for a visit, an act he regretted from the moment of her arrival—a day early. The visit was full of tensions and willful misunderstandings about the nature of the relationship. Shelley was still asking a lot more of Carl than he was prepared to give. As for Shelley's new lover, he evidently did not yet figure prominently in her plans.

How can we make sense of this situation? Shelley was an addict in the classical sense. Though she was a sensitive, capable woman, she did not seem to derive any real satisfactions from her work. She did not make friends easily and did not enjoy very many people's company. Whatever new opportunities came to her as a mature person, her early marriage continued to set the pattern for her life. Like her husband and previous lovers, Carl functioned as a symbol of certainty, tying everything together for her. By being willing to sacrifice all other possible connections and commitments in order to preserve—or invent—this sure focus for her existence, she became that much more needful of a crutch in order to live. Carl had become Shelley's only world, one which at least had an immediate, superficial reality while they were living together, but which was becoming increasingly flimsy.

Carl's addiction was more puzzling, for he was outwardly adventurous and good-natured and seemingly a self-assured person. He had a strong feeling for the prerogatives enjoyed by a young professional, and for the independent life that was open to him. But he couldn't come to grips with himself or organize his life in any larger sense. When any complicated personal emotions were introduced into his scheme of things, requiring him to establish his basic preferences, he had no idea of how to react. He became passive and showed an almost pathological tendency to vacillate. Unsure just what intimate relationships were all about, he took a detached approach to his life and to other people. Since he could not give his involvements a solid grounding, only a woman who was prepared, however perversely, to cling to him no matter what could form a lasting tie with him.

Carl's actions, in fact, made no more sense than did Shelley's. Very few men, feeling as he said he did, would have kept playing her game for so long. He could present himself as a calculating male who was using Shelley as a convenience, at the same time that he maintained the relationship long after it supposedly became burdensome to him. Or he could take the opposite line and say that he couldn't bring himself to hurt Shelley by cutting things off, while he was hurting her far more by permitting her to evade reality and thus not discover whether she could sink or swim on her own.

For all his savoir faire, Carl was adrift. A woman who saw to his superficial wants could make him feel as if he were being looked after in deeper ways—something he desired but was incapable of bringing about genuinely. Because he was so out of touch with real emotions in himself or others, he could only form a long-term relationship with a person like Shelley who bestowed affection without regard to whether or not it was mutual. Thus he needed her as much as she needed him. Whenever the desire for emotional security becomes primary over all else, for whatever reason, addiction sets in. And someone who consistently gratifies an addict's needs generally shows some matching weakness or uncertainty. Carl, too, was an addict. A month after the visit from Shelley which so annoyed him, he came up to Washington to spend the Christmas holidays with her, rather than taking up a number of invitations to visit other parts of the country. Whatever his opinion of this woman, he couldn't do without her.

It is fitting that Shelley, who was the prime mover in creating a relationship out of Carl's essential passivity, was also the one who, in a final paroxysm of frustration, broke it off. Even as her visits to Carl continued, her new lover began to assume real proportions. Shelley tentatively held off his advances while implicitly asking Carl to make a decision to resolve the situation, in the hope that he would affirm his commitment. Carl, meanwhile, waited with increasingly ill-concealed relief for things to be settled by this outside agent. Unable to move Carl by this one last effort, Shelley stormed out on him one weekend, but not before discharging her long-standing rage in a physical attack on him. Now she has transferred the burden of her dependency to a new relationship, just as she did when she first met Carl. As for Carl, being in Washington without looking up Shelley is for him like being a newly reformed alcoholic who winces every time he passes a bar.

A NOTE ON ONE-SIDED ADDICTIONS

Carl's case should make us think twice about labeling as "one-sided" an addictive relationship that lasts any length of time. An addict demands so much from a partner that only a person who, at bottom, seeks the same reassurance the addict wants will conveniently meet these demands. The partner has to have some strong reason for satisfying or tolerating an addict, and that reason must go beyond the mere acceptance of the guilt the addict spreads around.

There are one-sided addictions. As all interpersonal addictions involve delusions, a one-sided addiction is based on outright fantasy. We all know of cases where, on the basis of a short acquaintanceship and some misunderstood signals, one person falls in love with another and imagines the feeling to be mutual. The infatuated lover then reconstructs his or her inner world to prepare a leading role for this new person, who in reality is no more a part of his life than a figure in a dream. More often than not, the object of these attentions is bewildered and uncomfortable to learn of the place he or she occupies in the lover's emotional life. Such fantasies break down when the loved object is asked to act out the role the lover has envisioned, and the addict's disillusionment is usually precipitous.

There are instances, though, where a fantasy relationship does go on for a time in reality, with one partner being addicted and seriously overestimating the other's commitment. For the nonaddicted partner, there may be motivations which temporarily cause him or her to agree to things he or she does not ultimately want in a relationship. Perhaps this person has been placed in a stressful or otherwise unfriendly situation—say through working in an unpleasant setting or coming to live in a strange city. The person might then have need for a clinging affair which does not really represent how he or she approaches life in calmer or more congenial circumstances. But this, by definition, would not be a permanent arrangement. Otherwise the person would be letting a transitory unhappiness create a long-term dependency, and would be letting negative motivations determine the basic course of his or her life: in short, he or she would be addicted. There are also special cases of one-sided addiction where the nonaddicted partner knowingly manipulates the addicted lover in order to gain some specific end, such as money, sex, or a way out of an unpleasant family situation. While this may not be an attractive way to approach relationships, it is not by itself an addiction.

A partial, temporary addiction can even be a constructive, though costly, stage in a person's development. Take Joan, who benefited from being part of an addiction. When Joan got her mas-

ter's degree in business administration, she faced with great trepidation the trauma of finding her first responsible position as an
adult. She had either been attending school or working at modest,
low-level jobs for most of her twenty-eight years. Somehow, as her
last year at school went by, she didn't get around to signing up for
interviews with the large companies which came to her school to
recruit. She claimed that she didn't want to work for an impersonal,
profit-oriented firm, but she also didn't take any steps on her own
to find a job with a different sort of business, or with organizations
in the public sector or the arts.

Complicating the choices confronting Joan was her relationship
with Seth, with whom she had been living for over a year while attending business school. Joan very badly wanted to move to the West
Coast, while Seth was committed to staying in Boston, where in
Joan's opinion he was mired down. This relationship was the longest
and most satisfying Joan had ever had with a man, at the same time
that it was tempestuous and often disquieting to her. Seth, who was
extremely possessive, made requests of Joan that were often self-
serving or irrational. He wasn't vicious, but he was persistent, and
more or less got what he wanted from Joan by acting hurt, or sulk-
ing, or just doing things for her. But he was dedicated to the relationship, at least as long as it could take place in Boston, and he was
genuine in his love and devotion for Joan.

This was important to Joan. Her father had been incapable of
showing affection, and thus she had never learned that she could
inspire emotional loyalty in a man. When she had begun seriously to
relate to men outside her home, she had found that her desires for
this kind of fulfillment were too strong and ruined her relationships.
Seth was the first man who reciprocated her emotional need in all its
depth, and she loved him for it. But at the same time, she saw the
limitations of such a connection and the costs that it, and Seth, were
exacting from her. She wanted to go out on her own as a self-sufficient professional, and she wanted to do it in the part of the
country where she most enjoyed living. Her relationship with Seth
would not permit her to do this.

As she wavered over these considerations, her inaction decided
the issue. She didn't get a job on the West Coast or anywhere else,
and so she continued to live with Seth, taking art classes, seeing

friends, and generally filling her time with the not unpleasant pursuits available to her in the city. But as the summer following her graduation turned to winter, and she thought about continuing this existence indefinitely, the gratifications it provided began to pale for her. This time she systematically set about finding a job doing the kind of work she wanted for an organization she respected, and in an area where she wanted to live. She was still uncertain about what she would actually choose when the time came, but she nonetheless made sure to provide herself with some choices. For his part, Seth just bided his time, not interfering or complaining, but keeping up the demands he made on Joan, and secretly feeling that she would not be able to leave him.

In March, Joan was informed by the Oakland Museum that the job of business manager was hers. Joan was ecstatic. For the first time, the real world had shown that it respected her and wanted her to become a part of it. This occurred at a time when she also had been feeling better about the value she had within her relationship—as though Seth's long-standing affection had finally impressed on her that she was a lovable person. Yet the source of these good feelings, Seth, was indicating more and more clearly how strong his own needs were, and how they could not be met either by Joan's leaving him or by his leaving his secure job to follow her to California. The quandary was an agonizing one. Seth was no help in Joan's deliberations, as he remained aloof, stating simply that if she loved him, there would be no question of what choice to make. Finally, Joan decided to take the job.

She left Seth that summer, after two years of sharing her life with him, feeling freer and braver than she had ever felt. She also left with sadness. Seth had given her something that she had always wanted and had never before possessed. But with it came other emotional encumbrances that Joan could not in good faith accept. Seth's caring had created part of the psychological basis of her being able to leave him, and the paradox troubled her deeply. But she was also a person who had to grow, and with a true reverence for what they had had together, she left Seth. For the next couple of years they exchanged visits as lovers and friends. These visits became less frequent, and eventually Seth found another mate and informed Joan that he was going to marry this woman. Joan was relieved. Although she retained her warm feelings toward Seth, she was also extremely ambivalent toward him because of the way she had behaved around him in the past. She could not tell him this, however, as long as it would hurt him. Now she could congratulate him on his upcoming marriage, sincerely reaffirm her commitment to him as a lifelong friend, and turn at last to face the rest of her life fully and with eagerness.

Joan had addictive tendencies, but she was not an addict. While her relationship with Seth may have been a real addiction for a time, she sacrificed it for a broader notion of what was good for her emotional life and, perhaps, Seth's as well. In doing this, Joan had to confront very real aspects of herself—her feelings ran deep in both directions. This is why what she did cannot be labeled an expediency, even though she gained something from the relationship which caused her to leave it behind. The genuineness of her feelings toward this involvement, which enabled her to leap into an exciting and growing existence, also made it conceivable that she could be an addict. It was just that she came to base her life on feelings of joy, confidence, and love for herself rather than the feelings of pity, guilt, fear, and disrespect that were also within her.

Addiction is not based on calculated expediency. Rather it is rooted in an existential pain that is deeper than any calculations about sex or money or a need to make up for one's unattractiveness or low social standing. However, poverty, lack of career opportunities, or a bad home environment are closely tied up with addiction. If a person's life is strongly affected by these things, they can contribute to the overall sense of despair that leads to addiction. Thus a dependency based on bad objective circumstances can shade into addiction, so that there is no point in trying to tell them apart. Sometimes, though, we can distinguish between them in the disparate reasons two people can have for coming together.

Bea, for example, lived under a brutal, unpleasant regime in her parents' home, where she remained trapped by her lack of skills and education, along with her limited vision of the paths open to her. Unwilling or afraid to make the sacrifices involved in going out on her own, Bea met a well-to-do restaurateur and discerned that he was lacking something she could give him. For all his accomplishments, Mel did not take himself seriously as a man. By responding to him more fully than he would ever have hoped for, Bea won a proposal of marriage, which she welcomed even though she found Mel old-fashioned and not particularly attractive. In one stroke, she got away from her parents while gaining their approval. Her marriage supplied what she had always wanted—a degree of comfort and the freedom to spend her time as she wished. Bea merely chose what she felt to be the best of a limited set of options in life, and if she ever leaves Mel, that, too, will probably be a strictly pragmatic move.

Mel relies on the relationship for something more basic than does Bea. Thus, he is more truly addicted. The relationship is potentially volatile, in that either party could defect if they found a better way to satisfy their needs. But although Mel recognizes at some level Bea's grasping nature, it would take much more for him to call it quits than for her, because his need is less a function of external circumstance. Bea's lack of genuineness in the relationship is something she is not prepared to acknowledge fully to herself, let alone to Mel. This is not love on her part, but neither is it addiction. For Bea has a better understanding of the relationship than Mel does, and her compromise with life doesn't reach down to her soul.

For all their differences, what the couples in this chapter have in common is that they were driven to addictive relationships by family and other background factors. These factors are key points in the stories of all the individuals involved. If we want to understand why they and other people become addicted, we must turn, then, to the family patterns and the farther-reaching cultural influences that prevail in an addicted society.

The way they shut their doors, these married people, and shut themselves into their own exclusive alliance with each other, even in love, disgusted him. It was a whole community of mistrustful couples insulated in private houses or private rooms, always in couples, and no further life, no further immediate, no disinterested relationship admitted: a kaleidoscope of couples, disjoined, separatist, meaningless entities of married couples. —D. H. LAWRENCE, *Women in Love*

6

Growing Up Addicted

Let us take a closer look at Allen and Gail, who staked several years of their lives on a relationship that joined only their external selves. We have seen how this marriage shook beneath the surface, how it soon came apart. But why did it come about in the first place? Gail and Allen were attractive, physically and mentally able individuals. Why, then, did they feel pressed to commit themselves so precipitously to such an imperfect union?

Gail and Allen in a sense formed a father-daughter relationship so that they could play within their marriage the roles of assertive male and adored female which were denied them within their own families. But such standard psychoanalytic interpretations only go so far. Gail undoubtedly would trace her insecurities to the trauma of her parents' death and her uneasy position within a family where—however warmly she was welcomed—her cousin always knew the surest routes to her aunt's approval. Yet the cousin herself, with all the benefits of her real parents' love and a continuity of upbringing, brought no internal direction to the shifting social atmosphere which she entered when she left home. Her extreme changeability be-

115

trayed a search for security that was even more frantic than Gail's.

It would seem that childhood traumas such as death and divorce are not the sole or principal cause of addiction. Children from broken homes do not necessarily become addicts, and, as Allen shows, children can just as easily have severe difficulties when their homes are not disrupted by death—or divorce. Allen faced considerable emotional pressure from being expected to meet his father's standards and match his brother's achievements. These insecurities, too, were apparently not the root of his problems. For his brother, like Gail's cousin, ultimately gained little from his favored position in the family. A standout performer in every way up to his graduation with honors from law school, the brother lost his momentum and entered adulthood feeling as uncertain and pessimistic as did Allen. He never practiced law, but instead returned to school to study physics in a desultory manner. In fact, it turned out that *he* envied *Allen's* intellectual abilities. After marrying a beautiful and gracious woman, he was divorced at the age of thirty and started drinking heavily. He, too, has proved susceptible to addiction.

If anything, the resemblances between Gail and her cousin and between Allen and his brother are more striking than the differences, and these consistencies express the styles of their respective households. The two girls' instability reflects that family's uncertain social standing and the aunt's fearful propriety. The two brothers' fatalism, combined with their forced march toward academic and other achievements, is in keeping with the stuffy, yet cynical decorum under which they were raised. These instances and others like them strongly suggest that special circumstances like sibling rivalries, differential treatment by parents, and broken homes are not all that influential in shaping those aspects of children's personalities that are relevant to addiction. More important are the constants— the attitudes, beliefs, and orientations that are transmitted to all the children within a given family.

Furthermore, the attitudes which create addiction are not usually even specific to individual families, but stem in large part from broader cultural moods and predilections. In the home which produced stable children like Allen and his brother and the home which produced unstable children like Gail and her cousin, we can discern common elements of self-doubt, anxiety, and smoldering discontent on the part of the parents. The breadwinners' careers in both cases were frustrated for their entire working lives by circumstances beyond their control. The two mothers had no choice but to be housewives, despite their considerable personal resources—in Allen's mother, the intelligence she transmitted to her two boys; and in Gail's aunt, the sense of responsibility and the strength that enabled her to hold a large family together.

Perhaps owing to such forced narrowing of larger aspirations and talents, these were nervous people who insisted on keeping strict control of their homes, allowing little voice to their children. If Allen and his brother procrastinated indefinitely over both large and small moves, they did so under the remembered weight of their parents' insistence that every little thing in the house be in its place at all times. When Gail's uncle taught her to drive, he would lecture her condescendingly, and would take control of the car at the sight of a pedestrian crossing the road anywhere on the block ahead. His final instruction to her after she somehow got her license was that she should never drive the car more than ten miles alone. Worst of all, this protection cum harrassment continued past the age when Allen and Gail should have formed some independent judgment. In their parents' eyes, it seemed, they never ceased to be children.

As a result, they never developed into fully competent people— not even as competent, say, as their parents were beneath their neuroses. This was especially true of Gail, who seemed perpetually in a state of upset. Her jitteriness and her appeals for verbal reassurance may well have been less an expression of a need for love than of helplessness and a lack of confidence in herself. Considering that she married at a time when she hadn't established a personal identity, it is significant that she was later surprised when other people found her appealing and sought her out. She had been systematically taught at home to underestimate her own capacities. At Eugene Gail came to think differently about herself, but by then her marriage, and perhaps her basic personality, had already been formed.

Allen, too, was deeply affected by his parents' forebodings. Although he was mechanically adept, he always hesitated for weeks before tackling a broken household appliance. Then, as he worked on it, he would oscillate between claiming that the repair was as good as done and swearing that it would be impossible. Under the confident air he displayed to Gail was a deep strain of confusion and volatility. The same spirit characterized the couple's life together after their marriage. While Allen maintained order by restricting the scope of their activities, an uncertainty which approached hysteria was always threatening to erupt. During the two years they drove Allen's father's old car, they swore one week that he had been a fool to give such a good car away, the next week that it was about to fall apart. In their personal lives they seemed equally eager to declare things settled, and equally unsure that they were justified in doing so.

At their wedding, the minister repeatedly referred to the bride and groom as "children." He seemed to direct his remarks to their parents, who had given him his instructions and made all the wedding arrangements. Had the parents actually arranged the wedding in a larger sense as well? Initially, both sides had opposed the marriage, precisely because Gail and Allen were so young and inexperienced. But their opposition took the form of testing the strength of the young people's feeling for each other by seeing whether they would persist in their plans in the face of obstacles. Gail's aunt did not want her niece to have an intimate relationship with a man unless he was to be the man who took her out of the house forever. Friendships and varied experiences with men were not goals that the aunt valued, and so they weren't tolerated in Gail's life.

Nor were they encouraged by Gail and Allen's social milieu generally. The marriage was brought about by the couple's acquiescence in a widely held outlook about marriage, an outlook fostered by parents, peers, and circumstances. For Gail and Allen, marriage was the only proper state of being for an adult—the only alternative to intolerable conditions of personal isolation and parental domination and the most decisive way to bolster one's ego and complete one's identity. Allen was driven to marriage by the alienation which warped his relationships with other men, made real friendship impossible, and created a longing for some form of human closeness. Gail, having no avenues of independent activity open to her, had to attach herself to someone else to attain the intellectual standing she sought. In her approach to Allen, she was able to draw upon traditional models of feminine behavior—accentuating her helplessness, throwing herself at his mercy, appealing to his better nature. In offering him this commanding, masculine role in her life, she unknowingly appealed to his insufficiencies.

Interpersonal addiction would not be so "normal" were it not reinforced by the very nature of family life and life in society. Allen and Gail's upbringing left them, as it left many of their contemporaries, with a lack of self-integration and a lack of ability to handle their environment. What's more, it did not give them a chance to strengthen themselves through friendly and loving relationships with other human beings. When they looked around for relief from their oppressive aloneness and uncertainty, they saw that society offered them one escape, its rightness and propriety affirmed in every way—an exclusive love affair leading to marriage. It took years of self-deception and additional years of pain before they learned to confront their situations in more essential ways.

BACKDROP TO AN ADDICTED GENERATION

As the case of Allen and Gail illustrates, the families and the social settings in which we grow up have a lot to do with whether or not we become interpersonal addicts. The process works in two ways. Growing up without a sense of self-assurance and self-sufficiency, we become liable to addiction in any form. And the overemphasis placed on close ties with a few individuals, together with the unavailability of other avenues for making contact with people and things, causes love, marriage, and family to be the most likely objects of our addiction.

Consider the kind of family that produced Allen and Gail as well as most of the other addicted lovers whose stories are told in this book—the middle-class American family of the mid-twentieth century and the post-World War II period. This family usually consists of two parents and from one to three children, separated from other people including even close relatives. The isolation of the nuclear family has grown wherever the industrial age has left its mark, but it has never before been so extreme as in mid-twentieth-century America. For whatever reasons (affluence, a philosophy of personal independence, plenty of room to move around in), individual families have had less sustained contact with each other in America than elsewhere. In European countries there are well-established social forms for bringing people together, such as the cafe and the pub, but the average American family has looked out at the world increasingly from the vantage points of its own house and car.

After World War II, the mobility traditional in America took on a new form. Nationwide corporations began shifting personnel as efficiency dictated. A child might make friends at school and in the neighborhood only to lose them all at once when the father was transferred. The only people the child didn't leave behind were his or her parents, and brothers or sisters. The child of this era grew up in a world very different from the one his parents had known when they were young. The biggest difference for him was that the extended family did not have a place in his life. It used to be that a household was more than just parents and children. There might also be grandparents, aunts and uncles, and cousins around.

The extended family and the community of which it was a part had been a very handy thing in an earlier period. One did not have to face the same few people all the time, so that if the emotional going got rough, a child, or an adult, could turn to some peripheral figure in the family or neighborhood for love, consolation, and the particular wisdom that came from that person's experience. Growing up amid the clash of a number of very different personalities—some of them, perhaps, even unusual or bizarre—a child got a more rounded picture of human nature, and thus had a chance to learn that his parents' idiosyncrasies were not all there was to human conduct. The child was often out of his parents' sight, either being supervised by an aunt, say, or left to the free give-and-take with brothers, sisters, cousins, and friends of all ages. But in the modern nuclear family setup the child came under the continual surveillance of his parents. This intrusive attention undoubtedly kept many children from learning to solve problems and get things done on their own. In place of these abilities, though, it gave them a feeling of being at the center of someone else's world—an experience they were likely to look for again.

In the mid-twentieth century, parents were almost the sole figures of importance to a child. Who, then, were these people, and what past and present conditions were they reacting to as they brought up their children? To begin with, they were two people who interacted with each other very intensely, though not always peace-fully or constructively. Often, with the social pressures they were under, they had not had the luxury of searching out a suitable mate. Only now they did not have behind them the extended family, which traditionally served to take the strain off a marriage, especially at the outset. Yoked to each other in some cases practically by accident, husband and wife found themselves alone together in the world, and that could be scary. Whether the husband ran a small business with his wife's help, or whether he came home to her from a day of coldly impersonal contacts at an outside job, they had to find in each other all the warmth and support they were going to receive.

This man and woman were not likely to be tuned into the niceties of personal relationships; they had more pressing things to worry about. Thus, they carried many unresolved and unrecognized emo-tional problems with them into marriage and childrearing. Still it was paramount that they be able to count on a basic emotional, moral, and practical support from each other, even if they started out with very different habits and preferences. So they hammered themselves into the mold of a harmonious team. On the one hand, they sacrificed much that they individually held dear for the sake of the marriage or the children. On the other, they released their con-tained but unrelinquished desires by sniping at each other when their daily lives brought them too much strain.

Historical circumstances, too, had contributed to the discomfort of these people (some of whom were especially vulnerable as im-migrants or the children of immigrants). All of them, as young adults or as children, had felt the effects of the Depression, whether materially or psychologically. The Depression taught them that whatever they did, they could not determine their own economic fu-ture. Always they would be at the mercy of an impersonal and seem-ingly malevolent marketplace. Even if they were not directly threat-ened with being without food or shelter, they would never again be able to feel secure about their economic standing. When one thinks of the schoolteacher I once heard describe how he had qualified for his position in the 1930s, one can appreciate the stress on people as their plans for a career were thrown completely out of kilter. This man had been among 300 applicants competing for five jobs in a citywide examination. "I studied my guts out for weeks," he said, "and finished seventh. Afterward they opened up two more jobs, and I got in." That was how hard he had to fight to get into public school teaching at that time, and his success in that one examination put him in a place where he stayed for the rest of his working life.

On the heels of the Depression came the dislocations of World War II, and in the wake of the war came an accelerated growth in technology, especially household technology. Already people had found their work restricted by an institutional environment. Either they worked for a large organization, or, if they owned a business, it was usually on the order of a retail store, with a fixed place in the scheme of things and a limited potential for growth. Beyond this, their home life was being transformed by the mechanical age which had grown faster than any untrained individual could keep pace with. As central as the car was in America, James Flink in *America Adopts the Automobile* indicates that most people—especially in the cities—were not able to fix their own. When the washing machine, television, and all the home gadgetry of the postwar era appeared, people were already accustomed to depending on machines whose workings they did not understand. They had grown used to calling on expert technicians for mechanical repairs.

This reliance on expert authority was present even in something as personal as childrearing. Pediatricians and manuals were consulted in place of the grandparents who were no longer around the house. A baby's fever could be frightening to a mother when *her* mother wasn't there to say, "Oh, that's just a little upset. Let it take its course." Lacking such a voice of experience, the mother would naturally turn to a doctor, or a book. A sign of both the breakdown of the extended family and the triumph of the technological outlook was the extraordinary popularity of Dr. Spock's *Baby and Child Care*, which came out right after World War II. While Dr. Spock was a sound and a fairly sensitive adviser (things could have been a lot worse), the vacuum that was there for him to fill signified that the family's own resources were no longer adequate to the demands made on them. In a slightly later era, regular visits to a pediatrician would be de rigueur for obtaining the information and reassurance that used to be provided by grandmothers.

This new generation of parents was expressing its uneasiness about a world which seemed forever beyond its mastery. Out of this feeling came the vast, intangible fear which has characterized our age—anxiety; or, in Franklin Roosevelt's phrase, "nameless, unreasoning, unjustified terror." Since people didn't know what they were afraid of, they couldn't do anything concrete to allay their fear. Once they had checked the gas to make sure that it had been turned off, there was nothing functional left for them to do. But they still worried, and to assuage this feeling they fussed endlessly about matters over which they had no control, or where they had already done everything possible. Is the gas leaking? Did we leave an electrical appliance on? Will the car start this morning? And to their children: Did you remember to bring everything you need? Don't run around the block at night!

Chein found that adolescent heroin addicts were taught by their parents to feel an excessive concern with the dangers of life. Yet parents in the mainstream of society often communicated this same sort of anxiety, both through the way they handled everyday household problems, and through their direct admonitions. What permitted the parents to transmit their worries so freely? For one thing, in dealing with their children they reacted reflexively, driven by their own emotional imperatives; they couldn't help themselves. At the same time, they really cared about their children and wanted to prepare them for life's pitfalls as they saw them. Finally, a child gave them their only chance for exerting control in an otherwise chaotic world. Here was the one person and one place where they thought they should be in charge. Indeed, the frustrations they experienced elsewhere only fueled their irrationality at home, where they could express fears and demands with a lack of restraint that was not allowed them anywhere else.

The worldview children got from their families was one in which the comfort and security to be found in the nuclear family was sharply contrasted with the turmoil lurking outside it. The optimistic, confident spirit of the early industrial age had been replaced with an almost primitive, superstitious attitude toward technological and bureaucratic power. It was necessary to propitiate such forces, so that they would not harm you. In this swirl of suspicion and mistrust, the family was seen as a garrison, requiring strict loyalty and giving in return a safe haven. With most other people out to cheat you, it was vital to support family members in any potential conflict.

Family secrets were to be protected, for if any sign of weakness or instability leaked out, the information could be used against you. Both material and spiritual resources had to be hoarded.

For the children, at least in their early years, the sealing off of the home strictly limited what sense they could make of things on their own. They had to accept what their parents said and did as reasonable, because that was all they saw, all they heard, all they knew. This resulted in part from the parents' reluctance to let them out of sight to explore the world on their own, because then the children might not always be safe, or might grow and change unpredictably. In other words, the uncertainty which was so disconcerting to the parents might come at them from their children's direction, and that would be intolerable. To prevent this, parents often minutely directed a child's life, not realizing the danger of letting a young child's own judgment die stillborn.

AN ANXIOUS PARENT

Imagine the following scenario, which combines a number of the elements of childrearing which we have analyzed. Alice was a bookkeeper at a large downtown office in the early 1960s. Every day, precisely at 3:30 P.M., there was a phone call for her. It was from her ten-year-old son, informing her that he was home from school on time. She would make some quick inquiries—"did you talk to the teacher," "did you begin your homework," "did you buy the milk"—and give him instructions—"it's too dark to go out to play," "Bill's mother is busy so don't visit Bill," "stay away from the furnace. . . ." While scolding the child for taking up too much of her time, Alice still tried to deal with every contingency that might arise for him in the two hours before she got home. If he did not call, she put her work aside and frantically dialed people all over the neighborhood to track him down. Her tone of voice on the phone was generally overwrought, and she often communicated a sense of panic to her son, who would begin to cry out of fright while they spoke. Or he might cry because Alice's strictures seemed unfair, and he wanted to do something else. In those cases, Alice lowered her voice to a penetrating hush, and hissed, "Don't cry. I told you not to cry. You're making a fuss. I'm hanging up now, and I'll be home early. I'll talk to you then."

Often, the boy called back to apologize, and sometimes the entire scene would be repeated. Or he might call throughout the rest of the afternoon because he was lonely, or because he wanted more detailed advice from his mother about how to handle some problem in the house. Worried that the child was too "high-strung," Alice took him to a psychologist. Sometimes she reported to her co-workers what she and the psychologist had decided about him: "He is just too dependent. I try to get him to do things on his own, but he simply won't." Alice also expressed her frustration that having a child to support kept her at a job far below her capacities, although she had been in hot water at work because her attention was so often turned to her son.

In bringing up a child alone, Alice was faced with a difficult situation—one society doesn't make any easier. But her hysterical responses stemmed from her own problems in coping. Although she genuinely wanted what was best for her child, what she gave him mostly were her self-doubts and worries. Placing no check on the expression of her neurotic feelings, she molded his life in line with her anxieties. Her overprotectiveness, self-sacrifice, and resentment were reactions to incapacities and frustrations that she felt, and had nothing to do with what he needed. Their life together had no organization other than her neurosis.

The irrationality and self-defeat implicit in this closed system were in evidence every day at Alice's home. In order to have some peace and relaxation after a hard day's work, Alice put the boy to bed unusually early, which only meant that he was up earlier to bother her in the morning. She had told him "a million times" to play in his room with the door closed before she got up, but he seemed incapable of following that simple instruction. Instead, he carelessly left the door open, and as soon as Alice was awakened by his voice and movements she rushed in. Yet she was so little in command of herself that instead of straightforwardly telling him he was being inconsiderate, she smothered him with intrusive supervision. Even though she had announced that she didn't want to be bothered, as soon as she faced her son's actual living presence she immediately fell under the sway of her motherly impulses.

As for the boy, he seemed unable to learn a simple chain of cause-and-effect reasoning which would have told him how he could spare himself this constant, unpleasant carping. Or else his mother had already made him so dependent on her useless directions that he preferred hearing them to playing by himself. Alice's own dependency was based on her need to compensate for the undeveloped state of the rest of her life. She used her son to rationalize why she was not doing things that were feasible for her and that she wanted to do, such as taking night courses in painting, or, more crucially, finding a better job or way of life. In return, she taught him dependence, perhaps for life.

Whether a child like Alice's can grow up to be other than an addict depends on whether his later experiences can get beyond his mental and spiritual confusion and give him solid reserves of knowledge and strength. But the pattern of dependency which has been established in the child will take a lot of additional, constructive experience to break. For the patterned way of reacting to events that he has learned has a way of reinforcing itself. Just as parents create an image of the world for a child that matches what they see, so, too, may the child keep that image alive in his mind. The question is to what extent a different vision can intrude. For at least a general answer, we will trace what happens when children emerge from the house, go to school, meet friends and lovers, and become adults.

HOME, SCHOOL, AND THE OUTSIDE WORLD

The film *Lovers and Other Strangers* featured an exaggerated portrayal of a middle-aged Italian-American couple. "Who's happy?" they replied whenever their adult children expressed their discontents. To parents like these, life was a rough-and-tumble holding action, not a joyous affirmation. They did not seek adventure themselves, or encourage their children to sally fearlessly into the world. Rather they exhorted children to proceed eagerly, but cautiously, along the established channels for advancement in life. Success was to be gained in an orderly and circumspect manner, by advancing in school and other organizations, making connections, and not offending those who passed judgment on one's progress. Money was valued, but not as a means to influence society or to facilitate personal adventures. No, money was sought primarily for security—as the most substantial cushion against a dangerous world.

Perhaps the biggest lesson children learned from their parents was to avoid taking risks wherever possible. This had important consequences for the way these children developed, since a willingness to take calculated risks is essential for a person to be psychologically motivated to achieve. According to David McClelland and John Atkinson's theory of achievement motivation, a high achiever derives satisfaction from accomplishing a realistic goal, one which is challenging but feasible. Moving on to progressively harder tasks, he or she accepts a degree of uncertainty at each new level of difficulty. But a person whose need for achievement is submerged by fear of failure will instead attempt an impossible feat, so as to take the sting out of the failure he anticipates, or will stick to a sure thing, so as not to have the slightest chance of failing.

America traditionally was what McClelland calls an "achieving society." The twentieth century, however, has allowed less and less room for the independence and challenge on which the high achiever thrives. By the time the Horatio Alger stories came out, their inspirational message was already obsolete. Achievement motivation has declined since the turn of the century, and the motive to avoid failure has been on the rise. The parental attitudes that accompanied these developments have been documented by Daniel Miller and Guy Swanson in *The Changing American Parent.* Instead of teaching their children to go out and build something, post-World War II parents told them to "get along," and not "rock the boat." This going along with others was associated not with benign feelings toward them so much as with alienation and mistrust.

Of course, as children grew older, they spent more time away from home. But all too often they reacted to their experiences in new settings—school, in particular—with the guardedness they were taught at home. As Jules Henry has observed in *Culture Against Man,* children were primed to regard their classmates as competitors who should not be given too much assistance lest they gain an advantage. They were also taught an exaggerated respect for authority, as symbolized by the teacher. One's own judgment counted for little against what "the teacher said." The documentary film *High School* shows a father conferring with his daughter's teacher in the child's presence. He talks about her as though she weren't there, assuming as a matter of course that she is wrong and in need of correction, and that the teacher knows how she should act.

If a conflict arose between respect for authority and a child's self-respect, authority usually won out, no matter how obviously the child had been wronged. Consider the recommendations Haim Ginott gives in *Between Parent and Child,* one of America's most popular works of child psychology, for dealing with a ten-year-old boy's upset over an incident in school:

> Ten-year-old Harold came home cranky and complaining.
> Harold: What a miserable life! The teacher called me a liar, just because I told her that I forgot the homework. And she yelled. My goodness, did she yell! She said she'll write you a note.
> Mother: You had a very rough day.
> Harold: You can say that again.
> Mother: It must have been terribly embarrassing to be called a liar in front of the whole class.
> Harold: It sure was.
> Mother: I bet inside yourself you wished her a few things!
> Harold: Oh, yes! But how did you know?
> Mother: That's what we usually do when someone hurts us.
> Harold: That's a relief.

Here Ginott recommends the same platitudes to a mother that he offers her for dealing with a less consequential problem (e.g., when rain keeps a child indoors), where they may serve some purpose by allowing the child to vent his feelings. But in this story, Harold either has been unjustly accused, or, even if he did not tell the truth, has been subjected to a public humiliation that goes far beyond what his crime deserves. It would seem as though Harold's anger should be supported in some way by his mother, and that the two of them should take steps to make sure that he is treated more fairly and humanely in the future. Instead, Harold's mother gently brings him around to a self-examination which will enable him to defuse his bitterness and to accept the treatment that provoked it.

Beneath Ginott's up-to-date emphasis on expression of feelings and peaceful resolution of conflict, his underlying endorsement of submission and self-suppression bespeaks an attitude prevalent for some time now. Why has this been so? Why have parents wanted their children to subordinate themselves to institutional authority? We have to remember the special, talisman-like quality which school took on for the parents of the Depression era. To them, seeing their children properly educated was a way of making up for their own limitations and missed opportunities. If they themselves had never had a chance to go very far educationally, it was all the more important that their children not suffer from the same disadvantages. Later, parents carried on this heritage of deference to the sanctity of school. Teachers and school officials were powerful figures who held the key to something which parents prized so highly they could not be objective about it. There were parents who lived in perpetual fear that their docile middle-class children would "flunk out of school" or not get into college.

Most parents thus ended up undermining their own position. Although they really wanted their children to do well, the anxiety they expressed magnified the difficulties at hand and actually hurt the children's ability to perform. With schoolwork as with everything else, it was not uncommon for parents to adopt an accusatory tone that diminished a child's self-respect and self-sufficiency. They didn't want to disable their children; they were just giving a natural expression to their own feeling that life was no joke, and that you had to work hard and not mess around. Their denigration of their children came from their feeling that the children were too cocky because they hadn't taken their knocks yet, hadn't been cut down to size by the world the parents knew to be out there.

We have all heard parents harangue their children about homework:

> Fred, have you done your English paper?
>
> Well, I did well without working too long on the last one. I sort of work better . . .
>
> Never mind! You just think you did better on that last paper. You haven't gotten it back with the teacher's mark, have you? I'm not letting you go to the football game until you do it. You're never going to pass your exams and be accepted at the university at this rate.
>
> But, Dad, I told my friends I was coming this afternoon.
>
> Forget that. What's more important, this paper or a game?
>
> But I've got plenty of time to do it.
>
> You'll do it right now, and go to the game when you're done.

Fred's father is damaging his son's integrity and self-confidence, both by interfering with his commitments to other people and by throwing him off his natural stride for getting work done. In addition, Fred is being told that you can never be sure about the quality of what you are doing until it is certified by someone in authority. With training like this, he won't be able to assess coolly the requirements of a task in terms of his own ability and pace. Instead, he will look to someone else for direction from start to finish. Fred's father may have good reasons for being so excitable. What is irrational to us may make perfect sense in terms of his background. But that doesn't do Fred any good. His problem is to differentiate between unreasonable commands and his real needs, and to develop a view of himself that is impervious to his father's power to disrupt his activities. We see that Fred at least fights back. Somewhere within himself, he knows where things stand. If he can augment this side of himself as he grows up, he may develop a reasonable strategy for coping.

ADULTHOOD DENIED

The same parental and institutional regimes shaped life for Fred and his contemporaries when they reached adolescence. Old enough now to develop interests and initiate activities outside the home, they were cautioned not to do anything that might bring shame on themselves or their families. If they tried anything too offbeat, they faced chastisement from their parents along with ridicule that came from friends and schoolmates trained along the same lines as they were.

Even with adolescent children, many parents continued to have difficulty letting go emotionally, to the point where they treated their children as children long after such treatment became inappropriate. Here is what Ginott, in *Between Parent and Teenager,* considers a reasonable way of addressing a boy in his teens:

> Our response must differentiate between tolerance and sanction, between acceptance and approval. We tolerate much, but sanction little. . . .
> One father, irritated by his son's long hair said: "I'm sorry, son. It's your hair, but it's my guts. I can stand it after breakfast, but not before it. So, please have breakfast in your own room."
> This response was helpful. Father demonstrated respect for his own feelings. The son was left free to continue with his unpleasant but harmless revolt. . . .

It is questionable whether a man who speaks to someone else so disrespectfully is really respectful of his own feelings. What is certain is that his manner here is degrading to an emergent adult who is discovering his own style and identity. What is the youth himself to do? At his age, he may be able to reject his father's judgments as prejudiced. In their place, he can consult his own experience in order to evaluate himself and his actions.

One reason why it may be difficult for him to keep his bearings while under parental attack, however, is that the thoroughgoing respect for all authority which he has been taught does not disappear after childhood or adolescence. As a college student he will find it impossible to talk to professors naturally and on equal terms. Nearly all Americans today similarly show an outsized deference toward high government and business officials. This expansion of authority is symbolized by the evolution of the police from the ludicrously impotent Keystone Cops of 1910 to today's frightening specter of high-powered cars, searchlights, and ammunition. As for the disrespect attributed to student protestors of the 1960s, a number of radical leaders at that time confided to me that they felt uncomfortable standing up to college administrators. Indeed, the vaunted use of "pig" and other derogatory appellations when speaking directly to government and university officials was really very infrequent, especially when compared with the heckling considered normal and "within the system" at nineteenth-century political gatherings. It is odd that what was labeled as a growth of disregard for sanctioned authority was really just a feeble reaction against a relatively recent psychological bondage.

An awe of those in official positions goes with the doubting of one's own capacities. Young people who have been conditioned by their parents' nervous uneasiness can develop in one of two ways. Some, unable to separate the essential from the irrelevant, tune out their parents' warnings altogether and become unreliable and careless, unable to bear the thought of straining to accomplish anything. Other adolescents accept the warnings and rely on them in place of evaluating situations for themselves. When they no longer hear their parents' anxious remonstrances directly, they re-create them in their own minds. Their coping is a matter of constant vigilance: something can always go wrong without warning. The parents are forever a part of them, living within them. When parents request that an adolescent always call if he is going to be late getting in, they are tying him down spiritually even after he is physically autonomous. With the nagging thought of worried parents at the back of his mind, he can't think of losing himself for the evening, of having an affair, of taking a mad trip to New York. As his lips meet a woman's, he is overcome by the feeling that he should be making a phone call. Life is approached with grim concentration, and you don't take any shortcuts or scenic detours.

The adult who is produced by this training is left with a distorted approach to making decisions. Much of his behavior consists of ritualized worries or acts directed toward warding off some dreaded outcome which never materializes. Such neurotic behavior serves to reduce anxiety, at least momentarily. And because whatever the person fears does not in fact happen, he feels in some way that his compulsive reactions have helped him. Thus, he persists in them, irrational as they are. Equally irrational is his considering only the negative consequences that could come from a proposed course of action, such as changing jobs or trying to know someone. Ideally, one would take into account the likelihood of a positive or negative result, and then ask oneself how much one desires the positive result or wishes to avoid the negative. This would produce a balanced decision. But where initiative and risk are involved, it is all too common for a person to consider only the potential dangers, no matter how improbable or inconsequential. "Why take a chance?" is the credo he has learned. So he goes all his life missing experiences which he could easily obtain for himself, and which he is often delighted with when they are thrust upon him, as when he loses his job and is forced to look for a new and better one.

Take, for instance, the story of Nat, an ex-student who illustrates how the irresponsible and the overly responsible reactions to parental nagging and negativism merge. Nat thoroughly understood his father, an oppressively orderly man who had taken care to set himself up as early as possible with a job, a house, a wife, and even a car that he could keep for life. When Nat dropped out of college, he said something very poignant about his father's reaction. "My father is tremendously worried about what's going to happen to me," he said, "because he isn't sure what I'm going to do next. What my father really always wanted has been for me to hurry up and go through school, get a job, get married—and die." When I heard this story, I was struck by the truth in what Nat said. Just as the father had struggled to remove all uncertainty from his own existence, this man valued his son's experience only insofar as it served to nail the son down, and thus to eliminate any possible doubt for the father.

It was a tragic assessment of the older man, but what did it point to for Nat? Had his piercing insight into his father given him a better grip on his own life? Although, as the comment I quoted suggests, Nat was extremely gifted verbally, he never settled on a vocation. He always found his opportunities not sufficient to his tastes, thinking them laughable for their impurity and lack of meaning. Because all the careers he considered—and the people who filled them—were flawed in some way, Nat rejected entirely the possibility of fulfilling work. He made a few halfhearted attempts to establish himself away from home, but his unwillingness to put himself on the line, either with people or at some kind of work, always brought him back to his home town and reliance on his parents. By the time he reached his late twenties, he was left with nothing to fall back on but a disorderly version of his father's fearful, boxed-in existence.

THE MARRIAGE MATCH

So we enter upon adulthood—often anxious, wary of risk, vaguely distrustful of others, awed by powers outside ourselves, held back by external and internal constraints. To a greater or lesser extent, we are left in a weakened position psychologically, a position not different in kind from that of the addict. Where are we likely to find relief? The answer, for many, is in marriage.

Why has marriage been such a panacea for the postwar generations in America? Their childhood experiences taught them that only the family could enable them to feel comfortable and have some say over their surroundings. When their parents disrupted their plans with friends by insisting that they uphold family obligations, sometimes even imaginary ones, they learned that friendship came second to a more basic commitment. Their chances for developing strong friendships were hurt further when their parents taught them that people outside the house were not to be relied on. When a person is made to be cynical about "outsiders" and their intentions toward him, then only through the sanctioned ritual of marriage, with its legal provision for the sharing of property and its customary provision for the sharing of secrets, can he relax his caution to the point of trusting one other person.

The nuclear family in which today's young people grew up was a restrictive, inward-looking institution. Children observed that married couples spent all their free time together, that they went everywhere as one entity. For a husband or wife to have independent friendships and activities away from home would invite suspicion that the marriage was in trouble. Thus children sensed the boundaries clearly drawn around their families; economically, emotionally, sexually, that was where it was all supposed to be taking place.

All around them, children picked up prevailing attitudes about the primacy of social experience over personal experience. What they saw was that people are rarely secure in their own company, but always look for someone else to do things with. Even people who are interested in music or sports or movies usually don't find these interests so compelling as to be worth pursuing alone. Instead, they are preoccupied with the social considerations involved: who will they go with, who will they meet there, how will others react? Yet these social experiences, all-pervasive as they are, are not used to enrich a person's emotional life. They are screened through a filter of family solidarity and self-protection. Challenging new contacts—potential friendships—are ruled out, and the relationships that remain are most often casual and interchangeable. Deeper needs for human closeness can be channeled in one direction only.

Trained from an early age to look for one special person to share their lives with, young people direct the greatest part of their emotional energy toward finding this partner. High school and college life only reinforce this aim and confirm the artificial categories in terms of which people react to each other. With friends of the same sex, as well as those of the opposite sex who are not regarded as eligible partners (often because they are already attached to someone else), things go only so deep and no more. Friendships formed along the way to marriage serve as temporary measures, created out of convenience and exigency. A boy or girl can always cancel plans made long in advance with a friend in order to accept a last-minute date with someone of the opposite sex. And after a mate is found, friendships either disappear or become more superficial and limited than they were. Once settled down, a person might never again be alone with someone he or she formerly considered a close friend. So it is that in a society overly concerned with social relationships, genuine friendship is hard to come by.

But if people aren't serious enough about those individuals who are not available for mating, they are utterly preoccupied with those who are eligible mates. When boy looks at girl, or girl looks at boy, he or she sees not a unique human individual, but someone to fill a role, a potential husband or wife. This dehumanization is expressed in the social customs which keep men and women apart except in structured dating situations, and which block the natural mingling and person-to-person relating from which real experience may grow. Unable to involve oneself deeply with people of the same sex, one cannot really get to know people of the opposite sex. Instead, one sees the opposite sex as an abstract thing, as something needed to complete one's existence. In this objectification of other human beings lie the roots of addiction.

Some of the implications of this rigid classification of people into potential lovers and "others" appear in the case of two working women who roomed together. After having planned for some time to take an extended trip to Europe, they finally accumulated enough vacation time to do so. Suddenly, two weeks before they were scheduled to depart, one of them met a man and within days found herself engaged. With a speed that was shocking to her roommate and friend of many years' standing, she made daily announcements of old ties being cut and new plans being made to yoke her life to the man she had just encountered. The first casualty of this housecleaning was the trip with her roommate, who then had to readjust her vacation plans on short notice. What was so remarkable in this situation was that the woman who changed her plans so abruptly didn't for a moment stop to consider her friend's feelings. One can imagine different ways of handling the complexities of such a delicate situation, but to this woman society had given a clear-cut criterion: Men come first.

Society prescribes marriage as a cure for insecurity. "He'll be all right," they say, "once he finds somebody to settle down with." Studies by Floyd Martinson and by Nevitt Sanford have shown that people who marry early tend not to show full "ego-development." But more and more people are marrying early, and more and more of these marriages are ending in divorce, because the burden of meeting two people's entire range of emotional needs is too great for many marriages to bear. Even so, since people are marrying earlier and are more prone to remarry, Americans are spending more of their lives married now than ever before. In *Marriage and Divorce: A Social and Economic Study,* Hugh Carter and Paul Glick explain this seeming paradox:

> Marriage, as a way of life, is extraordinarily popular in the United States and appears to be growing more so. . . . So well accepted is marriage as the normal and approved status of maturity and adulthood that it seems probable that a considerable number of individuals who either are temperamentally unsuited to marriage or are incompatible with their prospective marital partners will nonetheless marry because it is "the thing to do." As a result, many of them will become separated for a while, and some of these separated persons will eventually become divorced.

Even among young people whose new cultural style supposedly repudiates the old stilted conception of dating, most appear to be carrying on in the same old way. It is true that young couples engage in sex more readily than did their precursors. But we should not expect such deeply ingrained cultural tenets as the significance attached to marriage—and sex—to be forgotten in a decade. Researchers have consistently found that sex on college campuses tends to be monogamous and is often associated with an ideal of eventual marriage. The psychologist Bernice Neugarten has noted that parents and children often differ little in their attitudes toward sex: the young people seem to suffer many of the same qualms and guilt about it that their parents felt, while the parents can accept their child's living with someone because this usually presages marriage. Greater sexual activity at a younger age in combination with conventional attitudes about sex can be found even in high school and junior high school, as shown in Robert Sorensen's book, *The Sorensen Report: Adolescent Sexuality in Contemporary America.*

So, ironically, while more sex is taking place, it seems that relationships are often more staid and confining than ever. Since sex is still usually rationalized by assuring oneself that one's lover is someone special, the pressures toward closing oneself off prematurely are actually increasing. In an atmosphere where people feel that they should be having sex, there is the constant danger that a casual affair may be turned into something far beyond what makes sense for the people involved, simply so that they can justify their behavior, mainly to themselves. The catalyst of sex can turn a first date into an exclusive and permanent relationship.

It used to be, at least, that people could date freely without such heavy implications automatically being attached. A guest at a recent wedding heard the bride's mother reminisce exuberantly about her own courting days. "My parents didn't let me go out with Harry unless I also went out with someone new that same week," she said. "So I always went out twice a week, and I had a whale of a time before I finally married Harry." The guest looked over at the bride, who, unlike her mother, had been living with her boyfriend for years before they were married at twenty-one. Also unlike her mother, she hadn't dated another man in all that time. She cut a pale figure next to the older woman. The greater self-determination that the daughter enjoyed had not brought with it a freer, more expansive social life. Attaching the same solemn meaning to sex that her mother had, she did not have external prods to prevent her from being tied down by that solemnity at the earliest possible moment. She also did not have the vitality to replace external constraint with self-generated energy, and the life she led was really extraordinarily conservative.

People who came of age after the sexual revolution supposedly transformed college life are no less subject to the pressure to couple than those who came before. Many of them, in fact, sweep themselves up into serious commitments at a more immature stage in life than they would previously have done. I think of the man and woman assigned to adjacent rooms in a coed dormitory who moved in with each other during their freshman year, never dated anyone else in college, married while seniors, and got divorced a year and a half after graduation. More commonly, a student immediately finds a boyfriend or girlfriend outside the dormitory, so as to be spared the challenge of getting to know a wide range of people of both sexes and choosing some among them to become close to. "I already have a girlfriend" serves as well as it ever did to excuse a person from interacting seriously with anyone else.

Once I went to a luncheon a friend of mine gave for a group of college students in his special summer seminar. I spoke to two personable women about how they were adjusting to life on the campus. They told me unself-consciously, "We're both living with lovers we met our first day here." I wondered that people could be casual or impersonal enough about intimate relationships to choose as a partner whoever was available on a given day, yet still be uptight enough to associate exclusively with this one partner. Somewhere at the back of these women's minds must have been the model of their parents fortifying themselves with a mate—choosing usually out of practical necessity, occasionally out of whim, rarely out of judgment and feeling. Changes in custom, I later thought, do not necessarily produce changes in consciousness. The sexual revolution brought about a degree of adaptation in behavior, but it couldn't be expected to liberate the spirits of an entire generation.

SIGNS FOR THE FUTURE

Now that so many addicted young people are themselves married, what will happen to the children they bring up? In the first place, we should observe that the hypothetical "post-World War II" family described in this chapter still exists, since no definite line marks off one generation from the next. Indeed, the survival of authoritarian assumptions about childrearing in so popular a modern counselor as Haim Ginott shows that many of the practices of the past extend into the present. The mid-twentieth-century family was the one that produced the addicts of our case histories. Now, under more palatable labels and with a more easygoing manner, many of the same attitudes toward living and relating are being transmitted.

It is true that since the forties and fifties there has been some evolution in parenthood. Many young parents express fewer overt neuroses than were the rule ten to thirty years ago, and place a greater emphasis on peaceful, harmonious relations within the family. In a time of greater affluence and higher educational levels, the young today pay more attention to their relationships generally, and, as parents, to their children's desires. However, there is a continuing pattern of addiction in young people, one which should make us cautious in attributing large significance to even the most attractive, well-intentioned changes in style. In Allen and Gail, in the young bride who shut herself off from experience much earlier than her mother had, in the students rushing to establish themselves securely with lovers on campus, we see evidence that people are still turning to each other out of the addictive need for security. Vicky's parents were understanding and nurturant in a way that many young couples aspire to be, yet also in a way that stifled their daughter's motivation to become a complete person in herself. Similarly, new parents today who are just as fearful as, though more temperate than, their own parents still pass on their fear to their children, in whom it will once again be a source of addiction. They do so because addictive tendencies are woven so very deeply into the fiber of our society.

Even entirely new social forms which strive to remedy the extreme insularity of conventional family life do not always serve to liberate the individual spirit. With communes or with single people living together on a semipermanent basis, self-protection can be the aim as easily as it can be with the nuclear family or sexual coupling. Roommates of the same sex may exclude others from their small society, and may lean on each other out of insecurity and a need for mutual support. Larger units of people, sometimes explicitly labeled families, can enable their members to lead asexual lives by effectively ruling out intense relationships between any member of the family and an outsider. A man who had dropped out of sight socially for a time met an old friend and invited him to the house he now lived in with a number of other very religious Christians. When asked how long he planned to stay with this group, he replied quite frankly, "Until I marry someone like us. For the present, this is the most secure setting I can find."

Countin' flowers on the wall
That don't bother me at all
Playin' solitaire till dawn
With a deck of fifty-one
Smokin' cigarettes and watchin' Captain Kangaroo
Now don't tell me
I've nothin' to do
—LEWIS DeWITT, *Flowers on the Wall*

7

The Addicted Society

A man with two teen-age daughters was fascinated and horrified by the Patricia Hearst story. He went around asking everyone he could, "What went wrong with that girl?" The paradox of Patricia Hearst has troubled many parents who worry that someday their children, too, may inexplicably turn on them. But the mystery surrounding this young woman is not impenetrable. Using the facts and impressions assembled by Andy Port and John Pascal of *Newsday* (in a syndicated series published in May 1974), we can look at the formative influences on her and at what she did when the direction of her life fell into her own hands.

Brought up in an atmosphere of "smothering overprotection," Patty Hearst was sent to a succession of strict Catholic girls' schools. The rules she was taught there were entirely external to her, so that she possessed no sure criteria of judgment. She was not experienced enough to know how she really felt about things. At times she seemed to recognize this lack, as when she took a clerical job "to do something different." Such gestures didn't have much substance, though, and she continued to organize her life around what were to her known quantities.

Chief among these was a young teacher, Steven Weed, whom she met at her school when she was sixteen. Weed immediately became the one factor Patty considered in every major decision she made. At the age of seventeen she enrolled at a small college in the town where Weed lived, and a year later she followed him to Berkeley. In her last year in high school, and still accountable to parents and teachers for the way she spent her time, she had been "an eager participant in several extracurricular activities." But the following year at Menlo College, where she was on her own, she "shunned the school's social life almost totally. With most of her time divided between schoolwork and Weed, Patty made few friends at Menlo."

Once at Berkeley, she and Weed single-mindedly drew a circle around themselves. "Patty was an extension of Steve and Steve of Patty," a friend recalled, adding that he saw one without the other only once in two years. Up to the time of Patty's abduction by the Symbionese Liberation Army, she and Steve were living a quietly hedonistic life, were still largely dependent financially on the Hearst family, and were preoccupied with their coming marriage. Patty herself was an unfocused undergraduate with no political inclinations, no compelling interests or philosophy, and no clear purpose for being in school. Her conversion, or "brainwashing," by the SLA was simply the substitution of one external structure for another, just as her conversion from family and school to a romantic-intellectual involvement with Weed had been.

Like other small, antisocial groups, the SLA was a world unto itself. The very fact of being fugitives from the law protected the group's members against contact with anyone who might challenge their beliefs. Interestingly, one of Patty's tapes reveals that a love affair with a man in the SLA was a catalyst for her acceptance of the group ideology. As always, she was molded by her immediate surroundings, whether or not she initially chose them for herself. This is the answer to that anxious father's question. Patricia Hearst had been prepared for the SLA by all the groups, institutions, and allegiances that she had previously accepted. The underlying similarity in the two kinds of membership is something the perplexed father doesn't understand and wouldn't want to face.

CULTURAL DRIFT

Beyond any particular phobias that a family transmits to its off-spring, beyond any special historical event that affects one generation or another, there is a disability that touches us all in modern Western society, and especially in America. It is a subtle feeling of drift, an assumption we make that many crucial things are beyond our control. In part, as others have observed, it stems from the loss of the stable social structures and religious beliefs that have traditionally provided a framework for individual lives. Most people are not and probably never were equipped to live comfortably in an existential void where they must create their own values and meanings. People have always found it easier to construct an ego out of larger certitudes—God, country, social position, and family. Today, however, we are not provided with viable versions of these constants at birth; we have to search for a makeshift certainty to hook on to. If addiction is a manifestation of a need for external structure, it is understandable that it is so much in evidence at present.

Still, our vulnerability to addiction is not simply a matter of having given up beliefs that we could no longer take seriously and social regulations that we were no longer willing to stand for. Something else, something unequivocally valuable, was lost in the transition to the modern age. This was an internal self-assurance that came from being in touch with daily life. Whatever our addictive potential has been through the ages, we were once much closer to the matter of our existence. The signs and patterns of nature were relatively clear to a farmer, woodsman, or hunter. Even machines could be quickly fitted into people's notions of how to get the things they wanted. The usefulness of early pieces of farm machinery was readily apparent to those who adopted them. Thus the machines were real for these people. A farmer felt comfortable using a tractor or a truck, dealing with its idiosyncrasies and making repairs on it.

Whether people lived on farms or in towns and villages, the universal requirement of hard work brought them down to earth and kept the uncertainty in their situations from overwhelming them. Institutional reality, too, was perhaps easier to apprehend: God's ways were mysterious, but the village minister was accessible. Now we find ourselves ill-prepared for dealing with the multitude of things that make up our environment and our society. Separated from physical reality by an abstract technology, we cannot cope with the mechanics of the technology itself, which for us is just as real and present as nature. On top of all this, there is our formidable system of institutions, from the simple forms of association that human beings have always practiced to giant organizations and bureaucracies like General Motors, the U.S. Government, and the universal school system.

Even as technology has grown in complexity, the rural person and the working-class person have retained some contact with and understanding of the machines that their lives depend on. The better-off urban and suburban—the middle-class—person regards these things with a crypto-magical aversion, as though they are enemies whose anarchic power is just barely harnessed. Where the middle-class person should and does have an advantage is in his ability to deal with institutions. Through education and daily familiarity, he knows better how to accomplish things in an institutionalized setting. He shies away less often than the working-class person from direct contact with the many bureaucracies and organizations that he encounters. Yet this may only be a difference of degree, for many individuals who spend their whole lives within large organizations are as reluctant to maneuver in the organizational environment as those who have little to do with it.

Even when we do see ourselves as capable of actively manipulating this part of our world, there are serious limitations to what we will attempt. In Kafka's *The Trial,* the protagonist is arrested and put through the judicial process. Although he knows of no crime he has committed, he accepts the rightness of the proceedings and bends all his efforts to getting advice from mysterious legal consultants and influencing minor bureaucrats. Somehow, as in a nightmare, he is unable to get to the basic question: what was the crime and why is he being brought to trial for it? Similarly, our manipulation of institutions is often limited to stratagems by which we can squeeze out benefits for ourselves: making connections, obtaining good positions, eliciting bureaucratic favors, bending the law in our interest. Our stance toward institutions is a passive one, in that we don't try to have any impact on the institution itself. Its rules, procedures, and goals are seen as totally immutable.

Unable, then, to assert ourselves against the dominating influence of institutions in our lives, we come to feel an even more basic sense of impotence. We find it hard to conceive of ourselves as prime movers in anything. We do not know or believe we can know how to do something original, whether that means constructing physical things or molding the organizations which are so much a part of our lives. Nowhere close around us can we find models of self-directed activity and creation. As a result, few of us imagine that we can write books or songs, make films, start businesses, design cars or build houses. The experts—people from a world apart—produce the edifices, art, and machinery for the rest of us, and we feel it is futile and silly to hope to participate in these endeavors.

When Marx spoke of mankind's becoming alienated from creative labor, he was emphasizing one feature of what has grown into a pervasive detachment from bedrock experience. Today we are fortunate if we are able to find work with which we can in any way identify; rarely can we initiate our own enterprises. In the process of "modernization," our alienation from nature has extended even to our own bodies, so that few of us have any sense of how to plan our diet and exercise to keep ourselves healthy. In earlier times, experience, sometimes tragic experience, was forced upon us. In the absence of this immediacy, we are losing our feeling for our own reality and the reality of our world. But the loss is not a necessary and irreversible function of technology. It is possible to come to grips with this era which, after all, has also given us unprecedented opportunities for pleasure and productivity.

Where it is so natural to insulate ourselves from experience, we must seek it out actively if we want to find it. Now as always, the best antidotes to addiction are joy and competence—joy as the capacity to take pleasure in the people, things, and activities that are available to us; competence as the ability to master relevant parts of our environment and the confidence that our actions make a difference for ourselves and others. Both joy and competence require a connectedness with life in the concrete. When this sense of a real grounding in life is lacking, feelings of self-doubt rush in to create a desire to escape from ourselves. This is where the search for solutions outside ourselves—addictive solutions—begins. The sources of addiction can be found in our institutional involvements and other artificial attachments. They act to replace the physical and emotional ties we have

left behind us. At the same time as they set a pattern of alienation and dependency for us to follow elsewhere, they are foci for
our dependency, and thus serve as addictions themselves. Taken
together, they form a picture of the addicted society.

EDUCATION FOR ADDICTION

Almost as formative an experience as family upbringing, school,
too, is severely distorted by needs for security and social identity that
are external to the experience of learning. Just as we see in many
men and women not the intrinsic person but a potential husband or
wife, lover or rival, so we all too often think of school not in terms of
what we learn there, but in terms of the reassurance that comes
from belonging to an institution and gaining its approval.

Nowadays we are so acclimatized to the presence of school in our
vision of things that we tend to equate education and schooling. But
schooling is not the only way to prepare people for adult life in society. In fact, the present-day format for education is of recent vin-
tage. Throughout history, people simply learned what they had to
do on the site where it was actually done. As late as the nineteenth
century, this kind of apprentice system was the dominant form of
education, even in specialized areas like architecture, medicine, and
engineering. Since then, more and more people have been spending
more and more time in school.

School shapes the perspectives of the people who pass through it,
even as it serves the perspective of the society from which it receives
its mandate. When Ivan Illich says in *Deschooling Society* that school
and other leading institutions are "either socially or psychologically
'addictive,' " he means that they feed on the insecurity which they
themselves create. School engenders insecurity by leaving people unsure what real experience is. Students must direct their attention to
the institutional requirements of the school, rather than to the
meaning and usefulness of the subject matter that is taught. They
are dependent on formal certification of competence within the system rather than practiced competence in dealing with actual problems. People are not asked to show what they can do, but only what
they have done in the artificial setting of school.

Unlike the practitioners who taught apprentices, schoolteachers often have little or no direct experience with their subjects. English instructors are rarely professional writers, government and political studies instructors rarely have held governmental or other administrative posts, business teachers rarely start or manage businesses. Rather, these people themselves are the products of layer upon layer of education, and so they simply continue the system that they have learned so well.

The integrity of learning is lost when school separates people from the resources of the community and the environment and substitutes a forced infusion of knowledge. The rewards and motivations are all pumped in from outside, rather than growing directly out of the process of learning. Even if something is intrinsically interesting to a person, studying it within a strict curriculum and on the basis of a teacher's approval and evaluation will quickly extinguish the person's desire to explore the material on his own. A study by Mark Lepper and his colleagues shows that if small children pursue some activity originally out of natural inclination and are then instructed and rewarded by a teacher to perform the same activity, they will stop performing when the teacher, and the external structure and approval he provides, are removed. Is it surprising, then, that when a student emerges from beneath the sanctions of school, he typically shows no desire to pursue the subjects he was taught in that context? Or that few adults do any systematic reading for the purpose of learning about something?

Children only know that they are supposed to learn because school, parents, and others say they should. Their parents may not care whether they ever read a book outside of school, come up with an original idea, or think things through for themselves. Grades and degrees are the only signs of performance that parents and prospective employers—and thus students—can recognize. The importance of these ratings is affirmed by the school and its faculty, which are concerned to justify their functions. These pressures create the disproportionate concern about grades which students develop. Anxiety and self-doubt are natural by-products of a system where success is seen as crucial to the individual, yet is felt to be beyond his or her determination. In the absence of real or self-regulated rewards, the student is thrown back exclusively on the judgment of his capabilities that one older person, the teacher, makes.

In *How Children Fail,* John Holt describes a common instance of what we have elsewhere called "fear of failure," a child's preoccupation with getting right answers (answers the teacher approves of) no matter how they are arrived at. The child looks to the teacher for hints as to what to say, instead of reasoning out a proper answer or one that reflects his or her own understanding of the question. Since this does not allow true intellectual processes to develop, the exercise is completely wasteful, except to confirm the habit of reliance on authority and the corresponding distrust of one's own thinking. In fact, one can hardly form thoughts at all. As the years go by, this dependence forces an individual to acknowledge the importance of expertise. Moreover, participation in school establishes the deferential patterns that his relationships with other authorities and institutions will assume. "Once we have learned to need school," according to Illich, "all our activities tend to take the shape of client relationships to other specialized institutions."

As we proceed through school, facing new teachers every year, our intellects must be malleable enough to encompass all the different styles of thought we encounter. As a result, we do not develop the habits of thought that generate internal intellectual standards and that make it possible to evaluate situations critically. By the time I arrived at a good university after a successful high school career, I was unable to see, when faced with a bad lecturer, that his presentation was muddled or inaccurate. Instead, I would wonder anxiously what was wrong with me that I could not follow what was being said. Besides looking toward years of schooling completed and degrees and honors bestowed as indices of whether another person is worth listening to, we rely on outside verification of whether or not our own thinking is valid.

This tendency to attribute inadequacy to oneself rather than to the situation is a primary factor in causing 40 percent of the students at American universities to fail to graduate. Further along, it prevents many doctoral candidates who clearly have the ability to complete their degrees from doing so. The students who drop out are not the most rebellious, but are among the most serious about (and therefore most tortured by) school's demands. The rest—the ones who are better adjusted to shattered nerves, their low status in the school hierarchy, and a program of diversionary chores in place of honest work—hang on, aided in many cases by the drugs of the student world, from Dexedrine to marijuana.

A person is now considered to be deprived if he or she does not go to college. Facing the economic burdens of their own increased size, colleges and universities have generally been expanding enrollments while lowering quality. The amount of work demanded from students and the standards applied to this work have declined sharply in recent years. What remains in many cases is merely a patina of education, where faculty indifference makes it hard for students to learn, while most students find the lack of attention and the absence of demands a relief. For many of these people, college is a continuation of childhood; they are glad to prolong their protective dependency on an institution that requires nothing tangible of them. Unfortunately, as students must go beyond college for the specialization that marks them as proficient at something, a liberal arts education does not remedy the immaturity and lack of knowledge and skills which lead students to it in the first place.

The people who emerge from this educational system, therefore, end up no more likely to do or think something new or independent than do those people who haven't received such educational advantages. Most are prepared to fill the narrow organizational positions that society has readied for them. Indeed, a good many of the best students elect to go to graduate or professional schools so as to obtain additional certification. This guarantees them an uninterrupted flow of positive reinforcement for what they do best: sitting in classrooms, taking notes, memorizing information, and following instructions.

Throughout the 1960s it was almost obligatory for an able-minded student to attain an academic or professional degree, with Ph.D.'s and academic careers being especially valued. A person who wanted to stop going to school after his bachelor's degree would be met with admonitions like, "Don't you want to learn any more?" The controversy that arose among families and friends did not entirely center around the practical economic consequences of earning or not earning a degree. Rather, there seemed to be a basic emotional uneasiness—Laing's "ontological insecurity"—about how one could possibly define oneself without having an advanced degree. The expression of this uneasiness was a sign of the depth of addiction to formal education.

By 1970 an unfavorable economic turn and the ending of draft deferments for graduate students brought an end to this mass movement for Ph.D.'s. In place of academic careers, students and the universities themselves became more interested in pragmatic courses of study that would enable people to get jobs when they graduated. This new trend, encouraging in itself, has continued the academic boom in a new guise. The now-favored "practical" career fields also are ones which are felt to require years of postgraduate education. These include medical, law, architecture, business, social work, and counseling programs. With so many certified professionals being turned out, we have a proliferation of highly trained people in not-so-demanding jobs, or at least in jobs which never demanded so much education as they now require. Besides the academic Ph.D.'s teaching in high school, we have functionaries who once held bachelor's degrees (and who really only needed good sense) but who now are getting degrees in law, business administration, or social work. A counselor or psychiatric nurse may have developed great skill in dealing with people, but many observers will ask only whether he or she has had sufficient "clinical training." The self-educated or naturally skilled person now has almost no place to go.

By detaching us from our environment and educating us into subservience and a sense of inadequacy, school undermines our natural defenses against addiction. In the way we cling to the family, many of us are left clinging to school as the only world we feel comfortable in. Illich would remedy this condition by reestablishing the connection between education and the worlds of work and play. People would learn more effectively if they learned from immediate personal and economic motivations and if the learning process had a direct bearing on their lives.

School systems have been going through a period of self-examination for some time. One series of reforms involved "opening up" classrooms—that is, allowing children greater freedom to find out what they liked to do within the school and to pursue it on their own. Later, the discovery that fundamental skills such as reading were declining drastically led some schools to cut back on such reforms in favor of a disciplined approach to the three R's. These divergent movements have been rushing all around the question without being able to meet it directly. The real issue is whether or not children can draw a connection between what they are taught, or exposed to, and their own lives and the world outside them. If school does not reflect this world and this need in a convincing way, then no method will be more successful than another in engaging a child's attention and abilities.

Wherever practical opportunities have arisen for exposing students and teachers alike to the outside world and its responsibilities, both educators and students have been gratified by the results. A federally funded program which enables underprivileged high school dropouts to take jobs while reporting back to school for guidance and a few required courses has been so successful that it gets applications from students who don't qualify. Some high schools are rearranging their class schedules so that any interested student may participate in on-the-site training programs. What still remains is for future changes in education to reflect this growing awareness that institutionalized unreality is harmful to us all. This can only be done by making real experience the primary theme around which education is organized.

MEDICINE AND PSYCHIATRY

Our attitude toward medicine is the most portentous example of society's misguided reliance on outside expertise. Relinquishing the management of our physical selves affects our psychological strength and self-confidence in the most direct way. It happens as the result of a misunderstanding of the nature of medicine. The regulation of bodily functions is not an exact technology, but something much more subtle. Consider, for example, the placebo effect, whereby a substance without active chemical or medicinal properties appears to relieve physical ailments. People are cured of everything from minor complaints to major disabilities by treatments (e.g., hot baths, faith healing) which seemingly have no direct effect on the body. We tend to view these miracles as artifacts of earlier times, when medicine was not so advanced, or of primitive cultures or minds, which can be misled by anything. But even modern medicine is predicated on faith in the medical process and the doctor. In *Persuasion and Healing,* Jerome Frank explains that in all cultures, a group of people are seen as having the ability to heal the sick. Because of the confidence placed in them, these physicians are often able to perform their function successfully.

Today we think of medical science as having reached an objectively advanced state, but there are many, many areas of health and illness—ranging from the common cold to cancer—that our medical knowledge cannot come to grips with at all. A striking illustration of confusion in medicine has to do with an operation most children undergo, tonsillectomy, which many surgeons now feel has been a medical fad. As a demonstration of what a vague diagnosis tonsillitis is, and how unclear is the necessity or value of treatment, consider the following study conducted by the American Child Health Association. Harry Bakwin chronicled the cases of 1,000 children who were sent to doctors for examination of their tonsils. Of these 1,000, 611 received a positive diagnosis, indicating they should have an operation. The other 389 were then examined by different physicians, who recommended tonsillectomies for 174 of them. The process was repeated with the remaining 215 children—who had now been diagnosed as healthy by two physicians each—and 99 were found to require the operation. Finally, a fourth group of doctors saw the rest of the children, and scheduled nearly half of them for surgery. No matter how many times a child had been cleared before, each new examination carried with it a 50-50 chance that he or she would be declared in need of a tonsillectomy.

It is not such a simple matter to decide when a medical problem exists and what should be done about it, as Eliot Freidson makes clear in *Profession of Medicine.* Dr. Lawrence P. Williams, author of *How to Avoid Unnecessary Surgery,* shows that many operations carried out in the United States are unnecessary. Indeed, some have been proven to be positively harmful. Diagnosis and treatment of most diseases are very heavily influenced by cultural and medical trends, individual variations among doctors and patients, and chance. Yet the average person has become more and more trusting of medical infallibility and omniscience.

What is worse is that this aura of all-knowingness has crept farther and deeper into people's lives in recent times. Irving Kenneth

Zola, in "Medicine as an Institution of Social Control," has enu-merated the many new areas of health and sickness to which the medical establishment has extended its domain. Medical authorities now instruct people—from grade school on—about how much sleep to get, what kind of exercise to do, how to react to menstrual periods or colds, and so on. They are not restrained by the fact, for example, that debates are going on about whether and how much people with viruses should rest, or that the range of individual needs for sleep, exercise, diet, and menstrual adjustments is so great as to defy prescription.

Obviously, for matters of everyday health, the soundest approach is to develop a good sense of what one's body needs, given one's physical makeup, history, and personal preferences. This is really the only way to be able to handle the flux of the human organism. Keeping healthy means knowing within oneself what one requires in dealing with the environment and with the demands of living. When this notion of appropriateness of behavior is absent, a person will fall into unhealthy habits, excesses, and deficiencies. In an article in *Science* entitled "Obesity and Eating," Stanley Schachter has shown that fat people, a growing portion of America's population, find it difficult to tell when they are hungry, and thus when they should eat. Instead, they react to external cues, such as the time of day and the setting of the table, to tell them how to behave. Eating too much, smoking too much, drinking too much, failing to exercise—all of which are related to one or another major medical killer—are the things which doctors should most want to deal with in order to guard their patients' health. Yet simple medical advice or treatment is far from being helpful with these problems, which grow out of personalities and lifestyles.

The practice of medicine in the United States actually makes it more difficult for us to be in touch with our physical selves, since it portrays proper health care as a prescriptive rather than a natural process. In place of an understanding of nature's healing powers and a feeling for our own ability to deal with minor physical ir-regularities, medicine makes us think that only it has the answers. We thus overuse doctors grossly and cede them too much authority over ourselves. We would be far better off if we knew how to take care of our own health, and if, as Dr. Stanley Sagov recommends, we collaborated with our doctors in diagnosis and treatment. If we were critical about what we were told, and checked it against our own feelings, we would be much less likely to suffer unnecessary operations, incorrect diagnoses, and wrongheaded treatments. From the standpoint of addiction, if being detached from any kind of direct experience is harmful, then detachment from the rhythms of our bodies is doubly so. Such an attitude influences everything we do.

The addictive implications of our dependence on medicine are most strikingly present in the psychiatry-psychology boom. Getting some kind of emotional counseling has become acceptable to the point where many typical Americans now do it. Among some groups, like young unmarried professionals in New York City, it is actually the rule. No doubt this comes in part from people's increased consciousness of their dissatisfactions and from their desire to remedy them. Nonetheless, as mental "illness" has been destigmatized by labeling it a disease, a false impression has been created that there are known malfunctions of either physiological or psychoanalytic origin which lead to emotional problems. These, it is believed, can be treated precisely and in good order through the application of psychiatric-medical principles. There is very little basis for these beliefs or for the belief that psychiatry is an especially effective tool for helping people gain emotional stability and contentedness.

In an imaginative study which made clear the inadequacy of the whole process for diagnosing mental health or sickness, David Rosenhan and his co-workers at Stanford University were able to get a number of normal, psychologically trained individuals committed to mental hospitals. Once there, they found it uniformly difficult to get out, no matter how they acted or what they said. Usually, however, the patients in these hospitals could see through the infiltrators' poses even before the latter revealed themselves. Earlier, in *Asylums*, Erving Goffman reported that doctors and other personnel in mental institutions expected patients to act as though they were crazy and unconsciously encouraged them to do so by looking for and rewarding clinical symptoms. In this way, the doctors reinforced their own roles at the institution by making sure the patients fit into theirs. Such roles are maintained to the exclusion of relationships based on human equality, even though these would seem to be helpful to patients. A nurse I knew of at a Midwestern mental hospital was discouraged from a friendship with a female patient by innuendos about her own "mental health," and was reported for unprofessional behavior.

In *The Myth of Mental Illness*, Thomas Szasz, himself a psychiatrist, attacks the misconceptions that stem generally from the over-legitimization of psychiatry, its diagnoses and its cures. Szasz feels that the increasing belief in the concreteness and specificity of mental illness is a result of the association of psychiatry with physical medicine, although, as we have seen, diagnosis and cure are far from infallible there as well. Where researchers, such as Albert Bandura and H. J. Eysenck, have attempted to evaluate the results of psychiatric treatment, they have found little reason to believe that such therapy is any more effective than the simple passage of time or just having the opportunity to talk to someone. Many people who are happy with psychotherapy agree that the chance to unburden themselves is the main benefit of their treatment. It is so difficult for them to gain anyone else's ear that they are willing to pay for a sympathetic listener.

Why do so many outwardly normal people think they need psychiatrists? Consider the man who, when his wife died of cancer, turned to an older sister for emotional support. The only way she could respond was to suggest that he see a psychiatrist and to offer him a loan to pay for his therapy. Although brother and sister thought of themselves as being close, they could not really deal with each other at a difficult moment in the life of one of them. Psychiatry has grown popular at a time when genuine human communication is hard to achieve. Psychiatry can never fully substitute for this communication, however, since the only real solutions to a person's problems are those which become a part of his life structure. Among other things, a person has to have regular ways of expressing his feelings to the people near to him.

Since almost every functioning individual has some quirk that can be called neurotic (as did over 80 percent of the New Yorkers interviewed in the famous "Midtown Manhattan Study" by Leo Srole and his colleagues), everyone is a candidate for professional counseling if he or she so chooses, but that choice has serious implications for the person making it. In the first place, simply regarding a personal characteristic or style as a problem makes it one. Second, deciding that you cannot cope with the problem in the normal course of living means giving up on your own resources and turning yourself over to an outside agent who cannot know as much as you do about your own life and feelings.

The prevalent form of psychological vulnerability that we have been dealing with in this book is the absence of a sure sense of personal control. In this light, the very act of consulting with a psychological expert may itself be part of the neurotic pattern, and may actually reinforce it. It is a helpful and often necessary step to acknowledge your weaknesses and to try to deal with them. But at the same time, it is crucial for a healthy person to maintain control of that process. The things that have to be done are things you ultimately have to do yourself, whether or not you have been helped by a psychiatrist. Consultation with a sensitive therapist may suggest areas for personal examination and thought and ways to pursue more fruitful avenues for dealing with life. But the danger of relying on the psychiatrist indefinitely for support in coping, and for alternative gratifications in place of real self-expression and satisfaction, is potentially present in every psychiatric relationship. This is why psychiatry is increasingly popular in an addicted society.

People often seek psychiatric help when a love affair is broken off, when they are unable to adjust to new surroundings, and, on a more permanent basis, when they have a continuing need for emotional support. This is compensatory rather than remedial behavior, and it may bring about greater, rather than less, reliance on the therapist than initially existed. In addition, the very setting of psychiatry may lead a patient to dwell on his fears and inadequacies. By reinforcing self-absorbed and negative modes of expression, psychiatry can actually lodge a person in a fixed pattern of complaint and self-questioning in the place of action. Of course, psychotherapy is predicated on the goal of eliminating its own reason for being. Yet quite frequently, as could only be expected, the very human people who practice it have motivations more complicated than this: through insecurity or their need for self-justification they may unconsciously encourage dependence.

Just when a therapeutic relationship should cease is a crucial question. One woman had been seeing her psychologist steadily for eleven years, since early adolescence. The prospect of "cure" seemed to have long since faded by the wayside. By spending much of her income to secure the companionship of her therapist, the woman acknowledged her great need for him. She often spoke of leaving the city where she was living, because it had bad associations for her and because she wanted to start anew. Then she would lament that she hadn't saved enough money to leave. Anyway, she reflected, moving would mean discontinuing her therapy, which had come along so far with this one psychologist. Fear of the unknown and the unwillingness to give up sure sources of nurturance—these are the ingredients of addiction.

Therapy must mean releasing emotional energy, energy which has previously been blocked or misdirected, so that it can express itself constructively. When, instead, therapy *diverts* energy from real-life issues and relationships, it stands the danger of being an addiction. While becoming more dependent on the psychiatrist's approval (or mere presence) for sustenance, the patient may be sacrificing the opportunity, and even any desire, for other satisfactions. Take, for example, the divorcée who broke off her social evenings early so as to be well-rested for her morning appointments with her therapist. This woman was unhappy without a boyfriend or a husband, but by devoting so much of her time and concentration to her psychiatrist, she didn't have much left for other relationships. Men found her treatment of them slighting, so that one of the principal problems which had motivated her to see a psychiatrist was exacerbated by her therapy. What seemed suspicious about her psychiatrist's role was his willingness to accept so much of his patient's attention. Once, when the woman became angry because he scheduled another woman client immediately after her own appointment, the psychiatrist asked her what her reaction revealed about her. He might also have considered what it indicated about their relationship.

Phyllis Chesler, in *Women and Madness*, views the institution of psychiatry as a form of social control that is applied with special force to keep women in their place. She notes that while 90 percent of psychiatrists are men, many more women than men undergo private therapy. According to Chesler, therapy resembles marriage in that it is a socially approved way for a female to gain direction from an authoritative male. In terms of addiction, a woman can have the reassurance of a stable relationship with a man without facing the normal demands of such relationships. She can voice her complaints regularly, expect her therapist always to respond to her, and not have to meet any requirements other than to pay the fee. While not usually as encompassing as a marriage or love affair, psychotherapy may still be the centerpiece of a person's life. It has the added advantage of being available to someone who is unable to offer another person as reliable a haven as she seeks from him. As for the man's role in this loaded situation, it is naïve to think that most therapists are ideally free of ego-involvement. The "commitment to therapy" that therapists demand of their patients turns out, in many cases, to mean fidelity to them as men.

To justify psychiatric dependencies, people can resort to vague explanations that place psychological functioning safely outside the individual's sphere of responsibility. That is, they can legitimize their difficulties by tracing them to psychoanalytic causes or to underlying malfunctions in their nervous systems. The woman who had been seeing her psychiatrist since adolescence believed that she had sustained minor brain damage in a childhood automobile accident. This reasoning became a crutch that impeded her progress toward dealing with her real anxieties. Her thinking, however, merely reflects widespread beliefs which are supplanting religious and other magical explanations for unhappiness and evil. These medico-psychological hobgoblins are as absurd and remote from our feelings as any other hobgoblins.

Newsweek (8 January 1973) had a cover story describing depression as a mysterious affliction that is only now being traced to its physiological roots. According to *Newsweek,* "there is no doubt that depression, long the leading mental illness in the U.S., is now virtually epidemic. . . ." The article does not say why the "disease," if it indeed does spring from physiological causes, would be getting worse, since presumably these causes would remain roughly constant over time. The article does go on to reassure readers that "the prognosis for the victims of depression is now brighter than ever before. In the last few years alone, a whole new pharmacopeia of anti-depressant drugs has come on the market. . . . Besides the promise of new drugs, there has been steady improvement in techniques of electroshock therapy." The thinking behind the article permits those who find themselves or their children distressed and confused to chalk up their unhappiness to some distant, esoteric source, and at the same time holds out the promise that drugs will be able to alleviate their problems.

The physiology of the brain and the nervous system is very little understood today, and our knowledge has certainly not reached the point where we can base realistic therapies on it. In the words of the neuropsychologist Bruce Masterton, "the working of the brain continues to elude us. . . . In the century that has seen light at the end of every other tunnel, this one remains black." There have been important efforts to explore such areas and to relate them to mental disorders (such as are summarized in Solomon Snyder's *Madness and the Brain*), but these are necessarily only preliminary steps. Where we do have valid and useful information is on the antecedents and conditions in life that produce psychological problems and emotional upsets. We also have a good idea of some of the patterns that these problems assume, so that we can recognize them and, hopefully, intervene.

What we now know points in quite a different direction from what the *Newsweek* article indicates. For example, Martin Seligman's research on "learned helplessness" has uncovered reliable indications that acute depression results from a person's feeling that his actions do not matter—that he cannot influence the course of his life. Seligman's data show that "a life without mastery may produce vulnerability to depression." By diverting our attention from discoveries like this which can help us, popular mythologies about mental problems actually worsen our plight.

Clamoring for answers we hope will make sense of our situations, we settle on solutions which are harmful. One example is the use of Ritalin and other "behavior modification" drugs to treat hyperkinetic (hyperactive) children, in some cases whole school systems full of them. This has been justified, in one interpretation, by the claim that the drugs simply increase alertness. In another interpretation, they somehow correct "minimal brain damage," although Dennis Cantwell reports that organic malfunctions have hardly ever been found to be associated with hyperkinesis. Actually, hyperactivity is a form of behavior that has many causes, from maladjustments in the school situation to outright boredom. And what is called hyperactivity may simply be a healthy abundance of energy. Through the use of drugs, a medical solution is being applied to nonexistent problems and problems which, at least on such a large scale, must be mainly social in origin. A more ominous example is psychosurgery, which operates from the fallacious assumption that one-to-one connections have been established between certain parts of the brain and specific kinds of behavior. Since this is not true, surgery intended to eradicate undesirable behavior will have side effects, up to and including the near extinction of normal human functioning.

Such extreme manifestations of medical repression as psychosurgery and drugging children are, in fact, controversial. In general, though, both lay and professional attitudes are growing more favorable toward quick, decisive, bludgeoning treatment of emotional disorders. On our part, this involves a sacrifice of our selves to experts and authorities who we think will tell us what we need. Perhaps we are not far from the day when we will all be willing to hire psychosurgeons to repair our psyches whenever we are sad or puzzled. We already seem to be going pretty far in this direction in our use of drugs.

DRUGS, MEDICINE, AND THE MEDIA

It has become commonplace to acknowledge that drug takers of the youth culture are simply following the example of their elders, who themselves lean so heavily on drugs like alcohol, medically prescribed stimulants and tranquilizers, and such everyday "uppers" as coffee and tobacco. The ready resort to drugs symbolizes culturally sanctioned methods for responding to the world. As Lasagna's placebo study showed, people who believe in the power of drugs over themselves are also more likely to take direction from established institutions—for example, hospitals and churches.

In *Mystification and Drug Misuse,* which deals with prescription as well as illicit drugs, Henry Lennard and his colleagues analyze the extravagant overuse of medically prescribed substances in our time. For example, according to Karen Dunnell and Ann Cartwright, in any given 24- to 36-hour period from 50 to 80 percent of the adult American population takes at least one medical drug. Lennard explains that both doctor and patient expect any medical consultation to end with a prescription whether or not it is at all useful—the patient, so that he will be reassured that his illness is being treated; the doctor, so that he can reaffirm his competence as a medical practitioner. In line with this, it is reported by Lennard and by Linda Fidell that doctors are more likely to prescribe medications for women than for men.

What's more, few doctors are fully aware of what the drugs they recommend actually do, or of the implications of their use of medicines generally. Dr. A. Dale Console, who served as medical director of the Squibb drug company, told a Senate subcommittee that "the average practitioner is the captive of the drug industry." That is, doctors do not normally learn about drugs from medical sources, but instead tend to get their information from pharmaceutical company advertisements and sales pitches, which often mislead and confuse them about newly introduced drugs and their consequences. As the most profitable of the pharmaceutical companies' products, tranquilizers especially are the object of a wide-ranging sales and publicity effort. A majority of the advertisements in AMA and other medical journals (which depend on drug advertising for financial support) are for tranquilizers. In the February 1972 issue of the *Archives of General Psychiatry,* a random example, there are nine consecutive full-page or double-page tranquilizer ads. Their messages are quite poignant, the one for Thorazine reading, "I go to pieces between visits [to the psychiatrist]."

Addiction as a drug-related experience is prominently associated with depressant drugs, such as alcohol and heroin. Yet despite the growing alarm of various medical and government authorities over the addictive potential of prescribed depressants, including tranquilizers as well as barbiturates, these drugs are rampant in our society, and they are put there by doctors and drug companies. Among the fifty most frequently prescribed drugs in the United States, listed in Richard Burack's *The New Handbook of Prescription Drugs,* are the following: Valium, Seconal, Librium, Equanil, Miltown, Thorazine, Doriden, Fiorinal, Butisol, Nembutal, and phenobarbital, all of which are barbiturates, sedatives, or tranquilizers.

How is the medical profession able to participate so easily in the drugging of society? Beyond simply being indebted to and consequently oversolicitous toward the drug industry, medicine is itself an established institution, one with political, economic, and social positions to uphold. In intransigently opposing heroin and marijuana while being inordinately slow to damn tobacco, the AMA and related bodies are standing up for the status quo, established habits, and favored social classes. Nor are they any more objective in evaluating evidence about the drugs they dispense. Prescription medicine is the basis of the medical profession's self-esteem. And this is something on which they will not allow themselves to be questioned.

Partly as a result of organized medicine's encouragement of drug use, people now see psychoactive drugs—and the altered states of consciousness they bring—as a normal part of life in society. Both stimulant and depressant addiction are widely present in America. The first, in the form of nicotine and caffeine, is accepted so casually that people have no idea what they are caught up in; the second, in the form of heroin and even barbiturates, is feared and denied. However society claims to feel about the various depressants, there has been a significant expansion in their illicit and recreational use. The sedative Quaalude (methaqualone) has become the most popular campus drug, replacing the more adventurous speed drugs and hallucinogens. Of course, the depressant drug which has traditionally been the choice of most students, and their elders, is alcohol. The rise in the use of alcohol among young people, even those in high school, is truly staggering. The 1974 report of the National Institute on Alcohol Abuse and Alcoholism includes the finding that one out of seven male high school seniors gets drunk at least once a week.

A major means for spreading this drug dependence, and the addictive attitude in general, is advertising and the media. Manufacturers of sedatives go directly to the public with advertising spots which suggest that normal human events, such as weddings, visits from relatives, and job interviews, can only be faced with the aid of some deadening drug. Generalizing from the popularity of drugs and drug experiences, there have also appeared psychedelic ads which endeavor to convince consumers that they can get "Dodge fever" from buying a car, or find "springtime" in the puff of a cigarette. These ads are part of a class of appeals which start from the premise that people's normal existence is unexciting, and that a purchase or series of purchases is necessary to rescue them from their malaise. Automobile, clothing, and cigarette advertisements are often of this type, depicting the product owner as a completely different person from what he used to be (or what we know ourselves to be); the buyer becomes self-confident, captivating to the other sex, and able to transcend the small world of which he is regularly a part. The imagery here is straightforwardly that of addiction, and advertisers mean it to be this way; there is no stronger motivation for or surer guarantee of buying something.

Such advertising emphasizes the deficiencies of the person who does not use or possess a given product. It focuses on insecurities that all of us have to some extent. Sensitive areas, like a person's wish to be accepted by others, are exploited with portrayals of social disasters resulting from unclean clothes or houses, dandruff or bad breath. People are regularly reminded that they cannot take their desirability for granted, that they must be constantly on guard against those human foibles that might turn other people off. These ads affect us all, as the sales of sweet-smelling but otherwise useless mouthwashes and harmful underarm deodorants show. The effects can reach pathological dimensions with some who are even more desperate about their social identities. For years one man's friends thought he had a throat problem, since he would periodically spray his mouth even while he was talking with people. They finally learned that he was using a breath freshener, and that this was his way of relieving his anxiety about the impression he was making.

For the person who feels deficient, advertising generates the impulse to seek in some bromide or lotion, or in his attire or from an automobile, additional worth as a human being. The possession or use of a product then becomes rewarding, as it reduces a person's anxieties and artificially buoys up his image of himself. The very act of buying can be reassuring as a temporary way to alleviate uneasy feelings about oneself. This same man, when he became depressed, would rush out to buy some beauty-health aid, or perhaps something more substantial. In this way, he believed somehow that he was coping with his interpersonal failures, while actually—in the true sense of an addiction—he was causing himself greater difficulties by getting into debt and by convincing people that he was rather odd. His behavior is similar to that of the woman who buys a dress when she is down in the dumps. This habit, too, serves as an addiction. It can reach such proportions that there are women who buy clothes day after day only to return most of their purchases so they can continue their perpetual shopping sprees.

For children growing up today, the media's effects are more severe than ever. Through television programming directed specifically at them, children are besieged by intrusive advertising from the moment they can understand it. Prominent athletes, television personalities, and cartoon characters recommend vitamin pills to make them strong and healthy, and toys and other products to make them the envy of other children. Between such commercials, the cartoon serials themselves stress reliance on heroic figures and magical solutions to the dilemmas faced by children's favorite characters. Despite the addictive effect of this and the stunting of normal childhood activity which comes from children's anesthetizing themselves in front of television sets, parents find it hard to resist an arrangement which pacifies children—leaving the house quiet and free of mess. This passive form of entertainment which young people have become used to is blamed by some, such as Lennard, for the simultaneous growth of drug use among the young.

Television, which brings models of addictive behavior into our very homes, impinges heavily on the consciousness of children and adults alike. Some individuals, disturbed at the role played by television in their lives, have been moved to kick the monster out, with the amusing and yet also frightening results that Colman McCarthy describes in a *Newsweek* article, "Ousting the Stranger from the House." He found that he had to reorganize his home and learn afresh what his wife and children were like. Family members discovered new things about each other and began to talk about important aspects of their family life that they had ignored.

Part of their shock came from their recognition that television can genuinely be an addiction. Who can doubt, when watching a child transfixed by whatever flashes before him on the screen, that a compulsive behavior pattern has been established? Adults, too, reveal their dependence when they come home with only enough energy and motivation to turn on their sets. They need television to pass the time, to oil their relationships with those around them, and to cloak the emptiness of their lives. Newspapers have noted the finding of The Society for Rational Psychology in Munich, Germany, that habitual television watchers who are denied their favorite pastime can experience withdrawal symptoms involving disorientation in major areas of personal life. They cannot deal with their families, they lose interest in sex, and so on; it is a funny news item, with implications that are not so funny.

OTHER ADDICTIONS

Can we legitimately label a pastime like watching television an addiction? And, if so, what makes it an addiction? Addiction takes place with an experience sufficiently safe, predictable, and repetitive to serve as a bulwark for a person's consciousness, allowing him an ever-present opportunity for escape and reassurance. Once immersed in such an experience, a person loses access to other people, things, and pursuits, and thus needs the addictive activity or relationship even more. At the point of addiction, where withdrawal from the activity would unravel the fiber of the person's whole life, he sees no choice but complete and total involvement with the thing which now controls him. All of this occurs with a person who focuses his attention on television to the extent of giving up any serious attempt to deal with his household. Television is a prime example of the way society not only tolerates addictions, but provides them for us and even urges them on us.

It is encouraging that people are beginning to label the range of addictive attachments in our culture for what they are. In "Are You an Addictive Personality?" Dr. Lawrence J. Hatterer draws attention to a number of addictions, including shopping and sex as well as household drugs and alcohol. Hatterer and others also label as addictions overeating, compulsive gambling, and overworking. Since these and other dependencies together make up the addicted society, it is informative to look at a couple of examples in order to examine their operation and function: who participates in them, how other people are affected, and what overall impact they have.

It is a sign of addiction when people persist in behavior which is detrimental to their well-being, the well-being of the objects of their attention, and, finally, the well-being of others. The keeping of pets in American cities is such an issue, as indicated by a poll in *Nation's Cities* in which 60 percent of the mayors who responded listed "dog and other pet control problems" as a source of frequent citizen complaints. These complaints (as documented by Alan Beck) stem from growing numbers of dog bites, the ugliness and hazard to health of dog shit, and the noise of barking or whining from large animals confined in yards and apartments. Yet the pet population increases daily in what the American Humane Association labels an epidemic population explosion, one to which they believe Americans are almost totally unresponsive.

Why are people so strongly attached to their pets? And why are so many large animals brought into an environment of crowded streets and small apartments for which they are totally unsuited? The answer is that pets are well-suited to be objects of the search for emotional certitude. Few things are as consistent and predictable as the behavior of a pet. Many devotees of pets attempt to minimize the distinction between the love of an animal and the love of a person (with the help of pet food advertisements which personify animals, and which make it seem cruel not to pamper them). Some people, in fact, *prefer* the company of animals. One man characterized his dog as "the only living thing who really cares for me; who would be despondent if I died; who would love me no matter what happened to me in the world, or how mean I was to him." To elicit this kind of devotion, it is necessary only to feed a dog and occasionally pat it. Even when a person becomes tired of or bored with the animal and ignores it, it will continue to center its life around its owner. It is appropriate that in our era of the widespread objectification of emotional attachments, where addictions and love are so commonly confused, people can characterize a relationship with an animal as love.

When people find the give-and-take of normal human interaction too much to handle, having a pet may be the only emotional arrangement they can come to grips with. Pets naturally appear where human relationships are difficult to form, as among the old and lonely, or where they are transient and uncertain, as in the hip youth culture. A pet, though, can actually distract a person from other emotional needs and make it less likely that these will be gratified. A college student who had difficulty sustaining her relationships with people bought a large dog for the house she shared with three other women. The animal's presence quickly alienated her housemates, and the constant attention she paid it—including long walks and one-sided conversations—made it unpleasant for people to visit her. The next year she took an apartment by herself. When people occasionally did come over, they found their conversations with the woman punctuated by her comments to and about the dog, and her periodic hugging and caressing of it.

The predictability of canine behavior may explain as well why dogs are popular in middle-class homes, sometimes as models or even replacements for children. In one home where the parents were terrifically anxious about their children's whereabouts and doings, they got a dog which they always kept tied to a railing outside the home. They exercised it on a leash (as law required), and once in a while took it to the park. But even there they didn't feel free to let it run loose because "it might get lost chasing a rabbit." Although these people were acting in line with public regulations and social consideration for others, it makes one speculate about their motivation for owning a pet. One's concern for an animal can be sporadic and selfish, and one's main basis for deciding what a pet needs may be colored by one's own convenience. While parents claim that having an animal teaches a child consideration for other living things, this seems an odd kind of relationship to use to exemplify the complexity of human interchange. In families where parents regularly deny their children liberties that make the parents nervous, the children in turn learn to mold or suppress their pets' impulses—for exercise, sex, or stimulation—to fit their own desires and schedules. A common interaction that we can observe between masters and pets in the streets is a reprimand for some act of disobedience. The addictive use of pets is a form of cruelty to animals that is not often recognized as such.

The extent to which pets are addictions depends on the degree to which they dominate people's lives. There are many households where a dog is regarded as a love object, is controlled so as to fit into existing household patterns, and at the same time is allowed to influence important family policies. One man constantly scolded and punished his dog, but he turned down a desirable job offer in England because it would mean quarantining the animal for six months. Here the domination and self-sacrifice which frequently go together in interpersonal addictions appeared in what we think of as a much more insignificant relationship.

Young people, who are heavily involved in addiction to pets—and lovers—also have a youthful version of addiction to religion. We have already mentioned a Jesus freak who equated faith in Jesus with drinking, hallucinogenic drugs, and psychiatry (although he claimed to find it more effective than any of these for his purposes). Former drug users are, in fact, prominent among the members of the extremist, often authoritarian religious communities that have sprung up around the youth culture. An article in *Society* by Robert Adams and Robert Fox, entitled "Mainlining Jesus," summarizes some of the addictive elements in the Jesus trip—the denial of past and future, the release from anxiety and effort, the evasion of sexual maturity, the unassailable group ideology. A total commitment to a religious sect negates everything a person has been and done and suffered and learned, and reconstructs his or her thinking along the rigid lines of doctrinaire faith. Order is imposed by the strictures of the group, assurance and integration are found in faith in an all-powerful God, and the threatening responsibility of self-assertion is removed.

Freeing youths from such indoctrination seems to require an equally totalitarian assault on their sensibilities. With this as their rationale, some parents have hired Ted Patrick to kidnap their own children (often legally adults) from religious communes and to subject them to traumatic marathon "deprogramming" sessions. Once persuaded that what they have been converted to is actually a perversion of Christianity, many of the young people immediately seek to join the deprogramming group so as to save others. Repudiating the ethos to which they have so recently dedicated their entire lives, they feel the intense negative reaction which invariably follows an addiction.

What makes parents so desperate that they will resort to a stranger's forcible intercession in order to regain some influence over their grown children? What do they expect from Ted Patrick? One mother said of him, "He is my savior." Disappointed to find that Patrick was an ordinary human being, she explained, "I thought he would be a giant—some kind of god that we just had to have." Calling on an outsider to solve the problem, parents are quick to blame the external menace of subversive sect leaders for what went wrong in the first place. In fact, their own reactions show the same confusion that drove their children to lose their balance. One father said, "I'm sure it will take two years to rebuild what those kids destroyed in a week." But what real stability, what grounding in life, could this man's daughter—or Randolph Hearst's daughter—have had if "those kids" could destroy it in a week? And how rebuild it—by sending her back to school and church, where her unsure sense of herself was nurtured?

The parents involved in the kidnapings seem only to want their children to revert to the outward normality, the acceptably disguised irresolution and dependency, that they displayed before their religious conversion. This brings us back, full cycle, to school and the family. By sanctioning children's acceptance of self-denying affiliations throughout their lives, parents and society have led them to the grotesque involvement with drugs and religion that so many adults despise. But they shouldn't be surprised, for the link between the two kinds of domination is direct and indisputable.

Love and marriage, home and school, medicine and psychiatry, drugs and religion—all of these, successively or simultaneously, can be addictions for the person who has to use them that way. On the other hand, none of them need be an addiction, for anything we do can be addictive or not addictive; the key is in how and why we do it. But with an overall cultural pattern of addiction enveloping so many of our activities, we are always left looking for the next degree, the next lover, the next visit to the shrink, the next fix. We are taught—in many cases by the institutions themselves—that we need school, need marriage, need a steady job, need medicines. What we really need is to be whole in ourselves, to take charge of our own health and education and emotional development. We need to be confident that we can cope with, learn from, and enjoy the people and things that make up our environment. Because that wholeness is so hard for us to achieve, addiction is not, as we like to think, an aberration from our way of life. Addiction is our way of life.

*She always felt vulnerable, vulnerable, there was always a secret chink in her ar-
mour. She did not know herself what it was. It was a lack of robust self, she had no
natural sufficiency, there was a terrible void, a lack, a deficiency of being within herself.*

And she wanted someone to close up the deficiency . . . to close it up forever.

—D. H. LAWRENCE, *Women in Love*

*Always a man must be considered as the broken-off fragment of a woman, and the sex
was the still aching scar of the laceration. Man must be added on to a woman, before
he had any real place or wholeness.* —D. H. LAWRENCE, *Women in Love*

8

Addicted Lovers Apart

When we enter into love relationships, we do so as men or as
women, and these sexual identities, like other social roles, influence
the form of our involvements in major ways. Men and women ex-
hibit addictive tendencies in roughly the same degrees. However, the
different forms addiction can take in men and women are worth
exploring, as they highlight some special problems that contribute to
addiction. In particular, the addiction model can give us insight into
woman's role in society, at the same time that an analysis of this role
can give us insight into addiction.

Because the case studies in this chapter are meant to show one
side or the other of the male-female bond, they are studies of individuals, rather than of couples. They illustrate the way one individual, as an individual, copes or fails to cope with romantic involvements. People who have many lovers, simultaneously or in succession, may be just as much addicted as those who are inextricably tied to one person. The stories that follow show, therefore, what
an interpersonal addict does when not involved in an exclusive, mutually addictive relationship.

WOMAN: THE BURDEN OF INSUFFICIENCY

The women's movement, recognizing that conventional female roles deny women the experience of psychological wholeness, has emphasized how important it is for a woman to be able to make it alone. In saying this, feminists are talking about addiction. Society labors to convince women of their insufficiency. It does so mainly by organizing people into couples, through which a woman's primary identity derives from her relationship with a man. Although we are all given the message that we can't make it alone—that we have to join up with someone or something else to survive—women nonetheless bear the heavier burden of the cultural belief that a person cannot exist successfully outside the structures of marriage and family. This is why woman's conventional position in society can serve as a symbol of the socially approved addicted state, and why the concept of addiction has such relevance for an appreciation of the psychological pressures on women.

Society's assumption that women are not capable of an independent economic existence is reflected in the parallel assumption that they are not even capable of an independent domestic existence. It is now more unusual than it used to be for a woman to live with her parents until her marriage. But in lieu of this direct movement from daughter to wife, the college dormitory or shared apartment may provide only a transit point between these two accepted roles for a woman. In dormitories or similar housing arrangements, parents can exert considerable control over their daughters, for whom "home" still means their parents' home. As evidence that most women are not considered to be adults capable of living on their own, consider that when a woman loses the active protection of her mate, she is traditionally expected to retreat into some other protective structure. When a young married man without children has to go away for an extended business trip or a tour of military duty, his wife often returns to her family to resume her former place as a dependent daughter. It is even more ludicrous when a young divorcée moves back in with her parents and meekly accepts their renewed direction of her personal life.

I knew of a graduate student of 27 who, after her husband's early death from a brain tumor, moved in with *his* parents. She did this so that they could all share their grief and accustom themselves together over a period of time to their horrible loss. Even under these circumstances, where the people involved were not her own parents, she let them preside over her the way parents normally do in the case of an adolescent girl. They interfered with her social life, as when they insisted that the men she dated not take her to certain places or keep her out too late. None of the principals, including the woman herself, could seemingly conceive of her living with her in-laws as an independent adult.

To consider the implications of this is to begin to appreciate what addiction is all about. The denial of financial independence and freedom of movement to women is, at bottom, a denial of emotional independence, which is what addiction springs from in women or in men. Thus, the measures being promoted for achieving the independence of women—greater economic opportunities, greater control over their own bodies, acceptance of the legitimacy of the single life—have a broader human validity than their application to women alone implies.

The role mapped out for a woman symbolizes the addict's lot because it is predicated on inadequacy. A woman is expected to be an empty, formless vessel, shaped by whoever or whatever comes along to fill her up. Any activity undertaken out of this lack of personal completeness is likely to become an addiction. Conventionally, women have been channeled into a few basic involvements—marriage, family, home. These personal relationships constitute women's assigned sphere of activity. It is not surprising if, lacking other outlets, a woman defines herself by such relationships and depends on them to the point of addiction.

Today, when a woman's life history is not so predictable, she may still find herself no better equipped by her upbringing to live decisively and effectively. Our more loosely defined social world may only offer her a greater number and variety of addictive attachments. Anne is a portrayal of what a woman's life can be like under such circumstances. Coming from a very staid background, she found her life taking some unconventional turns. But there was an underlying consistency in the nature of her many involvements.

Anne grew up in a fashionable suburb of a southern city. She hadn't found her life very exciting up to the point when she graduated from high school, except for the state swimming championship she won. Her main experiences with people were within the family, and these did not amount to much. Her father was taciturn and imperious, her mother slightly fey and prone to chatter on about trivial happenings in the community. She spoke about how Anne would have so much fun in college, as she herself had had. Though kind and sympathetic, she never had anything of importance to say to her daughter.

At home and in school, Anne was never given any consciousness of her full potentialities. Nobody particularly noticed her, and she didn't seem to be valued anywhere except for her pretty face and her athletic prowess. Her father and mother only talked at her, and no individual or subjective reactions were expected, so that her ability to define or express herself had atrophied at a rudimentary stage. In her swimming she turned herself over to a coach and a self-denying regimen of curfew, diet, and practice. Through all of this she never received the love, contact, and affection she knew must exist somewhere, and which she craved, but which she did not feel worthy to receive.

After high school, Anne moved on to a small two-year liberal arts college for women in Connecticut. Her parents had heard that it was a nice school, with a good swimming team, and thought it would be beneficial for her to live for a while in some other region of the country. Anne didn't find anything significantly different about this new experience except that she was forced to worry about exams and grades. Prep school had not prepared her very well for even these moderate academic demands. She soon found herself in a constant state of anxiety, and she began to eat compulsively and smoke cigarettes—both very bad for her swimming.

The weight she gained also hurt her social life, with which she was already inarticulately but markedly dissatisfied. Her submerged discontent crystallized into the desire for a romantic relationship, but this was difficult to find because the school was located about fifty miles from the nearest men's college or large city. The women were periodically loaded into buses and driven to one or another of the surrounding universities and colleges for a mixer. Nothing much happened, though, since they had to return around midnight. Apparently none of the men Anne kissed passionately outside the hall cared to drive the hundred-mile round trip to repay her visit.

The general assumption at this small college was that the women could not look after themselves. Their existence was bounded by chaperoned dances, rules against male visitors in dormitory rooms, and, on the academic side, attendance records, lectures, and prescribed readings. Anne's distrust of her self-control—or perhaps just her unfamiliarity with exercising it—was exacerbated. She was supposedly a mature person, but she had no idea how to regulate her time, her interests, or her feelings. She had had very little experience of any kind. Her loves had been infatuations from afar. Parents, rules, and distance had kept men away from her. She had never spent time alone fulfilling herself. Her parents' house had a well-stocked library, but it was considered her father's. She had never picked out a book on a subject she wanted to know more about, except for the time she had tried to find out about sex as a girl. She had been insulated from everything. Nothing contacted her directly without the intervention and protection of others.

As the two years drew to an end, Anne, at her parents' prompting, applied to several prestigious Eastern women's colleges. Secretly, though, she was glad when she couldn't gain admission to any of these, and instead went on to the University of California at Los Angeles. She felt somehow that she wanted to get away, far away.

She was disoriented when she began school in Los Angeles. Living in a dormitory, she didn't do anything except attend classes in the morning, go to swimming practice in the afternoon, and study in the evening. The women who stayed around on the weekends, and wanted to go to movies with her, were usually not the most attractive, and since she was pretty Anne did not feel she belonged with them. Most of the more interesting women from her classes were in sororities, but she wasn't asked to join. Her sights did not rise above the conception of social life represented by sororities and the routinized dating and party-going they stood for.

At UCLA as in junior college, Anne never came close to having an integrated educational experience. There seemed to be no connection between what she heard in class or the assignments she read and how she lived her life, just as her father's books had had no meaning for her as a child. At both the colleges she attended, the dominant social atmosphere at that time branded any woman too concerned with her studies as odd, so she never did any serious reading except when she had to. Nor did her free-time conversations with friends ever concern the subjects she studied at school—these conversations were given over to other topics, most often men. There was no place for intellectual or self-exploration when she did interact with men. Very rarely, in fact, did Anne try to understand anything in her environment by thinking and talking about it. Her parents had not encouraged her to do so, and nothing since had taught her any different.

In this college milieu Anne was primed to turn to personal relationships for solace and salvation. At UCLA she finally found an effective means for exposing herself to men—fraternity parties, where she learned that after a few drinks she could act without inhibition and become a part of the goings-on. She had been introduced to moderate social drinking at her junior college. Now, though, she was expected to abandon herself more fully to the spirit of the occasion.

So it was at a fraternity party about a month after she came to UCLA that she had her first sexual experience. One man seemed particularly interested in her. After dancing with her awhile, he took her to his room. They sat on his bed and began kissing, and then he laid her down and took her clothes off. At the time it didn't seem proper to make any objections, and Anne displayed an acquiescence which made the man express surprise that she was a virgin. He invited her to spend the weekend with him. She rushed joyfully to her dormitory to sign out, spent three days and nights with the man, and then never heard from him again.

Anne did not know how to react, but she supposed she had been deficient in some way and had been rejected because of it. Resolving to conduct herself more competently, she steeled herself for the next party. So began a new ritualized period in her life when she went to parties with vague sexual intentions, and used her intoxication as a means for taking up with whichever acceptable man approached her. During this stage in her development, she came to enjoy and desire sex in itself. But she also wanted very much to find acceptance from a man. Whenever a man made some effort to see her again, she became convinced she had found a lover, someone with whom she could form a deep attachment.

She was bound to be disappointed and hurt many times, but she knew of no alternative. So she endured this way of life, finding in it occasional flimsy gratifications, for the rest of the school year. After a particularly hollow and detached summer at home, she returned to Los Angeles sensing that she should try something else. The previous year she had agreed to live in an apartment with two other women. With them she began to smoke marijuana, not only as a staple of her social life but as a way to enliven evenings spent lying around in the apartment. Her free time increased when she quit the swimming team. Although she still acknowledged the demands of her schoolwork, she was becoming lax there, too, with a resultant feeling of tension that often made her want to avoid her classes.

At this time Anne started seeing a man regularly, a former student who had dropped out and who now lived off money from odd jobs and loans. Though just as self-centered and insensitive to Anne as her fraternity lovers had been, he at least sought some kind of consistent gratification from her. Still, there was something important missing, something she wanted that she wasn't getting. In its place, perhaps, she followed her boyfriend's example and began taking amphetamines. While Anne did not collapse entirely as many speed users do, she did snort regularly, and she was constantly high. She would snort in the morning when she got up, and then try to attend classes, but the doses of the drug she was taking interfered with her concentration. Soon, although she was still officially enrolled, she had to all purposes dropped out. She would snort at night, too, after having run around the city all day, and so she settled into a twice-a-day habit. By summer, she decided she could not go home. She resisted her parents' requests, then demands, until finally they stopped sending her money, and in the middle of the summer she returned East with a supply of meth. Once she got home, her parents saw a radical difference in her. When her college transcript arrived soon after with nothing but failures and incompletes, Anne admitted her drug habit.

After their initial shocked disbelief, the family set to putting their daughter right again. They hoped that now that Anne was away from that crowd and *that* man, everything could go back to the way it was before. Following a friend's recommendation, they sent their wayward child to a psychiatrist, who supervised her withdrawal during a brief stay at a local rest home. Pretty soon everything seemed right, but Anne didn't feel right. She was bored and oppressed. True, she was now abstaining from drugs, but that was mainly because of the constraints of the situation. After a while she decided she was sick of the whole scene and left by bus one morning while her parents were out.

Returning to Los Angeles did not provide the lift she wanted either. Her lover failed to comprehend her increased need for emotional support. She felt deprived and isolated, with her family no longer behind her and nothing lying before her. Faced with her father's refusal to finance another attempt at her senior year, she had to rely on herself for material support for the first time in her life. She applied for a job at UCLA and went to work as a typist in the Department of Fine Arts. Her job kept her in some minimal touch with reality, but it provided nothing positive for her. Just as it was when she was in school, her problem was not that she couldn't follow rules; all she could do was follow rules.

The year was spent in excruciatingly dull days and in abandoned nights and weekends. She fell away from her previous year's lover and returned to a multiple-affair scheme. Her loves were like her drug, furious in the first rush, then fading to a dry, enervating down. Always she thought she had found in a lover a new meaning in life; always it turned out to be meaningless. Her excesses with drugs and sex were attempts to simulate real feelings and wholeness of being. Intoxicated, she could believe that she was earning the attention and regard she had always wanted. By now she had been involved in any number of institutions and activities—home, swimming, school, liquor, sex, drugs, psychiatry, office work—and yet her relationship with all of them was external and passive. Things just happened to Anne. She did not contribute anything from her own character or spirit.

This emptiness was typified by her intense, yet erratic, pursuit of sex. Anne's desire to have lovers reflected an underlying need for human closeness. But because she could not actively shape the sexual situations she partook of, she was totally unsuccessful in her efforts to translate her affairs into something other than opportunistic, alienated, and generally transient encounters. Although she was a sensual person who genuinely enjoyed the physical release of lovemaking, she did not attempt to make these pleasures a regular part of her life. The fact that sometimes she got into a lot of sex and other times almost none suggests that sex was just one more thing that came to her accidentally, or by someone else's decision. In her sexual activity, where she had a potential inclination for organizing a part of her life around a positive interest, she instead formed another addiction, because her whole life was, after all, a series of passive responses. So it is not surprising that she readily sacrificed sexual excitement when she saw a chance for something she yearned for more—peace and contentment.

A year had gone by since she started to work as a typist. A graduate student in Near Eastern art sometimes stopped by her desk to talk to her. One day he asked her out. She accepted, although she had never thought about him in a romantic way because he seemed so stiff and academic and because she was used to dating men from the drug crowd with whom she spent her free time.

The steady affair that resulted was different from the others. It was less exciting, and more reassuring. David took drugs only casually, and he made love with approximately the same moderation. Still, he was considerate and reliable. He appeared when he said he would, he didn't ask her for money, and he showed a positive interest in her doings. He sincerely wanted to share his life with her. David expressed to Anne his own feelings of isolation within the university and the city, along with his uncertainty about his career. Anne found this surprising, because he seemed the model of determined progress toward a goal. An honor student at his undergraduate college, he had come to UCLA to be a teaching assistant in one of the best fine arts departments in the country. However, this apparent purposefulness did not reflect how David really felt, and the two young people shared a pained sense of alienation that drew them to each other.

Soon after they began living together, David concluded that he could not go on studying Near Eastern art, and that he didn't like what he was doing enough to put up with the rigors of writing a dissertation. He decided to return to his family homestead, a medium-sized dairy farm near Ithaca, New York. Anne didn't mind. In the past she had vaguely envisioned country life as an escape from the troubles of the city, and whatever David decided about his career seemed good enough to her. So they moved East, married, and eventually, with money Anne had inherited from her grandmother, were able to buy some land in the vicinity of the family farm.

Ironically, considering the distances she has traveled, Anne ended up being what her parents originally prepared her to be, a housewife, although the cooperative venture of farm life is undoubtedly more appealing to her than the suburban housewife's role would be. She maintains a small house where she cooks, cleans, and sews, and occasionally reads, while her husband looks after the cows and the daily business of the farm. Ithaca is far enough away, and its delights sparse enough, to tempt Anne and David into town only rarely. They have no real friends in the area, and only a few acquaintances. Evenings are spent over late and prolonged dinners and then tea, generally followed by a little television and an early bedtime. While Anne has long since given up speed, time is often lightened by marijuana and wine.

Anne's relationship with David is a resting place, perhaps for all time. It is so obviously preferable to what went before, that any critical comment seems gratuitous and mean. The marriage represents Anne's peace with life, and as a human being's solution it can't be disparaged. But it is a fragile peace. She herself senses its insecurity, its need for protection from the outside world, as she was reminded by the tension she felt at David's interest in a woman on a neighboring farm. How much pressure can their tie to each other withstand? They cannot afford to find out. Born out of their mutual need, the relationship never fully established its reason for being, and the greatest caution must always be exercised in handling it.

WORKING TOWARD SUFFICIENCY

Anne, who never was able to discipline her addictive reflexes, found that she had to settle for a reasonably palatable version of the traditional female role. Increasing numbers of women are concerned with working their way out of such roles, or, where possible, with avoiding them altogether. To do this inevitably means to come to terms with addiction. What if you have already committed yourself to the stereotyped women's occupations and activities? Where do you begin if you want to grow out of that bind? A person who has grown out of it—with nurturance, some initial ability, and a lot of desire—is Marie, a divorcée in her early thirties. Marie's family was comfortable economically (her father owned an independent supermarket), but did not have the advantages of position and education. Marie was not brought up to be anything other than what her mother, and her mother before her, had been.

Predictably, then, at the age of 19 Marie married Bob, who was stationed at a naval base in her home town. They then moved to Bob's home state in the Midwest. Marie devoted herself to marriage, home, and family for twelve years, and had two children along the way. Then Bob fell in love with his secretary, another 19-year-old girl, and left home. Marie was disconsolate, all the more so because she felt she must have been to blame for the breakup. Her husband had often told her she was too demanding when she tried to ask him questions and talk to him after he came home from work, while all he wanted was to relax with a few drinks.

This dilemma typified the major problem Marie faced in her marriage, and in her later dealings with men. She was an intense person, full of emotional and intellectual energy, who was forced by her limited options to channel all of this energy into her relationships with her husband and children. Too expansive a person for the boundaries within which she was confined, she made demands on her husband which were unrealistic, given what he (like most men in his social milieu) was prepared to accept. Her personality would not necessarily have led her into addiction under other circumstances, but without the tools to satisfy herself any other way, she was emotionally dependent on her marriage for more than it could offer her.

Nonetheless, despite her real need for commitment to a man, and her lack of models for life other than that represented by her relationship with Bob, Marie got over her distress, mainly because she was hardheaded enough to know she had to. Using the alimony she received from her husband, she went to a local community college with an eye toward making a career for herself. She quickly settled on nursing as both an attainable and a potentially satisfying goal, although later she was to question whether even this would take her as far as she wanted to go.

Her school experience was grueling, but enormously beneficial. Although she had never before learned in this kind of academic setting, she adapted well and soon began to think beyond her next day's assignments. For the first time she was getting some perspective on the limited role others had assigned her in life. She thought about people and the ways in which they acted, about the political implications of the organizational interactions in which she took part, and about how she as a nurse could help others.

When she graduated, Marie went to work at a large urban hospital in a black ghetto community. She had decided that this was where she would be most useful, and where she could learn the most. In fact, she was learning so much that it was making her extremely tense. After all, this was the first job she had ever held. But she excelled at her work. Energetic and bright, she attracted the notice of the doctors, who discussed their cases with her and thus gave her valuable additional knowledge.

Her main contribution to the hospital grew out of her contacts with the staff of attendants under her charge. Seeing that the attendants resented her as they resented all the nurses, she set out to win their confidence. She pitched in with their menial patient care tasks, solicited their viewpoints about what was happening on the floor, and ate with them and introduced them to the doctors they encountered in the cafeteria. Eventually she found the attendants volunteering to help her and staying late when emergencies arose. They even began to attend the shift meetings (where the outgoing shift brings the incoming personnel up to date on the condition of each patient on the floor), which they had heretofore avoided.

What Marie had done was to bring to life the intelligence and sensitivity that had always been hidden by her being a mere accoutrement to a male. As a parent, too, she made great headway. When she had been house-bound with her children, she had often directed an inordinate amount of attention to their activities. The result was a daughter who refused to do anything for herself and a son who reacted against any kind of management out of a fear of being stifled. When Marie applied her energies more widely and productively, she lost much of her impulse to dominate and supervise at home. Her children were the first to notice the change, as they somewhat belatedly struck out to explore the world on their own. They still turn to her for support and guidance, which she makes time to provide, but now these interactions are dictated by their needs rather than hers.

Marie's attempts to extend her growth to her social life have not produced as uniformly happy a picture. In the immediate aftermath of her separation, she had very much wanted a man, but was not in a good psychological or practical position to find one. For one thing, she was fearful that her dating might be used against her in the divorce proceedings. Eventually a legal settlement was reached (in fact, her husband lost his job just when she began to work, and her alimony stopped anyway), and she started to see some men from her neighborhood, usually middle-aged divorcés with children of their own. Again and again, though, she received from these men the same troubling message her husband had given her: "You want too much; can't you let up sometimes?"

It was true that Marie was an insistent, demanding person, but she became less so as she adjusted to her independence and focused her energy outside herself. After wondering for a while whether she was asking too much, or whether the men wanted too much sacrifice from her, she became less concerned with the whole issue. A Catholic, she had been driven into her first affairs a year after her separation by her need for sexual satisfaction even as she had felt great trepidation and guilt. Eventually she became more easygoing, needing less sex, but at the same time finding that she could have it without guilt and derive pleasure from less than the deeply intimate relationships she had always felt she required.

As her awareness grew, Marie began to see a pattern in the men who were available to her. They all expected her to be a mother to their children, demanded loyalty and devotion (especially sexually) while reluctant to promise it themselves, and wanted her to meet their needs rather than express her own. They found her changing opinions about sex, race, and politics disturbing. In growing beyond her original definition as a wife, Marie had placed herself outside the social environment in which she had lived all her life. She was a displaced person! Now, besides building a new life structure, she had to locate new ground to build it on.

This realization led to a period of confusion and indecision from which she is just emerging. Her professional training and involvement have given her the opportunity and the confidence to relate to men besides those who offer the comfort and familiarity of a background similar to her own. Her better self-definition has made her less worried about having men around at all. Thus she is finding, somewhat to her surprise, that she can choose partners more on her own terms—where, when, and if she wants them. She would still like to find one man whom she can consider a partner for life, but now she wants one who values—and can match—her independent thought and contributions as a person. She is prepared to let her own will and the natural flow of her life, rather than the deadly combination of desperation and happenstance, determine the possibilities for such an involvement.

Marie would have been locked forever into an addictive syndrome were it not for the breakup of her marriage, and the powerful drive for self-preservation this released. For years her marriage was the focal point of her existence. She sacrificed all of herself in order to preserve the arrangement at any cost. Only her development afterward showed her not to be an addict. When forced to behave independently, she was able to, and this was the demonstration and the fact of her growth into nonaddiction. Even so, she was often tempted to recoil into another relationship, and she frequently yearned for a man to give her completeness. When she did not find one on her own terms of emerging self-respect, however, she always regained her composure. This, in the eyes of the outside world, defined her as a strong person. When her unhappy friends, both married and single, marveled at Marie's resiliency, she felt like a hypocrite, but all she could do was smile.

MAN: THE MAKESHIFT EGO

Society twists men, too, into distorted images of themselves, only the distortion is complementary to that which women experience. Forced to be inhumanly tough and invulnerable in just the way women are forced to be childlike and weak, men have no more of a chance than women to develop themselves as full human beings. At the same time, men face precisely the same assaults on their integrity and self-confidence that women do. In addition to the social pressures on a man to marry, find a steady job, "settle down"—and the inculcation of a sense of weakness and dependency through encounters with parents, teachers, doctors, employers, experts, and institutions generally—men face the special injunction that they always show a strong face to the world. The effort to maintain this difficult equilibrium creates the style of addiction found commonly in males.

It is a woman's privilege to express her uncertainties and to acknowledge her emotional attachments. In men, the same needs often appear, but less openly. Many men live in a world which demands much from them emotionally and gives them little in return. A man is expected to develop a highly positive self-image—"the male ego"—and project his belief in himself to the outside world. If he is unsure about the validity of his self-image, he is certainly going to find other males disposed to challenge it. At work, he receives little nurturance from men and women who are trained into the same competitive aloofness he feels he must display. So the conflicting burdens of his male need for reinforcement of his self-image, and his human need to share his self-doubts, fall on his wife or lover.

Guy typifies the kind of man who badly wants a total love experience to resolve the contradictions in his psyche and cure his unease with himself. Guy's search was thwarted by the vastness and complexity of his emotional needs, which no one woman could really satisfy. As a result, he was thrown back on the blatantly self-gratifying use of women that made him seem to many to be a Don Juan. The ideal he had in mind, though, was something quite different from the transient, sex-centered affairs he often got into.

Guy grew up, outwardly comfortable and complacent, in a suburb of Chicago. His father was a prominent corporate lawyer, his mother a passive, helpless person. The inequality of stature between his parents was a source of considerable instability in the family and within Guy himself. When Guy was a child, his father did not spend enough time around the house to give his son much positive direction. In addition, when he was present he tried to make Guy measure up to unrealistic standards of successful performance. He did this by belittling Guy's successes and implying that whatever he did was not quite enough. Yet Guy never learned to turn elsewhere, or inward, for his rewards.

His mother, on the other hand, lavished on Guy the respect she herself lacked. She met all of Guy's needs for esteem as well as she could with the few personal resources she had. Although she was indiscriminate in her praise and admiration, her trivial position in the home made these practically meaningless. She did teach Guy that, in the absence of what he regarded as true accomplishment and acknowledgment, he could rely on the sympathy of a woman.

With a father who wouldn't respond to the most exceptional performance, and a mother who effused about him no matter what he did, Guy soon did not bother to extend himself in school. In fact, with no models of purposeful activity before him (except for his father, whose goals seemed so remote to Guy), nothing seemed worthy of sincere and diligent pursuit. Rather, he cultivated an attractive personality, particularly a quick verbal ability, as a means of impressing people and winning affection to substitute for the love he most needed. Still, he was clever enough to do well academically as long as school was at the center of his life.

Away at college, Guy relentlessly sought close relationships with women. Even in his first year there, when most of his classmates limited themselves to weekend dating, Guy was known for having a girlfriend. The keynote to Guy's relationships was devotion. Feeling that he deserved loving attention, yet insecure about whether he could earn it, Guy did not leave the matter to chance. He made explicit, detailed, and often abrasive demands for the care and concern he wanted from his girlfriends. While he was still seeing high school girls, he got away with it. But it would no longer be as easy as it had been in his father's time to find an educated woman who would unthinkingly commit herself to a man who imposed himself so much, even if he was as attractive as Guy.

Just as Guy was about to graduate, his father suddenly died. The family seemed to fall apart, as if everyone had been held together solely by their connection to the head of the house. Guy's brother went to Europe; his mother sold the family home and moved to Florida. Meanwhile, Guy looked forward to returning to Chicago in the fall and rejoining a new girlfriend whom he had met during his spring vacation and who would now be entering the University of Chicago. It was to be near her, as well as to be in a position to exploit his father's connections in the legal world, that Guy had applied to law school at the university. But by the time he arrived, the girlfriend had dropped him. She made the curt announcement in the middle of a phone call in which he had been berating her for her carelessness (an act typifying a relationship which she could hardly have found enjoyable), and Guy's last emotional contact in Chicago was destroyed. He found himself alone and unloved—and about to start an unappealing trek through law school.

Why was he there? For one thing, because he preferred to go on living the student's life, which enabled him to devote much of his attention to women. For another, because he expected to be able to go into a corporate law career on his father's coattails. While he lacked the specific interests that might have directed him into some academic field, law school would still give him the opportunity to exercise his considerable verbal and mental abilities. To the intellectual friends with whom Guy shared his gifted conversational style, law seemed both too bourgeois and too diffuse a vocation, one which expressed no genuine heartfelt inclinations. Guy himself revealed no such inclinations, however, and to the conventional, careerist boyhood pals around whom much of his life still revolved, law seemed as suitable as anything else. All told, Guy had not thought much about it one way or the other. His ill-considered career choice reflected the shallowness and lack of integration that had marked his life.

The main problem he faced on his arrival at the university was more immediate. His spirit was broken in the aftermath of his rejection at the hands of the girl he loved. Denied even a modicum of emotional support, Guy had no energy for work. He made futile visits to his ex-girlfriend's apartment to win back her affection, and took up his classmates' time with tales of despair. He spoke of leaving school to join the army, or of committing suicide. But he pulled through. Intelligent, personable, and outgoing, he brought together a new group of friends who stood by him in his misery. Studying very little during his first two semesters, he managed to take his exams, and even do well—with a little help from his friends. Distracted as he was, he was still able to manipulate the academic environment.

The same love cycle was to repeat itself several more times in the next few years. Guy would throw himself into a relationship totally, and it would last for three months, six months, a year. Then the woman would grow tired and angry, and Guy would cling desperately to dying emotion, once more trying the patience of his friends as they attended him. Each time a woman left him, he complained that he would never again find someone who would love him. Gradually, though, he learned to adjust more realistically to his fate. Seeing that he couldn't attain the complete love he sought, he looked for women who would just keep him company for a while. So he began, opportunistically, to accept the consolation of transitory affairs. These did not fully meet his needs, though, and there was still a part of himself that greeted each new affair with the hope that he would never have to search for another.

What went wrong with these relationships? Guy was involved with many different women under a wide range of circumstances, and many of the breakups occurred for the usual variety of reasons. Because of its frenzy, Guy's social life appeared to be chaotic. But in retrospect it is possible to discern a recurrent pattern of futility and self-defeat in his love affairs, a pattern that stemmed from the way he viewed women in relation to himself.

With the legacy of low self-esteem left him by his father, despite his acknowledged intelligence and competence, Guy was uncertain about whether people could like him, and thus whether he had any real reason for being. So he sought reassurance wherever he could find it. To him, a friend, male or female, was someone who would listen to and support his posturings and his complaints. But it was only from women that he felt he could demand the total allegiance he craved. Sex was the symbol of their adoration, and Guy's continual banter with his friends was full of competitive, sexist overtones: "Do you think I'll get to make that girl with the big tits?" Actually, Guy's talk about sex conveyed his deeper need for acceptance, and he was ready to fall in love at the slightest pretext. Lacking any other consuming interests, he gave women a disproportionate place in his life. A married woman who kept trying to arrange dates for him with friends of hers remarked, "Guy talks about women as though they were different from people."

Women always came first for Guy. When he didn't have one, he plodded dejectedly through the events of his life. Intellectual stimulation, dispassionate interests, good times with friends—these things all were secondary. His unhappiness was never far from the surface, and his threshold for expressing his longing was low. This was when he made the greatest claims on his friends, but all the while he let them know that he wanted something more than what they could provide, and that he was with them only under a good-natured but insistent protest.

When Guy met an eligible woman, he wasn't able to be objective about her as a person, since he had so much hope wrapped up in her. Though insecure about being rejected, he would plunge right ahead, sparing nothing in his initial self-presentation while telling his friends what a superlative catch he had on the line. A brilliant, witty man, Guy would go through all his routines in an effort to make his appeal irresistible. With his ability to put himself forward, he was almost irresistible, except that in this supercharged state he often went too far. For a time he was known to relate his entire life story during his first evening out with a woman. This unrestrained approach alienated women who respected themselves. To such a woman there seemed something ignoble about a man whose life had so little meaning that she could immediately become its central focus.

To Guy's detriment, the women who did accept him were often passive, easily ruled (at least for a time), and uncertain of themselves and their own wants. At the outset, these qualities were well-suited to Guy's repeated demands, which made themselves felt once he had established himself with a woman. Far from being a casual swinger, Guy was a serious person who tried to invest every affair with great depth of concern. He articulated everything he was thinking and feeling and everything he thought was happening in the relationship. Unfortunately, though, his requests and criticisms were all directed toward making his woman friend more responsive to him alone. He took a nagging tone and imposed a judgmental outlook on what should have been a spontaneous experience. What he was after was complete control of the woman—physical, mental, emotional. There was something persistently inappropriate about Guy's manner, which signified an urge to dehumanize that went beyond mere preoccupation with sex.

The women who acquiesced to these demands were, in some cases, those who had fewer other options open to them because they had less appeal for men, or less confidence in their appeal. For this reason, given the self-serving nature of his desire, Guy soon tired of them. At the same time, in what seems a paradox, Guy despised these women for their very responsiveness to him. Fritz Heider's balance theory holds that it is easier to like people who value the same things you do, and vice versa. In this way, your view of the world is balanced. Since Guy did not have enough respect for himself, he was forced to denigrate those people who valued him and accepted his requests as legitimate. It pained him to realize that as he gained a woman's love, he ceased to regard her (just as he never could regard his mother) as a meaningful source of esteem and support. And once he was no longer excited by a woman, he became querulous with her.

Thus a woman who became involved with Guy in the hope of getting close to him found herself in the midst of irresolvable pressures. The lovers who remained desirable to him were those who held back from him emotionally while they accepted his attentions, usually because they were self-centered themselves. Often they could be aloof because they were physically attractive, and this, too, added to their appeal for Guy. With these women Guy initiated sustained campaigns to break through their alluring psychological reserve— the ultimate conquest that always eluded him. A woman who became one of Guy's obsessions found herself increasingly isolated from the rest of the world. They would spend a lot of time alone together, and some with his friends, but rarely any time with her friends. The centering of the affair around Guy's interests and Guy's world, and mostly his private world, derived from the priority he gave his own values and needs. Consciously or not, he selected women who were, for some reason, temporarily or permanently open to this domination.

There had to be a breaking point. Guy's overbearing, authoritarian style eventually became intolerable both to mature, experienced women, and to younger women who valued freedom and spontaneity. The outward compliance he exacted from the callow girls he most often fell in love with was usually made possible by their childish irresolution, and that in turn made for volatile relationships. More than once Guy unwittingly served as a father-figure, to be discarded when the girl found a new boyfriend. This occurred, for instance, with a college student whom he had been seeing for about a year and who finally left him for "a kid like me, who I can just have fun with." When such a woman built up the strength to call it quits, the break was usually sudden and irrevocable, although Guy would prolong the agony by imploring her for another chance. The bewildered woman found her former tormentor clinging to her for dear life. As Guy's feelings of inadequacy emerged once again with the crumbling of the relationship, he had all the more need for this or some other woman's concern. An addict, he had to seek more of what was destroying him.

In time, though, he would regain his grip, and a degree of balance would be restored to his life as he gathered reassurance from the circle of male and female friends he kept in reserve for these periods. In fact, underneath his depressing, adolescent litany of big tits without bras, Guy was a person of good impulses. His loyalty toward his friends, if sometimes overridden by more powerful drives, was real. With his women friends, too, he would talk of being "friends for life," and while he frequently had little in common with many of the women he happened to get involved with, he did keep up with his ex-lovers whenever this was actually a possibility. At times he sought renewed sexual ties with these women, but his friendships with them were often carried on at a more uncomplicated level of affection and unsolicited kindness.

Guy was a scrupulous person, though one whose moral sense was forever being compromised by passivity and egocentrism. As he got older, he began to nurture more systematically qualities that he had always possessed in some undeveloped form: an openness to the environment, an ability to relate enthusiastically to people, and a feeling for where the world was going. By the time he was in law school, his aesthetic and political orientations had evolved in a direction very different from that of most of his classmates. He was genuinely responsive to the moral concerns of his generation. This often left him at odds with his chosen career, although in his inertia and self-preoccupation, he was not ready to act on his changing awareness.

There was to be no place for Guy in the rigid organizational structure of corporate law, as he first learned during the summer vacations when he clerked for his father's old firm. Over such minor matters as his beard and a loosened necktie he came to be derisively referred to as "the hippie lawyer," and he was eased out of the company as the memory of his father receded into the past. It was now up to him to find a full-time position after graduation. For the first time he was left to do something important on his own resources.

He surprised himself by getting a job with another prominent law firm. But going to work as a corporate lawyer marked a major change in Guy's life. Hedonist that he was, he did not adjust happily to ten-hour days as a titled errand boy. At first, the strain of his new routine and the limitations it imposed on his social life intensified his need for a loyal woman friend. At the same time, though, by forcing him to see himself as a responsible adult, it put a brake on his tendency to disintegrate under emotional pressure. With colleagues and clients depending on him to produce on a daily basis, he no longer could afford the indulgence of histrionic collapses before an audience of sympathetic friends. Meanwhile, he was compelled to evaluate the purpose of what he was doing, for the simple reason that it was unpleasant and demanded a substantial commitment of himself. He resented his position as an inferior in the firm's hierarchy. Yet he wasn't motivated to do the things he would have to do if he wanted to move up, and he had real doubts about the meaning and value of corporate law.

Finally he resigned from the firm and took a position in government where he could participate in social planning alongside people less myopic than his former colleagues. Through this job he has integrated his moderately left-wing impulses into a stable lifestyle. In so doing, he has broken out of his father's mold and his earlier professional passivity. Most important, he enjoys his work. It is easier for him to resist addictive involvements now that his daily life is no longer a source of dissatisfaction.

Guy's development out of the excesses of his addiction has been more a natural process of growing up—or maturing out—than a deliberate therapeutic endeavor. For several years he has been cultivating an independent interest in books and movies and an ability to enjoy these things wholeheartedly. He has actively sought new friendships without expecting sexual benefits to flow from them. As he became more at ease with himself, he began to experience and enjoy longer and longer periods of self-containment until an opportunity for a reasonable relationship arose. After a while, this practice enabled him to approach women with something less than his old frenzy, and his overtures took on a new and appealing element of restraint and casualness.

On this basis, after going through a number of inconsequential relationships as before, he has formed a stable involvement which has lasted for two years. In direct contrast to the unrealistic initial buildups he had always given women, Guy did not at first find Nancy glamorous or sexually overpowering. Their contact was friendly and casual and went on simultaneously with other affairs on both sides. But somehow it outlasted the others, and in six months they were living together. The relationship developed with dignity, and the lovers' mutual feeling grew naturally rather than being pumped up at the outset and then left to deflate.

Nancy is the first woman Guy has ever lived with. His relationship with her is hard to figure out, so different are their inclinations, but it seems to be working. Nancy is more emotionally expressive than Guy, and considerably more energetic and outgoing. She is mature enough to be serious about her personal dealings, this being perhaps the primary trait that she and Guy share. Confident of her ability to attract people, whether lovers or friends, she has a well-established group of companions who are as important in the couple's life as Guy's friends are. When she wants to go out and do something, she doesn't depend on Guy to set things up. She makes plans with her friends and leaves Guy home to watch television if that is his preference. They do fight, since Nancy is troubled by the same things in Guy that have bothered other women, but the tough give-and-take demonstrates that she is fully engaged with him, and he appreciates this. Nancy has made him more warmly human and more secure, though it is not yet clear how deeply he has changed. When she travels alone to see friends in other parts of the country, he can still become moody and display glimpses of his old behavior.

In general, Guy's growth has been marked by increased self-control, but also perhaps by a more entrenched fatalism. The self-knowledge he has gained has apparently not been such as to give him a more extended scope and greater power in the world. Instead, he has moderated his demands on life, and his personality and habits have taken on some of the conventional attributes of getting older. He is less open, less vulnerable with his friends now. Recognizing that no one relationship can give him everything he needs, he has taken up time-filling hobbies that Nancy does not participate in, such as playing cards. These, rather than his existential anguish, have become his avenues for interaction with friends. He is a more pleasant, gracious person to be with than before, but also a less exciting one, for what made him stimulating was in large part the expression of his immaturity. The nonaddictive ideal of excitement *with* maturity is something he may never have been cut out to strive for.

THE DON JUAN: MALE OR FEMALE

As with the illustrations of Anne and Guy, a person can bring an addictive disposition to a number of successive or simultaneous relationships. From these examples, though, we might infer that such is not a natural state for the interpersonal addict. Anne and Guy, at any rate, ended up in conventionally stable relationships, and their stories suggest that this was what they were looking for all along.

Multiple sexual contacts (at least as an open and widespread phenomenon) have appeared relatively recently within the middle class. They derive from patterns in the lower class and in the most privileged classes, where transitory but passionate relationships more frequently occur. This volatile style of coupling has entered mainstream society via the youth culture, along with drugs and hip mannerisms. In a chaotic world it gives many individuals a series of temporary props, but the underlying middle-class desire for a permanent connection remains strong. When that search is successful, as both Anne and Guy illustrate, the basis of the connection tends to be something other than sexual attraction.

Although Anne and Guy had this in common, as lovers they looked as if they were playing different roles. Guy actively ensnared women, while Anne was passive, driven by fate and circumstance. This difference is more apparent than real, since Guy was being exploited even as he exploited others—a condition not uncommon for an addict. A role like Guy's is also often played by women. Sybil, like Guy, had a string of lovers while being unable to manage herself. Her case shows that the woman is not always the passive partner in addiction and that the "Don Juan" addict is not always a man. Sybil was much more manipulative in response to her desperation than Anne, and even more so than Guy. She differed from both, however, in being so detached from her need for love that she looked to men for little more than the time-filling oblivion that is the most universal component of addiction.

Born in a rural area in Western England, Sybil studied historic preservation at a red brick university. She came to London as an intern on an urban redevelopment project. Before she decided definitely to accept the position, however, she had kept her supervisor waiting for several months. This same irresolution, puzzling in a person of her ability, extended to her frenetic personal life as well. Never spending any free time by herself, Sybil went out every night, whether on a date with a man or to play tennis or volleyball with friends. She had an ill-matched assortment of boyfriends who were generally not as bright as she and who in many cases felt inferior to her. For her part, Sybil openly expressed disrespect for them, but continued to see them nonetheless. Her cutting remarks about these individual men never grew into a larger awareness of the pattern her life had assumed. "I just let these things happen," she said about her affairs.

The men who became Sybil's boyfriends were those who were willing to put up with her treatment of them for a long enough period of time. She made herself available to all while avoiding commitments to any. Most of these men as a matter of course made sexual advances, and Sybil as a matter of course accepted them. The only one she said she didn't "sleep with," apparently because he didn't ask, was a quiet, intelligent chap who, oddly enough, friends thought was the special, long-term romantic attachment in her life. When asked whether she felt especially close to any of her lovers, she seemed not to comprehend the question. Each of them just served as her fix for the night.

In her social life and elsewhere, Sybil could not sort things out. Her passivity and indecisiveness combined to carry her on, a spectator to her own existence. While she showed flashes of insight, her manner of speaking was detached, and her conversation became interesting only when it took the form of superficial word play. Neither she nor the people with whom she associated gave much importance to the things she said, which were often meaningless or inconsistent. During a period of labor unrest in the building industry a local newspaper interviewed some young professionals in government and industry, including Sybil, who were thought to bridge the ideological gap between the construction workers and business interests. After endorsing the union's position on all the issues, Sybil completely undercut her stand by saying that she was glad that management maintained the upper hand. "It certainly is good that they're not letting them have their way totally," she concluded. "Where would we be then?"

Sybil had not begun to resolve the clash of values between her traditional family background and the young, freewheeling crowd she ran with in London. Out of the composite of beliefs and opinions that she picked up here and there, she did not know which were really her own. A sexually active person, she abruptly shifted to chastity whenever her mother, a stern fundamentalist, came for an extended visit. Yet this was no real sacrifice for Sybil, since she didn't seem to value sex inherently (friends found her manner distinctly asexual), and since her mother's presence provided the ballast which, when left to her own devices, she sought from lovers. Beyond this, she even expressed agreement with her mother's strictures against premarital sex. In the swirl of her thoughtless and diffuse existence, she inwardly craved repression.

Suspiciously urbane to her family, inexplicably shallow to her colleagues, Sybil found herself in an intellectual role for which she had the requisite ability but not the slightest predilection. It was as though a partial brain transplant had been performed on a farm girl, giving her the knowledge and sophistication of a city planner, but none of the concomitant interests or habits. Sybil longed to do something different, but she could not gather the momentum to break away from her professional life as long as she could remain in a subordinate position where major decisions were left to someone else.

Whenever she sat quietly alone, as when she tried to read, Sybil would soon get tense. The energy she generated in her unceasing social life became an unendurably disruptive force when turned in upon her own vulnerable being. So she would "get together" with somebody. That only put her further out of touch with her work and herself, and caused her additional anxiety. She sought further escape in the one direction she knew—misuse of people. At the expiration of her internship she married the one boyfriend she hadn't been sexually involved with. With this support, she gave up her career while continuing the round of socializing that was her life. No one was close enough to her—not even herself—to be able to say whether she conceived her marriage to be an expression of love.

Anne, Guy, and Sybil used people indiscriminately as objects of addiction, but all of them eventually settled down with one person. Sybil did so out of the same uncontrolled self-centeredness that led her to make use of men in other ways. Anne, searching for a sure emotional object, ended up in a relationship which resembled the one from which Marie escaped, at least in terms of the similar outlooks and needs the two women brought to their marriages. Guy has tried to forge a growing awareness of his unhappiness and failure into changed patterns of behavior. For him, possibly, self-recognition and help from others will lead to ultimate growth out of addiction. More than any of the others, Marie, whose addictive involvement ended with her divorce, seems to be on a sure path to psychological freedom. Perhaps this is because her addiction was socially ordained rather than the result of an addictive personality.

For all these people, issues of survival were very close to the surface. With so much at stake, how can growth come about? Should the dangers of change be risked when a person's existence is in question? And how, in such a precarious and delicate area, can change be carried out constructively?

Where was the hope of making reason and the will of God prevail among people who had a routine which they had christened reason and the will of God, in which they were inextricably bound, and beyond which they had no power of looking?
—MATTHEW ARNOLD, *Culture and Anarchy*

9

Society and Personal Growth

Addiction is an individual pattern molded by social and cultural forces. The addictive drift of society tends to sweep along anyone who does not make an effort to understand and control his or her destiny. Conversely, growing out of addiction means making changes both within oneself and in one's relationship to society.

These themes are captured, with the urgent significance which they have for our time, in D. H. Lawrence's *Women in Love*. Lawrence understood a great deal about addiction—the precarious psychological stability of some individuals, the factors that make for inner strength and weakness, the social roots of personal alienation, and, finally, the relationship between addiction and love. In *Women in Love* he combined a critique of the modern social context of addiction with a contrasting vision of personal autonomy and growth. Love figures centrally in that vision; it is seen as part of a conscious and yet spontaneous way of living and growing. To Lawrence, love is the spiritual antithesis of addiction.

Women in Love is about two sisters, Ursula and Gudrun Brangwen, and their relationships with men—Ursula's with Rupert Birkin,

199

Gudrun's with Gerald Crich. The two relationships go off in opposite paths because the people involved approach life in fundamentally different ways. Gerald and Gudrun, with their concern for appearances, try to model themselves after a socially proper image. In so doing they repress any discordant impulses they feel, which must then find expression in inappropriate or destructive ways, as when Gerald and Gudrun torture a rabbit together and are wounded by it. Gerald and Gudrun are comfortable at the surface levels of social interaction, but at some level they are uncomfortable with themselves, and thus they shy away from emotional intimacy with others. Gerald, for instance, out of his conventional male inhibitions, can only respond defensively to Birkin's offering himself to him in friendship.

Birkin and Ursula, on the other hand, express themselves more freely, but also with a deeper purpose. While they do seemingly flighty things which disconcert their friends, their erratic self-expression is part of a process of getting to know themselves, so that they eventually achieve a stability and contentment that eludes Gerald and Gudrun. They are serious people who deeply respect living things and living impulses, as they show by their reverence toward the catkins Ursula is teaching about when Birkin visits her classroom in his role as school inspector. Birkin and Ursula do not suppress themselves, and nothing within them grows to unhealthy proportions, to become a life-defeating eruption of need. Since they are each whole and independent in themselves—Gudrun enviously characterizes Ursula as "strong and unquestioned at the centre of her own universe"—they can come together in a relationship where they do not threaten or feel threatened by each other's wholeness.

This existential poise is what is lacking in Gerald and Gudrun, neither of whom is self-sufficient. For Gerald, after his father's death, life is "a noise in which he participated externally, and inside this hollow shell was all the darkness and fearful space of death." Gudrun's feeling that she is "outside of life" causes her "to suffer from a sense of her own negation." Just as Gerald "knew he would have to find reinforcements, otherwise he would collapse inwards," so, too, Gudrun "must always demand the other to be aware of her, to be in connection with her." These addicted lovers can only seek completion, a death in life, so that Gudrun yearns, "Oh, why wasn't there somebody to take her in their arms and fold her safe and perfect, for sleep."

While Gerald and Gudrun want to seal off their lives, defensively bottling up their desires until these explode, Ursula and Birkin strive to remain naked to experience. Birkin pledges to Ursula, "I deliver *myself* over to the unknown, in coming to you, I am without reserves or defences, stripped entirely, into the unknown." Ursula eventually breaks with her sister because she sees that Gudrun "finished life off so thoroughly, she made things so ugly and so final."

Gerald, meanwhile, is put off by Birkin's changeability. "I feel," he says to Birkin, "that there is always an element of uncertainty about you—perhaps you are uncertain about yourself. But I'm never sure of you. You can go away and change as easily as if you had no soul." Birkin is not at all inconsistent or unreliable in his friendship with Gerald. The "uncertainty" Gerald sees in him is his willingness to be flexible, to accept imperfection and the need to search and change. "You must leave your surroundings sketchy, unfinished," Birkin says, "so that you are never contained, never confined, never dominated from the outside."

Gerald's relationship with Gudrun begins when he walks through the night to come to her. Having lost his father, Gerald now needs another focus for his collapsing identity:

> "I came—because I must," he said. "Why do you ask?"
> She looked at him in doubt and wonder.
> "I must ask," she said.
> He shook his head slightly.
> "There is no answer," he replied, with strange vacancy.
> There was about him a curious and almost godlike air of simplicity and naïve directness. He reminded her of an apparition, the young Hermes.
> "But why did you come to me?" she persisted.
> "Because—it has to be so. If there weren't you in the world, then *I* shouldn't be in the world, either."

Gerald here is a sleepwalker, practically an automaton. There is no communication, no relatedness, between him and Gudrun. They are driven individuals, talking past each other because they "must" give expression to drives they can neither understand nor control. Their relationship is a mutually possessive-destructive one, each trying to bolster himself or herself by bringing the other under the domination of his or her will. Simultaneously, each reacts against this enclosure by yearning to be free from the connection, while resenting any sign of independence in the other. At the end of the novel, the two of them brutally turn on each other. During a vacation in the Alps, Gudrun takes another lover, an unsavory and nihilistic artist. After being goaded into a fight with him, Gerald again walks trance-like— this time to his death in the snow.

In contrast to the mindless, compulsive behavior of Gudrun and Gerald, Ursula and Birkin tentatively examine their feelings and actions in order to discover what they really want and don't want for themselves and their relationship. Here Birkin tries to harmonize his various desires:

> The next day, however, he felt wistful and yearning. He thought he had been wrong, perhaps. Perhaps he had been wrong to go to her [Ursula] with an idea of what he wanted. Was it really only an idea, or was it the interpretation of a profound yearning? If the latter, how was it he was always talking about sensual fulfilment? The two did not agree very well.

What distinguishes Birkin and Ursula from Gerald and Gudrun is the ability to think about themselves and about the effect they have on each other.

While Birkin and Ursula are unfettered and autonomous, able to go where they will as they work out their own set of values, Gerald and Gudrun are trapped not only inside themselves, but by society. Normally bound and choked by their social roles, they at other times react against these roles in an extreme, negativistic way. At such moments "they both felt the subterranean desire to let go, to fling away everything, and lapse into a sheer unrestraint, brutal and licentious." Gerald, as the industrial magnate, lives with the whole weight of the past, of "social England," of tradition and convention, pressing down on him. But while in London he participates in an orgiastic scene with a group of bohemians. "He was so conventional at home, that when he was really away, and on the loose, as now, he enjoyed nothing so much as full outrageousness."

Gudrun's vacillations are even more apparent. For while she, in the artist's role she affects, frequently disparages materialism and conventionality, she just as frequently accepts them, especially when it comes to the artificial way in which she conceives of marriage. Announcing that she is looking for "a highly attractive individual of sufficient means," she cannot visualize what Birkin and Ursula attempt—marriage as a spiritual union. Gudrun's failure to reach a stable equilibium is exposed in her inability to work out a free life within the framework of the society in which she lives. "One could never feel [free] in England," she laments, "for the simple reason that the damper is *never* lifted off one, there. It is quite impossible really to let go, in England, of that I am assured." Thus she finally runs off to nowhere with her artist friend.

To Birkin and Ursula, freedom doesn't mean an encompassing repudiation of all social conventions. It is to attain something more real than what society customarily offers that they desire freedom. Already largely separated from their families, they symbolically abandon the conventional order by quitting their jobs when they marry; but they do marry, because marriage is one social institution they believe they can make into something personal, something living. Birkin and Ursula's relationship, however unreinforced by other social contacts, is not an addiction. They show a consistently outgoing face to the world, even though they are usually rebuffed. They remain intensely concerned about Gerald and Gudrun, and when Gerald dies they cut short their trip and carry out the social forms demanded by the situation with a grace and sense of responsibility that prove their good faith in questioning these same forms. On the last page of the novel, Birkin reiterates to Ursula his insistence on the value of male friendships like the one he had wanted with Gerald. Birkin and Ursula's open self-questioning, balanced by self-respect, is the contrasting image to addiction, and an image of the way out of addiction.

APPLYING ADDICTION TO OURSELVES

The stark, almost abstract contrast between self-destructiveness and personal fulfillment which Lawrence presents in *Women in Love* closely parallels the distinction between addiction and nonaddiction which we have developed throughout this book. But in applying these models to ourselves in order to make practical use of them, we must be aware that none of us fits either extreme. Being human, we all fall somewhere in between. We all have more or less addictive tendencies in our makeup, along with positive, life-seeking tendencies. The question we face is what we as individuals can do to help ourselves in present-day society. The first thing we can do is to evaluate honestly and yet realistically where we are. While a degree of addiction is inevitable—and some addictions are more damaging than others—we have to recognize that something is always lost in addiction.

In the case of Anne, we saw an addiction which is so understandable that it is almost reasonable. Although Anne had the so-called advantages of birth—money and social position—her upbringing deprived her of all life-sustaining forces. She was given little self-respect, was discouraged from finding skills in herself and interests in her world, and was blinded to what human contact could be. Her discovering another soul to keep her company is a relief to herself and to any sensitive onlooker, and perhaps this will be sufficient to anchor her existence and bring her continuing and expanding pleasure. Her addiction is centered around another human being, so that there should always be the chance for emotional sharing, for growing together, and for helping one another out.

But paradoxically, this is where addictive relationships are most wanting, and often in very deceptive ways. The sharing may derive from a feeling of exigency which can disappear in a moment, and which is too desperate to allow genuine understanding or appreciation. The growing together can also be artificial, predicated on the other person's immediate presence, and having no meaning outside that context. And the desire to help can be submerged by a stronger desire to possess, even if that means sabotaging a loved one emotionally, socially, and practically. So what is actually missing in addictions like Anne's is what appears to be the ready chance they offer to explore and know another person, intimately and yet in relation to a larger world. This missed opportunity is the greatest loss from interpersonal addiction.

What makes these truths difficult to come to grips with is that people who are involved in addictive relationships are often those who congratulate themselves on their romantic breakthroughs, and who resist self-examination or questioning by others. Indeed, they intimate that those who think about and question love cannot know what it is. In this, they are supported by an entire culture, and by well-meaning observers who don't see that a destructive exploitation of oneself and others can take the name of love.

This social support explains why Anne was not likely to emerge, or to want to emerge, from addiction. But if she ever could replace addiction with a more substantial relationship to life, she would almost certainly welcome the change. Ultimately, addiction is an unrewarding condition to find oneself in. Especially when an addict is involuntarily separated from the object of his addiction—and cannot say anything good about it in retrospect—he will be hard-pressed to justify the experience to himself.

There are people who acknowledge the weakness, deprivation, and destructiveness in addictive relationships, yet who then ask, "If that's the only way many people can deal with life, why bother them with ideas about being more active or exuberant?" This is, of course, a difficult argument to answer. I have no wish to impose my values on anyone else. But I would find it easier to accept the contention that some people prefer addiction if those people were more honest and forthcoming in their preference. If someone said, "I am an addict, and I am contented to be one," then while he would be giving up a lot, he would be expressing a distinct choice. Most people don't want to be addicts, though, and especially don't want to have to think of themselves as addicts. When they *are* addicted, they are evidently trapped in a way of life that they themselves do not respect.

Yet most addicts are in just this position because they affirm the value our culture abstractly places on independence, activity, and growth. People don't want to have to say that they cannot live life fully. There is the uniform admiration for those who are adventurous, and who do realize themselves. There is the search for these qualities in movie heroes, artists, sports figures, and political leaders. And there is the constant wondering many people do about the chances not taken up, the whole life not lived. Most people wouldn't mind opening up their horizons, in small ways and large, if only they knew how and could feel secure enough in themselves to make a beginning. To these people, overcoming addiction would be like knocking down walls which have contained them and their destinies. Where people in the case studies in this book have accepted the portraits of themselves with equanimity, it has been because they feel and have shown that they are capable of growth—that they are not addicts anymore—and thus are not bound by any past description of themselves.

As time goes on, there are only two directions in which we can travel; it is impossible to stand still. Either we broaden our perceptions, our knowledge, our experience, or we seal ourselves up and wither away within our self-imposed boundaries. We keep ourselves open to life, or we close ourselves to it—which is just another way of dying. Some people, for example, do this by sleeping to excess, the closest simulation of death in life. And many people opt for death in various ways throughout their lives. This is the passive drift of addiction. If we cannot begin to fathom our motivations and see the patterns our relationships assume, then we are bound to follow a predetermined course which may be destructive to ourselves and others. The alternative is to understand what is given and what is changeable in our personalities and our society, and to act on that understanding.

SOCIETY, THE FAMILY, AND CHILDREARING

The real cure for addiction lies in a social change which reorients our major institutions and the types of experience people have within them. If we are to do more than to liberate ourselves one by one—beginning with those who are already most whole and slowly working to include others less well off—then we have to change our institutions, and ultimately our society. Just as we cannot begin to understand addiction without understanding people's relationship to their social setting, so we cannot begin to cure it in the absence of a more universal access to our society's resources, and to its political power. If addiction is based on a feeling of helplessness, it will be with us until we create a social structure that is sensitive to people's desires and their efforts at influence.

The interdependency of all individuals and organizations makes the elimination of addiction contingent upon basic social change. But this same interdependency means that if we work to influence those institutions that we normally deal with, we can make a contribution which will be felt throughout the entire system. In particular, the family is a place where any individual can be an immediate force for change. When we find new ways to relate to our parents, our mates, and our children—say, by making those relationships less exclusive and obligatory—we have an impact on all aspects of our social structure. We give nonsexual friendships more of a chance, lessen the strains of marriage, and, most important, modify the way children grow up and learn to see the world. We give our offspring new opportunities for life and love.

The commune is a social form which embodies an effort at changing modern family life. Groups of individuals, and even whole countries, have adopted it in an effort to counteract the confining pressures of the nuclear family. Since it gives individuals a broader exposure to others in an intimate setting, a commune ideally is a return to the spirit of the extended family and the neighborhood community. For adults, the commune can be an alternative to the standard organization of society into groups of two. By enabling people to have a number of trusting relationships simultaneously, it offers them the promise of a richer emotional life, and frees them from the need to find one person to satisfy every need. For children, the commune can provide a diverse set of adult models—along with other children of all ages to relate to—so that they will not simply grow up imitating their parents and learning one set of reactions to life. Communes, of course, whether or not they are organized on ideological principles, can be as much a total enclosure as marriages. But there are also many instances where the open dealings practiced within a commune extend to its members' relations with the outside world as well.

How well do communes work in reality? Investigations of collective upbringing in Russia by Urie Bronfenbrenner, and in Israel by Bruno Bettelheim, indicate that children in these nations are adept at relating to others and at acting independently to accomplish group goals. These strengths are achieved through emphasis at an early age on cooperation, initiative, responsibility, and peer-group, rather than adult, supervision. They are achieved, however, at the expense of a high degree of group conformity. Perhaps in America and other Western countries, where communes are voluntary rather than institutionalized, a greater variety of communal forms and values will develop. These might include some which are more capable of encouraging and supporting individual deviations than is possible within more uniform or totalitarian cultures.

Right now, the problem in America is not one of excessive communalization, but of its opposite, as Urie Bronfenbrenner indicates in his article, "The Origins of Alienation." Bronfenbrenner finds that many signs of social instability and family psychopathology—including divorce, child desertion and abuse, juvenile drug addiction, alcoholism, and crime—are more common than ever before. His conclusion is that a child's normal lot is one of isolation from meaningful human contact as well as meaningful work. To counter this trend, he advocates reforms in education and family structure that resemble Ivan Illich's proposals for bringing schoolchildren into reality. For example, he finds that model housing developments could be vastly improved by not only allowing children room to play, but also designing into residential and play areas the opportunity to interact with children of different ages and adults at work and leisure.

Bronfenbrenner is pessimistic, as is justified by the social conditions he observes. There are, though, an increasing number of people who are trying to sort out these issues of alienation and isolation for themselves, as by arranging to work intermittently or on a freelance basis while devoting more time to their personal lives and families. Others are creating more open households—households which, while not organized formally as communes, welcome visitors and sometimes invite them to be temporary members of the family.

With the occupational mobility that is commonplace today, many people in academic and other professions have no permanent homes, and they do not have a chance to form enduring relationships out of daily contacts with people over the years. In this there is a loss, which Bronfenbrenner is acknowledging when he says that personal alienation is more severe than ever. But there is also a gain, in that many individuals and couples are actively maintaining the friendships they do make across barriers of distance and time. Extended live-in visits by friends compensate for what used to be the regular traffic of neighbors through the house. Children can see that even in their stable household, people come and go, and come again. From such experiences they can learn to live with a fluid environment while learning to value and expect continuity in friendship.

Sex role evolution also is changing the home atmosphere. Bronfenbrenner sees a negative side to this, insofar as some mothers are neglecting their children in their search for other gratifications. That happens when women imitate an unenlightened male pattern of blind self-assertion. There are other families in which the readjustment of the mother's role goes along with a heightened personal awareness in both parents, and here the impact on children can be positive. With the father spending more time with the children, and the mother presenting herself as a fully developed, self-respecting person, children are exposed to two adults for equal amounts of time, and both parents are able to give fully what they have to offer.

The questions of social structure and custom which we have been considering are basically questions of the degree to which a child is exposed to his or her parents and various other individuals—questions of whom, how many, and how much. These are important issues, but so is the character of the interactions between parents and children. Whether a child's environment is a commune, open household, or unaltered nuclear family, the criteria for addictive versus nonaddictive childrearing are essentially the same. The opportunities for constructive breakthroughs are great, even where parents are themselves struggling within a conventional setting to overcome their own addictive hangups.

We must be careful, however, to isolate what really matters in producing nonaddicted children, since in this area people are so confused about what lessons to draw from experience. Many people, for example, look at the story of Patricia Hearst and put the blame on the permissive dormitory policies which enabled her to spend nights at Steven Weed's apartment while still a college freshman. Seeking a "rational" explanation for her later adoption of an antisocial ideology, they infer that her exposure to marijuana and the politics of Berkeley radicalized her. This explanation is invalidated by the fact that she lived a secluded, apolitical, self-centered life in Berkeley. Explosive changes were to be expected in Patricia Hearst's life because she didn't have a coherent idea of who she was and what she wanted. The moral of her story is not that being strict with children will somehow fortify them against disintegration later on. It is that people will fall apart whenever they are removed from the shelter of external control, if that is what they rely on to regulate themselves. The alternatives for our children, then, are for them to spend *all* their lives within the confines of a strict social structure (which generally doesn't exist anymore), or to be taught self-discipline and self-determination when they are young. This teaching can only be accomplished through an exposure to life in all its contours, all its difficulties.

This is not a manual, but we can derive some guidelines for childrearing from what we have seen to be the true causes of addiction. The strict regulation of children which emphasizes their limitations and disrespects their status and abilities deprives them of the wherewithal for effective self-management. But personal futility also results from what is called permissiveness—an avoidance of confrontation by parents that reflects their own unsureness about values and their fear of losing their children's allegiance. When unaccompanied by any concept of helping children grow, such parental avoidance forms people who are careless of their responsibilities to others because they basically don't care about themselves. The children develop no precise sense of the value of their efforts or their words or thoughts, and so they discount the words and actions of others. Thus the permissiveness-directiveness battle is to a great extent a phony issue. The real issue is the active encouragement of life and growth.

Obviously, the attitudes people have about themselves have a lot to do with whether their children will grow up addicted. When parents are involved in meaningful activity and have some investment in life beyond having children, they are more likely to nurture their children's independence, joy, and competence, instead of constricting their growth with fear, guilt, or excessive supervision. When parents don't need to begrudge a child his or her identity, the child can develop a respect for his autonomy and the autonomy of others, instead of the exploitative urge that is part of addiction. Nonaddicted parents are the best models a child can have, for a joyous spirit (just like its opposite) is catching. Even if we have addictions of our own that we are insecure about, we can still show our children our most positive, constructive face, teaching them ideals that we may not be quite able to live up to, provided that we don't try to deny the disparity or act ashamed of it. In circumstances like this it can be valuable, too, for children to have other models besides their parents. Still, considering how seriously children take their parents' example and how little else they have to go on in the early years, it is worthwhile to restrain the expression of worries which may be very natural, but which are not constructive either as a model for a child to emulate, or as a guide for his or her behavior.

Children have a natural exuberance and an instinct to explore. Bringing up children to be nonaddicted means supporting and rewarding their explorations, thereby passing on to them a spirit of adventurousness that will persist through their adult years. It means granting them as much autonomy as possible at any given age, without interfering with the response—even when it is painful—that they get from the outside world. It means encouraging them to complete self-initiated enterprises which give them a sense of their own worth. It means allowing them joint, and eventually full, responsibility for managing their own lives, as well as for accomplishing work that has real value in the family or elsewhere. It means welcoming spontaneous impulses and new personal directions which will take them beyond the sphere of parental observation and influence. It means treating them with a respect that teaches them to respect themselves and others. And finally, it means establishing a relationship of mutuality in which their communications are part of a genuine interchange. When you take seriously what you tell a child and do what you say you will, when you listen seriously to him and give him a real opportunity to influence you, then he or she has the best chance of becoming a real person. He can count on himself and others, and he knows that he can make things happen in human relationships and practical affairs.

OVERCOMING ADDICTION AS INDIVIDUALS

In childrearing and in social change lie our main hopes for the future. But the key question in all of our minds is, What can we do for ourselves? What if we were brought up in a household where we were taught that we needed others to complete ourselves? What if we live in an institutionalized society which denies us the feeling of self-sufficiency while distracting us with unsatisfying substitutes? And what if, in consequence, we see that we are fundamentally unsure of ourselves? Can we do something about our addictions? I believe that most of us can, though the process won't be quick and it won't be total.

If we want to free ourselves from addictive patterns of living, the first thing we have to do is to break the chain of reciprocal dependency that locks us into our past. In other words, once we understand the social and familial conditions that have in part created our problems, we have to move on. Staying preoccupied with the weaknesses we acquired when we were too young to defend ourselves is itself an escape that prevents us from dealing with our lives. Take Portnoy, in Philip Roth's *Portnoy's Complaint.* Portnoy wants us to see that his parents have placed a heavy burden on him by continuing to live through him even after he has reached adulthood. At the same time, he inhabits a nightmarish world where the bogeys of his parents are ever-present in the imagery of his life; thus, he is living through them. Always accepting his parents as a reference point for his actions—an excuse, an obstacle, a provocation—Portnoy cannot act autonomously. To live through someone else is addiction. To blame our parents, or society, for our failings is to fall back on the same passive orientation, the belief in outside control, that creates addiction. Acceptance of personal responsibility is the first step toward freedom from addiction.

We have good grounds for tracing the addictive bent of many of today's young adults to their home environment and upbringing. But it doesn't make any more sense to shift the blame for our problems back one generation, onto people who themselves had to react to circumstances that they did not create, than it does to blame ourselves for not being able to break out of those problems all at once. A more constructive alternative is to accept that we are each given our own set of psychic and personal limitations to resolve; these limitations are simply a condition of human existence. There is, of course, an ideal of autonomous self-realization that we are working toward when we analyze our dependencies and untangle oppressive involvements. But this is an ideal that we can only approach, not achieve, and it doesn't do *us* any good to blame past generations for having failed to achieve it.

We cannot flee from the past, or from modern society, addicted as it may be. But there is room in this society for us to gain a degree of control over our lives and over the nature of our involvements.

We may find it helpful to review some ways in which addictions are treated when they are recognized as such. These include not only heroin addiction, but alcoholism, overeating, and compulsive cigarette smoking. Many of us have suffered from one or more of these dependencies, perhaps in conjunction with interpersonal addiction. Since addictions are so closely related in their causes, the patterns they assume, and the people they afflict, we should be able to find in the treatment of commonly acknowledged addictions some constructive models for overcoming dependencies of all kinds.

We have to be careful, however, to distinguish between the productive and the futile in addiction treatment. In a culture whose view of addiction is so out of focus, it is not surprising that many addiction therapies fail to comprehend the problem. The most common mistake is for a treatment program to substitute one addiction for another, just as we ourselves do when we start smoking heavily to keep from overeating, say, or after the breakup of a relationship. The rationale behind methadone maintenance, for example, is to give a heroin addict a drug that is marginally less destructive (mainly because it is legal), even though it, too, is addictive. In an article in *Science* entitled "The Methadone Illusion," Henry Lennard and his colleagues discuss the therapeutic use of methadone as an example of a cultural tendency to resolve complex social problems with drugs and druglike panaceas. It seems that addiction runs so deep in our society that it is considered almost impossible, and not necessary, to cure it altogether.

Something akin to this substitution can take place in drug rehabilitation programs, even those which are otherwise constructive, when an addict is allowed to become so dependent on the support of the group that he transfers his addiction from the drug to it. Thus, if he is forced to leave the group, he is likely to resume taking drugs. The substituting of a social dependence for a drug dependence is commonly observed in Alcoholics Anonymous, a rehabilitation program which is explicitly social in nature. Members of AA gain strength both from receiving the encouragement of others and from seeing that they can play a positive part in a group setting. Alcoholics Anonymous has been a last refuge for people whose drinking habit has left them desperate, and its success in keeping many of these people from returning to drink is not to be denigrated. But the alcoholic is still left with the crucial task of expanding his new feelings of worth and self-control to other social contexts besides the AA group itself.

All addicts have to learn new ways of coping with life and of viewing themselves. For a drug addict, this may involve such elementary matters as learning a skill and cultivating sound work habits, along with more difficult reorientations such as coming to see himself as a contributing person. To accomplish these aims, responsible rehabilitation programs combine therapy with skill training and with group activities which prepare the addict for participation in the real world. At Daytop Village in New York, for example, addicts are given increasing responsibility within the group so that their competence may grow, and they are penalized with the loss of privileges when they fail at their assigned tasks. Group therapy is used to make these experiences meaningful and to help addicts turn their new competence into a permanent part of their being. More common addictions, such as smoking and overeating, require similar solutions. Many of us are addicted to food or cigarettes even while we have useful skills and a place in society. While these dependencies may not lead a person into prison or a full-time center like Daytop Village, they ultimately have to be attacked, within the confines of a normal everyday existence, in much the same way as heroin addiction.

In fact, it is precisely in these areas that addiction treatments have been most successful. Albert Stunkard and Hilde Bruch, among others, have devised behavior modification programs to change the eating habits of obese patients. These therapies attempt to give a person mastery over his or her compulsive reactions by making him conscious of them. A person may be asked to record when, where, what, and how much he eats, and how he feels at the time. In this way, he may discover that he eats mainly when he is angry, or that he overeats in certain locales. He can then act either to remove from his environment some of the cues that lead him to eat, or to question his own automatic responses to those cues. An analogous treatment program for smokers requires a person to rate the pleasure she anticipates whenever she reaches for a cigarette. If the rating is below a certain level (which is made higher every week), she is to forego the cigarette. This technique can wean a person away from cigarettes not so much by the direct regulation it entails as by causing the person to question her motivations for smoking generally. Armed with a consciousness of why he or she repeatedly indulges in something that is harmful and perhaps not all that pleasurable, the compulsive eater or smoker can think about his or her behavior and hopefully determine new patterns for it, instead of passively being directed by outside stimuli and unknown emotions.

For many addicts, whatever their addiction, such a resolution is a long step toward overcoming it. However behavioristic and mechanistic this and some drug programs may appear to us, they are what is called for in a wide range of situations. A person may, for whatever reason, merely have learned unhealthy responses in one area of life. Or he may have such basic problems that he cannot behave appropriately in the most elementary ways. In either case, it is necessary to bring about straightforward changes in behavior. There are also related existential issues involved. When someone is fat or addicted to heroin, he is expressing attitudes, not only about food or drugs, but about himself and his relation to the world. Thus, a rehabilitation program requires the development of insight into one's being and motivations, whether through group therapy, as at Daytop Village, or through careful self-examination, as in Stunkard's formula. Behavior has to be changed, but so do self-conceptions and consciousness of oneself. The one cannot proceed without the other. We cannot know what to control or how to do it without being deeply aware of our problems. At the same time, seeing ourselves change and acting more in touch with our needs cannot help but increase our self-regard. Getting a grasp on ourselves requires this combination of existential and behavioral analysis. Together, they offer us the key to turning addiction around.

The process of extricating ourselves from addictive relationships (and addiction generally) is modeled after the constructive drug and food addiction therapies, the ones which actually work. It is a process of examining every part of our lives and discovering where, how, and why we are addicted. It is also a process of clarifying our goals and initiating the behavior necessary to reach those goals. When we look at ourselves without pretense, we can begin to ask what we are and what we are dissatisfied with. At the same time, we can take our first steps toward getting where we want to be. Beyond the initial stage of insight, which may stun us, there comes a point where we have to carry over our self-assessment to a renewed involvement in life. For in using our understanding to guide an active interchange with reality, we can learn to expand ourselves and to deal more confidently—less addictively—with whatever has been limiting us.

Oh, if there is one thing men need to learn . . . it is to collect each man his own soul deep inside him, and to abide by it. —D. H. LAWRENCE, *The Plumed Serpent*

10

Getting Ourselves Together

Addiction in love is the primary concern of this book, but we cannot learn to cope with that kind of addiction, or any kind of addiction, by itself. Because addiction is a general predisposition, it cannot be cured without a basic personal regeneration. Love is possible only when we reach out to another person from our strengths rather than from our weaknesses. If we find ourselves in relationships based on weakness, these cannot be fixed without first, or at the same time, repairing our own spirits. This chapter considers the self-development that must provide the basis for nonaddictively relating to others, and lays the groundwork for the discussion on growth within relationships in the next chapter.

What can we do if we realize that we are addicted to people? Since we cannot abstain totally from the addictive object—in any case, abstinence does not cure an addiction—we must aim to become genuinely nonaddicted. We know that the problem of addiction is not in the addictive object, but in our orientation toward it. So the purpose of a period of abstinence is to relearn our orientation toward something which has become a dependency, but which can be enjoyed in a constructive way. To do this, we must fundamentally reshape our motivations, our methods of coping, and our sources of satisfaction. That alone will enable us to have increasingly healthy love relationships, instead of substituting one kind of addictive relationship for another.

In the self-examination which we hope will lead us to feel better about ourselves and to relate to others with integrity, we can anticipate some dangers. One is that we might evaluate our lives against some notion of idealized love and, necessarily finding our experience deficient, wistfully conclude that we have not fully lived. It is just this belief in idealized romantic love, of course, that engenders our desperate behavior and makes us liable to addictions. In its place, we should want to be able to feel the pleasure of being alive and of knowing who we are.

This feeling makes it possible to love, and also not to panic when love is not immediately available. What the addict wishes to escape from is the realization that it is impossible to be "all together" all the time. He thinks there must be some way, if only he can find it, to make things perfect always. Actually, when we are aware that we will have some unmet yearnings for love, and that it is normal at times to feel unfulfilled, then we can come to someone else with the realistic desires and expectations out of which truly stable relationships are forged. This emotional balance enables us to act in harmony with our larger interests and needs, along with those of other people. When we read about remarkably vital and enduring relationships, such as the one between Jean-Paul Sartre and Simone de Beauvoir, we see that two people cannot always give each other what they most need at a given moment. Instead, their own individual self-reliance allows them to maintain their confidence in and affection for each other.

Focusing our attention primarily on love is not the best way to attain it. The diagnosis of the state of our souls should not be conceived solely in terms of how well we get along with our lovers, husbands, or wives. Nor should we congratulate ourselves just because we obviously don't have addictive ties with members of the opposite sex. In assessing oneself and others, it is only natural to look critically at relationships between lovers which appear to be addictions, either because these relationships are exclusive or frenetic. But to imagine that addiction exists only between lovers is as mistaken as to think that only drugs can addict. It can lead to serious miscalculations about other types of involvements we have, or about our actual ability to deal with people or love. Since addictions can be formed to work, religion, friends, and social groups, as well as to drugs and lovers (whether heterosexual or homosexual), not having a steady lover or any meaningful sexual contact is no guarantee that one is not participating in some addiction. In fact, the absence of emotional involvement with others can be just as much a sign of the lack of wholeness and the fears that make up addiction as a clinging relationship can be.

If the concept of addiction is to be helpful to us, it cannot be used as a weapon—either for self-defense, self-flagellation, or the bludgeoning of others. If we see it as a way to tear down people we know, we are probably trying to turn attention away from ourselves, and we aren't being helpful to others. On the other hand, if we all too readily find in ourselves every symptom listed on these pages, and hastily resolve that everything about us must be changed, we manifest the panic and instability of response that are more a cause of addiction than part of its cure. But if we honestly apply the insight that addiction gives us into our own behavior, and use the concept to understand the behavior of others, we can begin to move ourselves and those we care for gradually but constantly toward self-realization.

IDEALS

Let us first set ourselves an ideal of nonaddiction. How does a person who is free from addiction think and act? The description that follows does not correspond in its entirety to any real person, and certainly it is not a standard we should compare ourselves with literally. But it is a standard that we can work toward, so long as we are committed to a belief in ourselves as changing and growing beings.

The key to nonaddiction is maturity. Winick's discovery that heroin addiction is often an artificial extension of adolescence, an evasion of adult responsibility, offers us a sound insight about addiction of all kinds. Addictive relationships, too, can be temporary refuges on the road to the clarity of thought and purposefulness of action that people should gain as they grow older. Addiction is discontinued when a person possesses an intangible sense of freedom and self-command—a sense of having the power to fashion the conditions of his or her life instead of being fashioned by them. It is hard to tell exactly when and why this change comes for any given person, for it isn't planned. It happens more as a result of accumulated experience and an evolving self-conception, a "growing into oneself."

An essential attribute of maturity is the ability to handle the inevitable conflict between our desire for connection with others and our own individual separateness. With this ability, we need no longer seek from others a whole life already made up for us. Rather, we can securely interact out of a firm sense of our humanity, and out of the realization that there is something in ourselves which does not disappear even if we fail at a relationship. This stability results from our having formed a variety of emotional contact points with life. When there is more than one thing we care about, more than one person through whom we are fulfilled and revivified, then we cannot be destroyed—no matter how much we are hurt—by the loss of one person.

The test of our secure being, of our connectedness, is the capacity to enjoy being alone. The person whose relationships are not compulsive is one who values his or her own company. It is easier to be comfortable with a self that is capable of creating satisfying attachments to life. We then welcome periods of solitude where we can exercise and express that self both in the real world and in imagination. We can take pride in a self-sustenance which, while never total, can withstand many pressures. This self-sustenance also serves as the bulwark for our relationships.

Consider how some people find it easier to get out and move confidently among others when they already have one relationship to start from. Being loved gives one a feeling of confidence, a feeling of not having one's whole being bound up in the outcome of every new contact. This lack of desperation communicates itself subtly but surely to others as an attractive and desirable quality, for people generally find it reassuring to relate to those who are already certain of their own value. By the same token, though, why can't the person whose acceptance and support is so vital to this feeling of value be yourself? Your relationship with yourself and your surroundings, rather than any external confirmation of worth, is the most secure anchor against perpetual uncertainty and escapism. It is also the best underpinning for the formation of the relationships which complete an emotionally mature person's life.

Essential as it is, however, self-acceptance is only a start. A full description of the nonaddicted person must include that person's relationship to his environment. This relationship is one which balances a sensitivity to outside stimuli and events with a strong self-identity. In *The Lonely Crowd,* David Riesman contrasts the "inner-directed" with the "other-directed" personality. Inner-directed people determine their course by means of an internal guidance system, while other-directed people rely on outside cues—especially those provided by other people—to decide what path to follow. In recent years, Riesman believes, the other-directed personality has become prevalent in America. But Riesman also speaks of a composite type which he feels may be evolving today—the "autonomous" person who is attuned to external stimuli, but not in a purely reactive way. This autonomous person is able to take in information about the appropriateness and likely consequences of any course of action without being totally constrained by current attitudes and other people's opinions.

We can picture the autonomous person as a competent man or woman who is not afraid of his or her individuality and who relates to the environment freely, enjoying the interaction rather than being intimidated by it. Such persons, secure in their worth, welcome feedback from the outside world, even when it is critical, rather than suppressing it or blocking it out. They see this information not as an assault on their self-esteem, but as an aid in becoming a better person. For example, when rejected by a lover, the autonomous person can consider seriously the lover's critical observations, not simply to get back in the other's good graces, but to learn how to deal better with people.

Up to now, our picture of the nonaddicted person has been an abstract one which does not give us much of the flavor of autonomous behavior. After all, in the areas where he or she is most self-assured, a healthy person expresses a spontaneity and a depth of feeling that cannot be conveyed by the categories I have used, however helpful these may be for formulating ideas. When I had the most trouble I have ever had in performing a professional duty that revolved around my style of working with people, I turned to a concrete example for aid. I had just begun teaching at the Harvard Business School, where I faced the demands of teaching an unfamiliar subject in a new setting. The instructor's role was the nondirective one of guiding a discussion among eighty students, and in it I became nervous and ill at ease. I was helped in this situation by a model of skilled performance in the person of the basketball player Walt Frazier.

Frazier, as playmaker and guiding force for the New York Knickerbockers, effortlessly combined self-assured control with fluidity and exuberance. As he roamed down the court, directing and moving his team, he reacted to everything before him, seemingly without taking notice. He could respond appropriately to any combination of circumstances, and yet he did it all with a relaxed ease that showed he was in complete command of himself and the situation.

Basketball, along with some other performing activities, like jazz, exemplifies a group enterprise in which a participant must be continuously aware of what others are doing, while simultaneously playing an active part himself. The individual's role is adaptive and cooperative without being self-denying; it is assertive without being anarchic. A great jazz musician or basketball player conveys an obvious impression that he is comfortable in what he is doing as he takes in and molds the apparent chaos around him. His confident bearing comes from practicing his skill before knowledgeable onlookers and with fellow artists who appreciate and are affected by his performance. He knows that he can excel in terms of the rules of the discipline; he also knows that he can go beyond these rules, expanding and reinterpreting them to achieve a genuinely personal form of expression.

This level of self-realization—this excellence and intensity which at the same time carries with it an ease and flexibility of style—is often given the name of "soul." Unfortunately, soul in the worlds of basketball and jazz is no guarantee of general adequacy as a person, for athletes and musicians are notoriously susceptible to the addictions of our society: sex, drugs, money, and public adulation. But the spirit of soul, so much the antithesis of addiction in its self-possession and freedom from external constraint, is something that has almost limitless applications. We can even make use of it in our approach to such commonplace daily exercises as driving a car and cooking.

What can give driving or cooking soul is the confidence, based on experience and ability, that we can handle just about anything we might encounter when we perform these tasks. In driving, this means knowing the road and the automobile so as to be able to adjust more readily to emergencies or unusual conditions. In cooking it is the ability to deviate from a recipe when a different taste is desired, or to put together a dish out of an idea and whatever ingredients are available. These skills involve a heightened awareness of the components of the setting one works in—the evolving traffic patterns, the taste of the meal as it develops. The outstanding cook or driver is calm and responsive, ready to improvise when he or she sees the need for it. But while he does not panic when strange or unexpected conditions present themselves, he is not emotionless. An activity accomplished with a mastery and flair gives a continuous pleasure in its exercise.

Minor as they are, driving and cooking are examples of the kinds of activities which, because they are performed directly and not under institutional supervision, can carry our personal signatures. If they are done with a truly individual spirit, they can give us a sense of our own worth and potency. The trick is to extend these feelings more broadly through our lives.

HOW DO WE KNOW WHEN WE ARE ADDICTED?

In the qualities we have noted—maturity, connectedness, self-acceptance, autonomy, soul—we have a model of nonaddiction that we can set against the image of the addict. Because addiction is to some degree a part of all of us, however, it is not always a simple matter to compare ourselves against the two extremes and to decide where we stand. In considering what is addictive and what is not, we find that we have to take up a few knotty questions, establish some commonsense qualifications and guidelines, and occasionally give ourselves the benefit of the doubt.

In the first place, we cannot always easily distinguish addiction from the normal and universal phenomenon of habit. An ordered life necessarily contains a good deal of structure and repetition; most of us go home each day to the same place and to the same people. So in trying to isolate our addictions we should be careful not to set unreasonable standards of total expansiveness, since we are creatures of finite capacity. At the same time, a nonaddicted life is one that tests, rather than takes for granted, the boundaries of our ability to take in new information and adapt to change.

There is also the more central issue of dependency. Since human beings are neither physically nor psychologically self-sufficient, we must have a degree of order, reassurance, and sustenance, especially from people and our social surroundings. It is natural that we need to feel a part of something larger than ourselves and that we seek to form attachments. But to acknowledge the ultimate insufficiency that comes with being mortal does not invalidate the designation of some dependencies as unhealthy. When someone overeats to the point where he shortens or limits his life, he is obviously eating too much, even though everyone must eat. In the same vein, it is only in infancy and in restricted settings like prisons that healthy people are totally dependent on one person or thing for sustenance. Adults in natural settings whose lives revolve around only one focus are in an unstable, precarious position. The behavior this leads to, either in clinging to the one object or in bewailing its loss, is a serious disruption of the living psyche. The difference between having one connecting point to the world and many (at a given time) is a difference of degree that amounts to a difference in kind.

If we accept the overwhelming, monomaniacal character of a dependency as a criterion for addiction, must we see the specter of addiction in any signs of intensity in our experience? Actually, quite the opposite is true. Addictive passions are not vivid or intense; they are passive, negative, indiscriminate, banal. Since the addict is satisfied by the most superficial qualities in an object or person—its ability to fill his time and occupy his attention—his passions never develop deeper meaning and feeling. Enthusiasm and joy in our activities are an answer to addiction. As with the scientist or the artist, when we find ourselves intrigued by something and pursue it seriously and with dedication, we are not expressing addiction.

An experience cannot be judged by the amount of time and energy it takes up. The criteria for evaluating any intense involvement of oneself are essentially the same as the criteria for evaluating a love relationship. Does the interest or activity make one feel better about oneself in a lasting way? Can a constructive life, even if it is an unusual one, be built around it? Does it improve one's body, or mind, or ability to relate to people? Does it make one a more interesting or useful person? Does it raise the level of one's aesthetic or spiritual existence? If it makes other involvements more difficult to achieve, is there enough substance in it to make the sacrifice worthwhile? Is it fun?

These criteria are hardly airtight, and it is clear that we will have to do a good deal of reflection and interpretation to apply them to our own situation. We cannot recognize addictions with absolute assurance or do away with them completely. Addictive yearnings are part of the human condition as well as the conditions of our era. Practically speaking, we can only make the personal decision to treat something as an addiction on the basis of how much we see it hurting us, and how much we want to be rid of it. More philosophically, we can accept a degree of ambiguity in our lives and relinquish the need for certainty and for perfect solutions that is itself a facet of addiction. Accepting ourselves in our imperfection, though with insight and determination to change, we are ready to become free, responsive beings.

A FRAMEWORK FOR GROWTH

We have envisioned the ideal of a nonaddicted stance toward life, and we have seen that this ideal can never be completely attained. Yet if we start with realistic goals and expectations, we can take some steps to develop the personal strength for which addiction is such a poor substitute. At the outset, doing so helps us give up, and continue to resist, addictions. Ultimately that strength, when we hold it securely, makes addiction seem unappealing, unrewarding, and altogether irrelevant to our lives.

In behavior therapy, personal development is conceived of as a process of increasing self-awareness in ways that lead directly to changes in behavior. It means understanding how we think about things, how we respond to them, where they fit into our emotional worlds. At the same time, it means putting ourselves into situations and training ourselves to react to them in new ways. While an improved awareness indicates where changes in our patterns of living are needed and what might be good ways to go about making these changes, actually taking the steps—and experiencing the rewards from them—teaches us the most vivid, enduring lessons.

It takes time, effort, and faith to mature out of an addictive disposition. In cases I have observed, the time it takes for change to occur, as well as the degree to which a person can realistically expect to change at all, are roughly the same whether or not the person enlists the help of psychotherapy. Therapy or no, the ultimate responsibility is still our own. Therapy can help us think clearly about ourselves, crystallize our aims, sound out our alternatives; it can provide incentives at key points. But these boosts only supplement a program of development that must take place primarily within our consciousness and through our actions. Also, the danger of forming a substitute addiction to the therapist or therapeutic program—that is, of using therapy as yet another external support rather than as a catalyst for internal change—calls for a degree of vigilance and energy that might better be put toward attacking the problem directly. Some people will find therapy useful or necessary, but they should always proceed with a point in mind at which they will leave the therapist's office for good, determined to work things out on their own.

In the same way, of course, nobody can gain much just from reading this book, beyond obtaining some initial insights. The only alternative to addiction is what is truly the opposite of addiction—active, personal involvement in our own destinies. A book can state general principles and provide illustrations, but the job of relating these principles to our personal situations, in order to come up with an individualized course of action, is part of what we all have to do for ourselves. In essence, we each have to write our own endings.

What suggestions might be helpful, then, to someone trying to outgrow addiction? Behavior therapy works on the idea that a person should examine why and under what conditions he turns to the addictive object, and then try to interrupt this pattern through whatever means are available. In doing so, the person will begin to be able to spend longer and longer periods without the addictive object. What will he or she do in this time? The deprivation will hopefully compel him to cultivate new interests and skills, provided that he focuses his released energies in this direction. Initially, these new activities may simply occupy the time taken from the addiction. Eventually they are meant to provide solid, positive gratifications of a sort that will replace the addictive tendency altogether.

So assuming—as is true for most of us—that we are not facing a major addiction that takes up all our time, let us go directly to the deeper aim of eliminating addictive tendencies through having a life that is complete and satisfying. Let us direct our therapeutic efforts toward bringing this about. We can start with learning to be comfortable and capable of enjoying ourselves when alone, since this is the epitome of nonaddiction.

For most of us, it may take something like a program of behavior therapy to get us to spend time in our own company constructively rather than to view that time with anxiety. For example, we can regularly set aside a few hours or an evening to do something alone that we have been meaning to do or that we think would be fun, looking forward to this not as a sacrifice but as a choice we have made. The activity might be reading a book, listening to music, writing letters to friends we have neglected, or seeing a film or show that we have been wanting to see. It might be some physical exertion like hiking or jogging, or a series of conditioning or yoga exercises. In carrying out these solitary appointments, we enable our bodies and spirits to recuperate from the world. We are resting from harrying interactions which have pressured us, perhaps in ways we are not always aware of, to go in directions which may not represent our inner desires. Through our solitude we can discover what we really prefer, and what our natural pace of living is. Out of this self-exploration an organic self can begin to take form which we can recognize as the self we are or would like to be.

For some people, the crucial issues of nonaddiction lie in learning to deal with others, or in simply meeting and getting to know them. Even if this is our major concern, it is important to start with an area of personal interest where we have established confidence in our abilities and our worth. Out of it we can derive constructive social interactions, say by joining a singing or theatrical or athletic group, or through participating in a food cooperative or a community action group or a day-care center or a women's consciousness-raising group. Since such contacts with others are thus a natural outgrowth of our self-expression, they are not forced, and we can approach them in a more relaxed way. These contacts should not be sought exclusively for some specific benefit we crave—for example, opportunities to meet members of the opposite sex—so much as for what they offer in the way of human association with compatible and stimulating people. Also, it is good to keep in mind the ultimate goals of self-expansion, rather than merely ferreting out a social niche into which we can escape. This makes it possible to avoid the sorts of group memberships that can come with drugs or playing bridge or any activity which tends to exclude outsiders and to make us less willing to meet other people on their own grounds.

Not all solitary activities are equally worthwhile as avenues of growth, of course. Some people spend their time alone drinking or playing solitaire. Self-renewal, on the other hand, requires the discipline that addictive aloneness seeks to avoid. To build our sense of strength and purpose, we have to apply ourselves in a concerted way to pursuits which may not always be completely pleasant, but which offer us something of substance when we master them. Time-filling hobbies do not exist on the same emotional plane as romantic involvements and other strong attachments, and it takes more than a hobby to remedy an addiction. Only through working hard at learning to do something well, something which is important to us and to other people, can we generate the competence and self-possession that will make a difference in our lives.

If there is one concept that represents the nature of people's relationship to their world, it is the idea of competence. Both McClelland and Atkinson's theory of achievement motivation and Robert White's work on ego-development portray the human organism as striving to expand itself through mastery of its environment. A child starts its progress to adulthood by spontaneously exploring its surroundings to find out how things work. By the time a person has gone through school, however, this impulse has been blunted and may be almost entirely suppressed. Yet it is both being competent in a specific area and having a general feeling of competence which offer the best antidotes to the hesitancy and doubt which characterize addiction. This means that we often have to pick up a thread that was dropped in our childhood to further our growth as adults.

When we know or do something well, we gain an image of ourselves as being able to come to grips with our world. The elements of that self-image—the confidence, the lack of anxiety, the adventurousness—represent the way we should feel and act in every part of life. The more central a skill or competency is to our existence, the more easily the feelings that come with it will generalize. For these reasons, following through on incipient interests or overcoming our inertia so as to become engrossed in an enterprise is at the heart of curing addictions.

If you do not already have a compelling focus that you wish to intensify, you can start with anything which has intrigued you at a distance, but with which you have never managed to become familiar. It could be scuba diving, growing plants, building an extension to a house, fixing cars or stereos, studying the history of World War II, or anything which strikes you as attractive and valuable to know about. It is surprising how gratifying a first step of this sort can be, and how quickly you can see yourself and be seen by others as being well-versed on a topic. An initial attempt at making something, a beginning effort to use your body, a preliminary encounter with a field through reading a book or two and asking some questions, and you often find yourself quite knowledgeable or skillful—or, at least, more so than average.

One example of a life-regenerating activity which most people can try is running. Kenneth Cooper, the U.S. Air Force physician who wrote *Aerobics,* found that besides improving the functioning of the heart and lungs, running also had a healing effect on the psyche. Among his subjects were pilots who were no longer flying, and whose psychological and physical condition had deteriorated as a result of their idleness. Many of them were drinking and smoking too much, were overweight, and seemed generally lacking in energy. After undertaking a serious program of running, they often experienced a remarkable resurgence. They took pride in themselves, reestablished their physical condition, and gained a whole new outlook on how they could spend their time.

What are the features of running as an experience that bring such benefits? When you begin a campaign of running, you may anticipate with anxiety the pain that will accompany the exertion; you may fear the prospect of not performing well, or of overextending yourself physically. After you actually finish a run, you are too winded to take any pleasure out of what you have done. When you persist long enough to master the activity, however, you begin to approach it with a confident alertness and to feel exhilarated and triumphant in the aftermath. Moreover, while actually running, you no longer think of what you are doing as taking one painful step after another. Instead, you have a sense of fluidity, of being able to cover a distance as if in flight. Once you have got yourself into shape, you are drawn to repeat the exercise regularly for the opposite motivation from that of an addict—the sense of accomplishment and good health that comes from your effort.

Of course, there is ever the danger of a one-sided development, which can become a kind of addiction. There is also the danger that as a runner—or a mechanic, or a musician, or a chess player—you may stop developing, and may stagnate at some comfortable level of proficiency. In that case, your satisfactions will be different and less internal than those which result from the accomplishment of extending your capacities. You will have found another level of stasis which is ultimately no less deadening.

To get beyond these dangers, you should never limit what you hope to achieve through an activity, and you should never confine your efforts at personal progress to the activity alone. With running, for example, you will probably find along the way that you are not as prone to overeat, or to engage in such addictions as cigarettes and alcohol. You may also have found that you have more energy and a better feeling about yourself. The final connection to be made is the realization that in the same way that you have converted an unpleasant exertion to a mastery, you can do almost anything else you choose. The sureness with which you tackle running, the confidence that you can attain something once considered out of reach, is a feeling you now know well enough to bring to the rest of your life.

PITFALLS IN GROWING

Overcoming addiction is as much a matter of encouraging positive involvements with one's environment as it is of withdrawing oneself from addictive attachments. Many of the problems that occur with the one process also occur with the other. In each case there is the emotional struggle of accepting the need to change. Then there is the resolve to launch oneself on a new course, whether it be to live without a drug or a lover or to undertake new enterprises or new kinds of relationships. This is followed by stages of being discouraged with one's progress, and of weathering the realization that improvement will sometimes be slow and that backsliding is inevitable. Finally, a new sense of self evolves, whereby in some subtle way one has grown into a more wholesome and responsible way of life.

To admit that there is some significant part of ourselves that we would like to change, especially when we have been avoiding that recognition for a long time, is bound to be painful. Even if we have been dissatisfied with ourselves, isolating some mode of behavior or thought as having brought about our discontent is a shock to our self-conception. If this shock hits us in an overwhelming way, our determination to change is bound to be short-lived: the pain is simply not bearable. For this very important reason, self-development has to be a gradual process. It has to carry with it as much respect for what we already are as can legitimately be maintained, and it has to stay clear of self-disgust or shame.

There are ready reasons not to fall prey to a sense of utter worthlessness when we confront our own problems. Many, many people have similar problems; like them, we are functioning individuals, no matter how severe our shortcomings. We are hoping merely to improve what has been at least a partially viable face to the world—that is, to become better people. It is paradoxical that when we can convince ourselves of our basic worth, we are most willing to change. When we acknowledge our weaknesses, we see that other people admire us no less than they did before. We feel almost relieved to be dealing with people on a new, honest basis, where we no longer think of our flaws as dark secrets which must be kept covered. In fact, nondefensiveness and openness become a positive part of our self-image, so that we will never again have to feel guilty about our weaknesses or our lack of compensating strengths. This is because we will be more able to gauge where we stand, to draw closer to other people who can provide us with critical guidance even as they support us emotionally, and to recognize the need for change within a framework of a stable existence.

It may help us to persevere if we remember that the only instant gratifications are in addiction. Being addicted means we are trying to get something essential but are afraid to work for it. Substantial pursuits, on the other hand, will at moments be unpleasant, messy, or frustrating, but they grow into experiences that amount to more than the sum of their parts. This is as true of dieting and giving up smoking as it is of acquiring a skill and completing complicated projects. In the early stages, when our incapacities are more apparent than our strengths, it may be hard to get going without considerable willpower. As we become firmly committed to a course of action, our doubts are submerged by the engagement in our efforts, until we reach the point where those efforts are clearly rewarded. Up to that point, to some extent, we are performing an act of faith—faith in the value of what we are trying to accomplish, and faith in ourselves.

The fat person, for example, sustains his emotional balance by overeating, perhaps as a way to reduce anxiety, or as a sign that somebody (if only himself) cares for him. Even though he is aware that he would be happier if he could replace his overeating with constructive endeavors, he cannot bring himself to do what he knows is best in the long run because he is so unused to getting positive reinforcements for his gestures in that direction. These are places where a therapist or a program such as Weight Watchers may help by giving the addict encouragement or even concrete rewards for new behavior patterns. Such rewards, which take effect immediately, counteract the ingrained feelings that have reinforced the addiction, and thus foreshadow the real-life rewards the addict has not been persistent enough to earn yet. But the use of temporary crutches like these artificial rewards is risky, and can only succeed if they guide the addict to the point where he can begin to experience the natural, long-term benefits of his behavior. We may want a therapist initially to establish such ad hoc rewards for us. Or we can try to establish them ourselves.

Unfortunately, our environment does not always serve us so well. Not all the people we regularly deal with can or will assist us in our ambitions to improve ourselves. Some of them, in fact, may be comfortable with our weaknesses and may therefore not want to see them eliminated. Hemingway's Mrs. Macomber shoots her husband when he ceases to be a coward. When our friends, lovers, or families are used to seeing us in a predictable light, they may not want us to accomplish anything too grand, perhaps because it might expose their own feelings of inadequacy. In that case, they may reinforce the cues from within ourselves that hold us back. When such obstacles are present, it may be necessary to break away—at least partially—and make a new start in another setting, or among different people. Growth nearly always implies some such dislocation. A change of scene in itself cannot be taken as a definite sign of progress, but can be a prelude to finding new ways of doing things.

Ironically, there are many fewer ways to gain outside reinforcement when we want to try something new than when we simply want to cure an addiction. We don't have professional counselors or organized groups to go to when we want to build a cabin or start a newsletter on a topic we are interested in. Our friends more readily rush to help us when we are sick or troubled than when we are trying to break out of old boundaries. That is why some people get sick, or complain so much, or even attempt suicide: it is so hard for them to get attention through more constructive efforts. On projects which entail concentrating our abilities toward a distant goal, the need to develop our own resources for sustaining concentration is very apparent from the beginning. How can we withstand the incessant doubts about whether our labors will bear fruit? In an era which overpowers nearly everybody with its moral and technical complexities, we can all in some ways be said to lack confidence, to have low self-esteem. The issue becomes not how to do away with our various insecurities so much as how to make them less a focus of our attention.

The answer for most people is simply to get into things, and to find out through trial and error what the real requirements of a task are, as opposed to the forbidding standards we often have in our minds. If we stay at an abstract level of speculation and dwell on our past and present flaws, as some forms of psychotherapy encourage us to do, we are not breaking down the obstacles we face. One well-known educational psychologist said to a student who had turned down a good job out of a reluctance to discontinue his therapy, "Have you ever considered the therapeutic advantages of having a job?" The advantages are that we force ourselves to engage with reality, including the internal reality of our capacity for mental or physical accomplishment.

In tackling a craft or an enterprise one step at a time, we try to establish our bearings as we go along, while understanding that we will have moments of relapse. A professional doesn't evaluate every portion of his or her work to decide whether he should bother to continue. He or she works unselfconsciously, with the attitude that "I am trying to do what I do well, and the end will come of itself after a while." We have to have a larger sense of progress, attaching justified importance to positive moves, if we are to endure the setbacks and slips that we will also encounter. A young carpenter told me that he knew he was a professional when he began to react to oversights or mistakes by figuring out how to compensate for them. It is beyond human capacity to actualize a perfect conception in one stroke, but it is very much within human range to improve a piece of work by repeated and consistent application.

Beyond our own experience with the work, getting other people's evaluation of our performance can also dissipate vague self-doubts. When other people are depending on us to get something done, their basic acceptance of the product, together with their critique of it, can take us a long way toward understanding what, exactly, is important in a job. A newly hired artist worked all night on hand-lettered script for a magazine layout. Realizing that the spacing was not quite perfect, she presented her work the next morning with great trepidation. The art editor took one look at it, said, "That'll do fine," and inserted it into the layout. What the artist learned was not how to write script, but at what point to stop worrying about it.

Once a person is confident that he or she can do what he sets out to do and can meet the expectations of others, he will not be afraid to take things on. He will also be willing to make equivalent demands of others and expect these to be met. He or she will have become a reliable person, one who can be counted on to do what he or she says and who prefers to deal with people who are similarly responsible. This sense of responsibility is the most solid basis for professional *or* personal relationships there can be.

Let us take writing a book as an example of a mature skill which entails an interchange with others. A first draft of a given work is usually far from what would be acceptable as a finished manuscript, in style, organization, or content. An experienced writer recognizes this, and doesn't panic because he knows a book cannot be done all at once. He appreciates what he has accomplished, and realizes that it has brought him to a plateau from which he can take the next step toward achieving his aim. He knows when a book needs more work, and when he has something that others can respond to as a reasonable text. The novice who judges his first draft by the standards of the prose he sees in print won't get anywhere. The standard he has set is too high to be useful to him. What is true for a single book is true for a whole career—and a life. A writer can only do the best work he can at any given period of his life, however awkward it may seem even to him. By practicing at one level now, he may be able to perform at a higher level later on. If he magnifies any one task out of a misplaced striving for perfection—like the writer in Camus' *The Plague* who constantly is rewriting his opening sentence—he will never get started.

If we were merely talking about an avocation or a bit of technical expertise, it would seem offensive to try to compare it with the delicate process of personal growth. But if we conceive of writing, or whatever, as something that is deeply a part of our being, then we can begin to see a larger relevance in much of what we have spoken about—the inevitable hesitancy and insecurity, the cumulativeness of effort, the importance of being realistic and humane toward ourselves, and the value of attending to helpful criticism. Whether the issue is learning to be alone or to relate to others, we should just *do it, live it,* and don't try to monitor it on too short term a basis. Nobody is emotionally sure or socially confident from the start, so extending ourselves personally will not be any more natural at first than stretching muscles that have been unused for years. We have to plunge in and observe as well as we can what we are doing.

Maturity may be a matter of finding something worthwhile we can do well, and staking our place in the world on it. From there, whether as a carpenter trying to learn about literature or a writer trying to build something, it should become easier to reverse the conditions which made us weak in one area and strong in another. This is just as true if we are good at some professional task but weak at relating to people, or vice versa. Starting with our strengths, it is then a matter of flexibility, awareness of what we want, and the realization that our lives do not have to be static and that change does not have to be accidental. Overcoming addiction is work, but in a deeper, more permanent sense it is fun. It beats addiction, once we are in a position to compare. Drug addicts and alcoholics frequently relapse, but only because they have not removed themselves from addiction. When it comes to the real cure, nobody who has made it there has ever been tempted to go back.

A CASE OF CHANGE

Mitch came from a family dominated by an intelligent but unsuccessful businessman who was both pompous and self-pitying. The father dictated to his son how he should do things and how he should think about them, and emphasized the negative and cynical aspects of life. Mitch's mother, herself sensible and hardworking, tolerated her husband's abusive and erratic behavior to an incredible extent. She could endure stoically, but she was too traditional to resist. Worse, she counseled her children to the same course of submission and self-denial.

Mitch grew up not wishing to challenge the forces that controlled his world, namely his father and the external conditions against which his father railed. Instead, he propitiated these forces by establishing his own personal routines, and by giving in when any conflict with authority arose. Thus, only within his private domains—his room, his mind, the guitar playing which he had begun at an early age—was he able to be secure in his command of things. Although he was totally nonassertive, his orderly habits of thought and careful work brought him uninterrupted success throughout school. Because of his straightforwardness and seriousness, he was also able to form strong friendships in high school and college. Even while he was doing well in these institutions, however, he resented their impositions—as he had resented his father's—without being able to do anything about them.

When Mitch graduated, he pointedly rejected the course that everyone planned and anticipated for him. He chose not to go on to graduate school to study literature or music. Instead, to his friends' shock and his family's dismay, he announced that he was going to devote all his time to writing and performing his own songs. While

Mitch had carried on his music through college, and people knew him as someone who could entertain with his guitar, nobody conceived of him as a musician or songwriter. He certainly had not performed professionally up to this time, and had no connections in the music world.

But Mitch was resolute in his plans, however unrealistic they seemed to others. After serving in the army, he came out intending to establish his independence once and for all. Looking around for an area in which to settle and a place to stay, he decided to move in with a college friend who was an architecture student at Yale. There Mitch was provided with a ready-made social network by his roommate. His roommate was the one who actively kept up these social contacts, with Mitch usually tagging along. In return, Mitch acted as confidant for his friend. These roles extended to the two men's dealings with women. Many times Mitch would go along as a third when his roommate and his roommate's current girlfriend went out together, or else they would fix him up with a date, with whom he might have nothing in common.

As far as his career goals went, Mitch did little. He kept up his guitar practice and sporadically tried his hand at writing songs, though he did not complete many and was not willing to perform those he did finish. Neither did he try to get gigs or to join the local musicians' union. He preferred to keep to himself musically, and to work at odd jobs like the one he held in the music division of the university library. Going on this way, he never established a meaningful relationship either in regard to his work or with a woman.

After a few years of this kind of existence, Mitch came to the realization that he would have to find a more substantial modus vivendi. His roommate was about to move to a job in another city, and Mitch had to look for a new place to live. At this point, Mitch was forced to do some thinking. Had he established real friendships during his stay in New Haven? Not really. These had all mainly revolved around his roommate. What about his relationship with the roommate himself? Mitch saw that it was basically unsound, since each man had propped the other up without either helping the other come to grips with his weaknesses. Finally, Mitch had to conclude that he had done nothing to point himself toward a musical career, and at 25 he was no closer to being a self-sufficient, respected human being than he had been in college. He could no longer use his youth to excuse the lack of real involvement in his life.

Mitch saw that he was on the brink of either drastic change or disaster. His fear of putting himself forward had forced him into a sheltered existence that could not bring him anything of lasting value. Operating on this grim discovery, Mitch called an old college acquaintance with whom he had jammed (and who he knew liked his work), who had since become an impresario for rock and jazz bands in the Denver area. The friend told Mitch about a number of possibilities and suggested that he come to Denver to try them out. Mitch was made just as anxious by this answer as he had been by the prospect of the call itself (over which he had agonized for days). He couldn't play with real recording groups, he thought; what was he getting himself into?

But Mitch went, as much from the lack of alternatives as from any positive enthusiasm. When he arrived, he found considerably fewer opportunities available than he had been led to expect. After several unproductive appeals to his friend, Mitch got a job just before he would have had to return to live with his parents because of lack of funds. He did not want to give up the independence that having his own apartment in Denver afforded him, so he accepted a gig as a back-up man with a group that played Latin music. He labored for four long months at a type of music with which he felt no inner connection and which he thought himself inadequate to perform. The other band members seemed to accept him though, and Mitch started to feel comfortable in what he was doing. At least he stopped regarding his playing as an embarrassment.

Mitch was too exhausted in the mornings to do much independent work, but one day he ran into the man who had originally brought him to Denver, who now asked him if he had any tunes he could perform. Mitch thought, "Sure, why not," and he auditioned for a club owner who was looking for an entertainer to play for student audiences. Mitch got the job, quit his previous spot and worked at putting an act together. Just at this time, too, he had joined the musicians' local. He was quickly appointed treasurer because his habits of mind were more orderly than those of his fellow members. The union was embroiled in both an internal and external dispute about whether young, rock-oriented performers should be paid at the same scale as more "legitimate" entertainers. Many owners and producers made use of such musicians without paying them union scale. Into this fray Mitch threw himself with an interest which was both practically and ideologically motivated.

On the verge of becoming a full-fledged member of a professional community, Mitch saw in retrospect that his life had been an addiction, though not in all respects. Inwardly, he was not a desperate individual who needed to hold on to people or to artificial substances in order to exist. He lived an organized life, had an inquiring mind, and related to people at a generally high level. He almost always enjoyed newness and adventure, when they were brought to him by others. But he was reluctant to take on the full responsibilities of an adult, either in his work or with other people, especially women, because he didn't know how to handle an active role in relationships. His fear of provoking conflict or rejection caused him to draw a circle around himself and his comfortable pattern of living, and to be dependent on others for basic satisfactions he could not get for himself. In fact, only when his objective situation became obviously untenable was he able to change at all.

When he was forced to move—as many of us are at some time or another—he set about what he had to do with seriousness and dignity. He accepted whatever work he undertook as worth doing well, and he tried to master the situation he was faced with, however short of his ideal it was. Yet he did not get so bogged down in these concerns as to lose sight of other things he wanted to do, so that he was ready when a real opportunity presented itself. He did not yield to other viewpoints on questions that were important to him, such as maintaining his artistic integrity and giving his talents, once established, a proper valuation.

Mitch felt substantially better about himself. At a reunion with his former roommate and other old friends, he pulled back when he saw old patterns reemerging, and he insisted on being treated with respect. With the people he was now meeting in Denver, he started with the assumption that he was a worthwhile and reasonable person, one whom many people could like if he showed them what he was about. What about his relationships with women? Here Mitch had not progressed as far. His contacts with women remained transitory and somewhat stilted, since his personal style still lacked both the forcefulness and flexibility that an intimate relationship requires. But Mitch at least saw himself as a person capable of growing and modifying his behavior, so that although he was not happy about his situation, he was not unduly pessimistic. He believed that now he had something to offer a woman. And by living alone, his daily life no longer sustained by a roommate, he was getting in touch with sensations of loneliness that naturally pushed him to adopt a more active social posture.

With all his talents and personal strengths, Mitch was an individual in danger of being submerged by oppressive involvements. But, as he matured, he began to be able to turn himself around. Mitch was never a blatant addict, yet the concept of addiction has much to say about his life. His case is a good illustration of how universal addiction is, how subtle and diverse are its forms, and how long it may take a person to do something lasting about it.

"What I want is a strange conjunction with you—" he said quietly; "—not meeting and mingling; —you are quite right: —but an equilibrium, a pure balance of two single beings: —as the stars balance each other."   —D. H. LAWRENCE, *Women in Love*

11

From Addiction to Love

To come to grips with a relationship, you must be willing to analyze yourself and it. This is the first step. It may be difficult to figure out your own and another person's motivations, the distribution of power between you, the patterns your interactions assume, and just what kinds of people you both are. But if you are unwilling or unable to make the effort, it will not be possible to discover the sources of the problems in the relationship and the means by which to improve it. People avoid this uncomfortable self-confrontation by characterizing it as "cold," "unromantic," or even "immoral." Such attitudes, however, are often present in the most exploitative and hypocritical relationships, the ones in which the partners gloss over their own and perhaps each other's behavior to the point where the strains become unbearable, and the relationship—or one of its participants—breaks.

Some people, no doubt, can be happy within a relationship while remaining blissfully unaware or uncritical of its mechanics. More often, people chafe at and resent the unconscious imposition of another's will, which strikes them as selfish and disrespectful. They

241

close more and more of themselves off from each other, while they seeth in barely restrained anger. Many such relationships last for a long time; increasingly, in recent years, they do not last forever.

Despite the need for critical self-awareness, one must be careful not to overstate the "critical" or negative side. An examination of oneself and one's lovers and friends is likely to turn up as much good as bad. Being extremely negative is, after all, a hallmark of addiction. The answer to addiction lies in accepting and affirming what is strong in a relationship while questioning and repairing its weaknesses. Nor does being critical mean vacillating between ecstasy and disgust—another sign of addiction. You combat addiction by maintaining a calm, realistic view of yourself and your relationships while always seeking to make yourself and those you deal with better people.

Accordingly, before taking up the assessment of addictive tendencies within a relationship, I would like to praise the friendship and love that come from knowing a person for a long time. Addiction is an unstable state of being, marked by a compulsion to deny all that you are and have been in favor of some new and ecstatic experience. Love at first sight has much in common with immediate addiction to heroin or alcohol. This is not to say that sexual infatuation is not as sound a reason as any other to be drawn to someone. Intensity of attraction is a beautiful thing. But to mislabel it love is both foolish and dangerous. What love requires on top of instant emotion is time, shared experiences and feelings, and a long and tempered bond between two people.

A couple who have been together for some time but who see problems in the relationship should not discard the familiarity and intimacy they have established for a will-o'-the-wisp notion of something better. It may be wiser instead for them to adjust their expectations—to become more realistic within their relationship, to scale down desires which they cannot satisfy for each other, and which perhaps no partners could satisfy. Knowledge of a person and, more, acceptance of and by that person are hard to come by. A history of doing things together and helping one another can be the most solid groundwork for a loving relationship. There are also external constraints, like children, which may dictate staying with a relationship or finding some solution between total commitment and outright separation. On the whole, the readiness to judge harshly and reject another person can be as much of an impediment to fulfilling oneself in love as can an overcommitment to stability and an aversion to change. In either case, fear should not dictate the result—one should not cling to a relationship out of fear, nor should one end it out of fear.

For some people a history of stable association can be especially valuable. There are interpersonal addicts whose impulses have been shown to lead them repeatedly into unhealthy reactions. Like Guy, the seeming Don Juan, such individuals sometimes "back into" love by finding someone to whom they were not initially overly attracted, but with whom they enjoy spending time, and whom they can get to know in a leisurely and gradual manner. After a time, two people who have come together in this way may discover they have developed an affection and a respect for each other that cannot easily be replaced.

ASSESSING RELATIONSHIPS

We have already listed some broad criteria for distinguishing love from addiction. To translate these into useful tools, we must learn to frame questions out of them which are meaningful to us personally. Some examples of these, starting with the most direct, are: Can you bear to be without the person you love when it is necessary or desirable for him or her to be away? Have you maintained the interests and associations you had before you met your lover? Have you developed new ones? And more pointedly: How would you feel toward your lover if he or she went off on his or her own? Can you imagine still being friends with this person if you were no longer totally involved with each other? And, finally: Are you a better person, is your lover a better person, as a result of your relationship?

These questions, to whatever extent they are answered in the negative, should make you probe further. They lead naturally to questions about the feelings which underlie the relationship, and, in turn, about you and your lover as individuals. What motivates each of you; what is it that makes you anxious about your partner's absence, or his growth as a person? How do you convey your needs to your partner; how do you gain his conformity to the limits you want to place on him? How does he react; what sacrifice does he demand in return? The answers to all these questions will in some cases be relatively straightforward, in some cases extremely complicated. You may dread spending time alone because you have few interests. Or it may be because you are not at ease with yourself. Your motivations may include the wish to avoid boredom, or insecurity about whether or not your lover finds you desirable. You may complain when your partner wants to do something you don't want to do, or you may accede, but with the intent to sabotage. And you may give in to your partner's irrationalities and weaknesses in order to insure that he or she will do the same for you.

All these are normal human impulses. In themselves, they are not unhealthy or disastrous. But when they all point in the same direction, when they dictate the overall pattern of your life, and when you cannot acknowledge or deal with them, then you are in danger of allowing your relationship to be an addiction. The alternative is the kind of existential analysis which brings these mechanisms into the realm of consciousness, thus making them manageable. Along with it, as in individual change, a smaller-scale—almost trivial—kind of behavioral analysis is an essential step toward escaping addictive patterns in a relationship.

If your interactions unavoidably fall into a set routine—if a predictable act on your part guarantees an equally predetermined response from your partner—no progress can be made. The relationship is at a standstill. For example, say that every time a couple goes to a party the man ignores the woman because he feels she is overly effusive. When they get home the woman reacts angrily to his slighting behavior. For his part, the man may return the spirit of her attack, refusing to acknowledge his error and attacking her for her failures. Or he may be extremely apologetic and rush to make amends by flattering and cajoling her. The latter response often concludes with an "I love you" on both sides. Neither of these denouements changes the man's or woman's behavior, and they do the same things the next time they go out. Their interaction is static. Because they cannot overcome the inertia of the relationship to talk things through or work on their problems *except* when they are angry (at which time they do so superficially or antagonistically), they are doomed to reenact the scenario whenever similar circumstances occur.

More directly tied in with addiction is the example of a man living with or dating a woman until he becomes sickened or oppressed by the relationship. He then calls it off, only to find after a while that he is lonely and distraught without the woman. He returns, she accepts him, and they proceed to the next breakup. No matter how many times the cycle is repeated, they do not jointly change the nature of their relationship when they are together, either so as to make it more durable, or to limit it to the level of intensity that it can withstand. Nor does the man, on his own, anticipate the next stage of his discontent enough to temper his behavior either when he is seeing the woman or when he is not. She, on the other hand, refuses to demand from herself or the man any indications that she and the relationship have integrity. And so they persist, unhappily, until some arbitrary point where things may be finally resolved by outside events, often with great trauma for one or the other or both. It should be noted that this tumultuous cycle is just an extreme version of the mini-disillusionment, rejection, and uneasy rapprochement which is enacted by the bickering couple, and which appears so often in stable relationships.

What is required to interrupt these never-ending, repetitive patterns of interaction is, first, an awareness that they are occurring, and, second, an understanding of why and when they occur. These, in turn, are only possible if there is a commitment to the relationship and an ability to bear up under what self-analysis will reveal about it. Working against the possibility for change, even where understanding exists, is the tendency for unhealthy patterns to solidify with time. This is the negative side of longevity. The longer two people have been together, the more ingrained are the cues each sets up for the other, and the less flexibility there is in the responses to these cues. People learn standard ways of dealing with any situation, and that learning becomes an integral part of their face to the world. In the first case above, the man looks for his wife's usual social behavior at a party, and then is put off when he sees it. The woman herself knows well when her husband has withdrawn from her, and just as readily seeks refuge in her rage.

Expectations people have of those close to them are powerful, and work in subtle ways. The woman may anticipate her husband's disapproval, may feel that she has no chance not to confirm what he expects, and may act as she always does at parties even when she herself does not approve of her own behavior. Or she may resolve to act differently, but he, fixed in his perceptions of her, may not be capable of seeing anything but that vestige of her old conduct which could not possibly be eradicated in one outing. So the next time, she refuses to make any effort to move in her husband's direction. For this couple, a gathering like the one which provoked their last fight may be perceived as a continuation of the battleground, with each of the partners setting out for the evening with the intention of finding derogatory evidence to use in the next, imminent argument.

Wasteful, draining cycles of interaction do not have to be as overtly hostile as this. Two people can relate in an easy, harmonious way which still forces both into roles they would not endorse and cannot be totally happy with. A woman may invariably defer to a man, allowing him to make the decisions and permitting his opinions to prevail. Whenever a choice comes up, or whenever the two of them participate in a discussion with others, the woman shrinks back, almost with relief. The arrangement is a smooth one, yet it prevents the woman from asserting herself and the man from learning to accept an equal partner in life. With its inequities, the arrangement is also potentially explosive, because the woman may suddenly gather herself together and break out of it, much as Gail did after she and Allen moved to Eugene.

In fact, to counter the argument made earlier for preserving old connections, separation may be the only way for some people to change. It may only be by breaking away from old contacts that one can freely realize a new self-definition. With those who conceive of a person in a set way no longer around to send out signals reminding her of what they expect, and to force her to maintain their image of her even in her own mind, she has a better chance to try out a new, desired identity. Psychotherapists, for example, are now realizing that releasing a patient to the family environment which originally created that person's problem may be self-defeating. Sometimes it takes some running away, as it did for Mitch, to get to a place where a person can be who he feels he is, or wants to be.

Given the difficulty of weighing this consideration against the accumulated positive meaning and value in a relationship, two people may want to find a middle ground where they can continue to relate to each other at a lower level of intimacy, if this solution lies within their emotional capabilities. They may preserve their involvement as a long-term friendship, while acknowledging that they will have more intense romantic attachments elsewhere. On the other hand, the imperative need to break down ingrained expectations often makes it desirable for a couple to separate for a time, thereby serving warning that they will be renewing the relationship as changed individuals coming to each other afresh. But it may be impossible ever to have strongly positive feelings again without having the negative feelings return as well.

Thus, individuals and couples who find themselves mired in limiting, unproductive relationships do have a range of options to consider. All constructive paths, however, begin with recognizing the nature of the addictive patterns in the relationship. The examples in this book have ranged from very antagonistic styles of relating to styles that are quite comfortable in their certitude and predetermination. The absence of overt disruptions is most typical of complacent couples like Vicky and Bruce, who, when presented with any novel opportunities, burrow back into each other like two kids in a bunk. All of these patterns can be classified as addictive. Because the interaction holds each of the partners back from expanding themselves, because it operates to constrain them through regular, repetitive mechanisms, and because the lovers accept these limitations out of a need for the reassurance that the constancy of the relationship provides, addiction is present. To want to change within a relationship, or to want to change the relationship, is to oppose addiction. To be able to do so is to overcome addiction.

CORRECTING RELATIONSHIPS

Translating awareness into action is a matter of personal resolve. You know certain things about yourself—what you don't like, how you would prefer to be—and you must force yourself to act upon this knowledge. However, as our review of addiction treatments indicated, certain methods are more efficacious than others for modifying behavior, feelings, and ultimately self-conceptions. These methods strike at various links in the cyclical chain of behavior that constitutes addiction.

By understanding why you feel as you do under a given set of circumstances, you can begin to come to terms with the behavior tied to this feeling. You can start to control what were once reflexive actions and emotions. The man who disapproves of his wife's effusive behavior at parties can ask himself why: does it reflect badly on him as a man, does it remind him of other people he doesn't respect, is it behavior that he encourages in her in private but can't stand to have paraded before others? He can isolate that which is irrational in his response, or at least that which serves no good purpose, and either eliminate it or make it the basis for further self-examination (perhaps with the help of his wife). As for the rest—that which he can identify as rightly annoying to him and which is potentially under his wife's control, and which he therefore may reasonably approach her about—he should present it to his wife for her reactions at a time when he knows he is not doing it out of pique or resentment.

The difference between interpersonal addictions and those having to do with inanimate objects like food and drugs is that there is a whole other perspective, another conscious, sentient being to consider. In working on an unhealthy interaction cycle, it is necessary to take into account the other person, without at the same time concentrating on how much he or she is to blame for the things you don't like about yourself and the relationship. When you can identify your role in a pattern, and wish to stop playing it, you should discuss it with your mate from the standpoint of explaining why you wish to cease, in order to elicit his or her help in executing your resolve. Thus if a woman finds that she always consents to a boyfriend's wish to be with her, even when she has other things she wants to do or has made other plans, she can begin by articulating to herself the insecurities which cause her to be anxious about refusing her lover. She might then explain these to the man, and tell him that she does not believe that giving in to them is helpful either to her or to him. By presenting this in terms of personal development, especially her own, she can minimize *his* anxieties about being loved and respected, especially if she can do it without being abrasive.

After you have started out on a new path—at least by breaking some old habits—evaluate your lover's reactions. You may find that he or she has responded to the changes as positively as you yourself have. "Why didn't we see this was better all along?" you may both agree. At that point, your partner may begin to contribute suggestions for change on his own. If, on the other hand, your partner is resentful and negative, even after continued efforts at persuasion and example, then perhaps he doesn't want you to be the person you would prefer yourself to be. In this case, your path becomes more difficult, since you have to give at least some consideration to the question of whether or not you can continue to know this person on an intimate basis. It is possible that some of the steps you have taken have been wrong-headed or extreme, and that your lover has valuable suggestions and criticisms for you to take into account. It is also possible that he or she is not prepared to accept what it is you want to be, in which case he is simply not the person for you. Ultimately, this must be your decision, a prerogative not recognized by the man in the Stevie Wonder song, "Mary Wants to be a Super-Woman," who feels he knows the woman "very well," while he wishes she could understand him as well as he does her. It is likely that his conceit is simply an admission that he is not prepared to let the woman take control of her own destiny.

Of course, a determination to change a relationship can, and hopefully will, be more cooperatively arrived at. This is especially true in the case where a couple is comfortable together but stalled in a dead-end interaction which is cutting them off from life. If they can begin by recalling other possibilities they could have explored, individually or together, especially those that were actively offered to them, then they can reflect on how they felt when they refused. Were they frightened, or lazy? Was each nervous about how the other would feel, or were they simply inert? Then they can discuss the value of taking up such prospects, anticipate that they each will actually be doing so, and look for chances to enlarge and enliven their existences. It is interesting to consider what people mean when they say they don't feel like doing anything else besides being with one person. It indicates that they do not visualize enough benefits in the alternatives to make it worth their effort. A good part of their deprecation of other opportunities is likely to be defensive, stemming from fear of one sort or another. By pushing themselves and their lovers a bit, they can embark on an activity or interaction that, once experienced, will encourage further explorations by virtue of the fun and variety it has brought.

It is worthwhile, if you mean to carry out such a program of life expansion, to set aside time specifically for talking out what that means. It may seem funny to enter into your appointment calendar, "Talk to Bob about how dull we are becoming," but, by definition, this is almost the only way to escape from the lethargy and inertia that sometimes descend on a relationship. No change comes about unless the people involved mean to bring it off, and nothing will be done unless some planning and attention are devoted to setting up the actual steps such change will entail. That is why it can be helpful to set exact goals for what you want to accomplish and when you hope to see the changes made. If your goals are not met, you should ask yourself whether enough progress has been made to justify continued efforts in the same directions or whether more drastic steps are necessary. Of course, it is best for you and your partner to set these goals jointly, but if this is impossible, it is your responsibility to set them yourself.

This process of articulation—of forcing things to the surface—will enable you to get to the bottom of some conflicts and anxieties in the relationship that may be surprising, given the patina of domesticity that has long been covering them up. "Honey," a wife may say, "I'd be jealous if you went over to your friend's house to talk over new ideas for your business, because I'd be afraid that you would see how little I can help you with things like that." Whether your response will be to refute or to acknowledge your partner's impression, and then to work the situation out, it can be the most valuable thing you will do for yourselves.

Both the fuel and the flame of these efforts will be the changes, however small or painful, that are actually made in the ways you interact. These will show you that improvement is possible and that you can bring it off, and will reward the moves toward improvement that you have made together. If you can escape the boring or irritating treadmill, all sorts of new possibilities can open up. You can feel a new glow about yourselves and your capacity to deal with each other more pleasurably and meaningfully. If you can both go outside the relationship for good times and new meanings, you will return to it invigorated and freshly able to give of yourselves. Or you may want to shake up your daily routine or introduce a new element into your experience. A middle-aged mother of three reported:

> In his bid to solve the "generation-gap" our middle son brought a packet of marijuana to us for a Christmas present. . . . [eventually] I tried it as did his father, brother and sister. . . . It was really marvellous. Everyone managed to talk together, about trivialities mainly, there was no tendency to put down anyone. Opportunities to complain or dig at the lack of academic diligence that was always part of the previous conversations with this boy were ignored, and father in particular listened to some of his ideas with a semblance of civility. That alone made the experience worthwhile. The family that night was closer together than anytime I can recall. . . .
>
> [Alone together, later that night] For the first time in years my husband talked for an hour or more about work, plans, memories, problems and possible solutions. . . . The miracle is that he seemed also to be a human being, and not only a work machine that ignored people, and particularly his family. I must have seemed somewhat more reasonable to him too, as he did not try to depreciate my interests. The real miracle followed when we had intercourse. Instead of the dull, perfunctory act it had become, usually indulged in on my part because it made it possible to get out of it the next night, sex was something splendid.
>
> [submitted to the Canadian Government Commission of Inquiry into the Non-Medical Use of Drugs, 1971]

What obviously happened to these people was that they got out of their very set, depressed patterns of relating to each other, and found out how much fun they could have. Hopefully, the pleasure this produced will cause them to continue to look for more constructive things to do together. I believe that the function of marijuana in this discovery was, although necessary, tangential. Without it the family would never have been moved off the course they had set for themselves. They still have a lot to do besides getting high to incorporate their new insights into a regular approach for dealing with each other. There are, of course, other means, aside from smoking dope, for people to begin to break the molds into which they have poured their lives. That is one way, however. The continued use of such an aid should be evaluated for its ability to inject fresh contributions into the household, and not as the one stock way to bring about good feelings there.

I believe there is also a need to think about relationships away from home (as the woman quoted did go on to do). The malaise this family felt had much to do with the larger social setting in which the family existed. In the same way, its members' treatment of each other was related to their accustomed ways of treating others not in the family. In the case of a couple, it would be immoral and ultimately unsuccessful for them to go out into the world purely for the purpose of improving their own relationship. Such excursions, if they are to have any lasting value, have to be true emotional experiences in themselves. We quoted Marx as saying, "It is nonsense to believe . . . one could satisfy one passion separated from all others. . . ." It is also nonsense to believe that you can relate to one person in a wholesome way while dealing with everyone else superficially. This is the message the addiction concept has for love. It says that we must aim to expand our honesty, intimacy, and trust to include others besides just one person. To do so would carry us farther—to a consideration of organizations, relating to other couples, and loving more than one person at a time. But these things are beyond the scope of this book.

LEAVING ADDICTION BEHIND

When my work on addiction in interpersonal relationships first became known, I began hearing from people about their concerns and problems in this area. Often, a married person or someone very involved in a relationship would tell me that my ideas had caused him to reflect on his and his mate's behavior. As a result of this thinking, these people told me, they were trying to exercise caution in avoiding the pitfalls of overdependency and isolation from others. Sometimes a person would confide to me that he or she had been or was a part of a deep addiction, and was trying to break loose from it. Most often, however, messages of quiet desperation have come to me from people who have failed at a series of relationships as a result of what they now saw to be addictive tendencies in their personalities. These are the people whose requests for help have been the most urgent. I respond to these people with mixed feelings, because I am not overly optimistic about the potential of outside therapy. Still, while warning them of the dangers of seeking answers from someone outside themselves or their normal lives, I have tried to give them some perspectives which seem regularly to emerge in the course of people's efforts to outgrow interpersonal addiction.

A man in Omaha wrote to me as follows:

> I heard about your work while I was experiencing the withdrawal symptoms from love that you describe. I am a divorced 43-year-old male who has gone through a repeating cycle of such experiences in my "love" relationships with women. Each time, I have developed a little more awareness about the problem; however, your ideas really put it together for me.

> My question at this point is, what can I do about my addiction? I seem to be able to have women friends, but when these become love relationships, I move into the same old pattern of behavior that you have described. In other types of addictions, I understand one is required to abstain totally from contact with the object of the addiction. Is this what is required for love addicts?

I began my reply by reminding the man that any solutions to his problems would have to be expressions of his own consciousness. They would thus have to come from his efforts at development, toward which my thoughts could perhaps make some contribution. I then explained to him that he was wrong to believe that total abstention could cure addiction. Obviously, this would be especially inappropriate as a way of treating difficulties in dealing with women. But it would be valuable for him to take some time away from romantic involvements so as to rethink and rework the way he behaved with women. Since he was already acutely aware of where his behavior was off base, and how he was consistently going wrong, I asked him to use his knowledge to recognize and offset addictive reflexes when he saw himself acting them out. I told him to try to do this in any way he saw possible, even if his methods seemed artificial, as by simply pulling up when he felt like making a demand of a woman which he knew would be wrong, or by not calling her when he felt some strong but unhealthy need to do so.

In what he had written to me, I saw specific positive signs, and points of departure for expanding his healthy contacts with women. I wrote back:

> Your less intense friendships with women are a good basis for fighting addiction. If you keep them going at the same time that you become romantically involved with someone, you will find yourself better grounded in people and life, so that you will be less tempted to be irrational and overconcerned with a lover. Continue to turn to your friends for company and warmth, and fit a lover into these established relationships. Then you can let your feelings and your interaction with her grow more naturally. Of course, the same goes for the other interests you already have [the man was a successful professional]. You should always retain in your perspective a sense of the importance of these interests to you.
>
> Your ability to deal easily with women whom you don't characterize as lovers may be helpful in other ways, too. After a time, friendship can grow into an emotional experience which is very satisfying, especially if past romances have been unhappy. Along these lines, think of how you act with a woman whom you regard as a longstanding friend, and try to behave around a lover with this same equanimity, no matter what your emotional response to her is at the outset.

I ended my letter to this man with a further expression of confidence that he seemed already to be gaining a better hold on himself. I said I hoped he would interpret my recommendations in a way which made sense to him and which would thus become an actual aid to him in his program for self-development. He wrote me again to say that my thoughts had been helpful, and to outline some steps he was taking in line with them and with his own thinking. His analysis of why he acted as he did gave me the impression that he could assimilate my advice into his own personal framework.

A letter to which I replied with a great many more misgivings came from a woman living in Atlanta. She wrote:

> I felt I needed to write directly to you. Your work made me think that you had researched my own "love-style" as data.
>
> Ever since my first "love" at sixteen, things haven't been right. Many loves and years later, I married a guy whom I knew I didn't love, but who showered me with the affection and security I CRAVED. It was a short marriage, due to a number of causes. It broke up three years ago. Since that time I have not heard one, single, solitary male say those three

magic words: "I LOVE YOU." So I fall in love with whoever shows the slightest signs of longevity in a relationship; and then I tell him of my undying love for him. When he replies that my feeling is not returned, I react in an appropriately dramatic manner. It is only recently that I became aware of these games. Within the past eight months, I have come to the realization that something is desperately wrong. In my new enlightenment, I know that I haven't loved these men at all.

The reason I'm writing this letter is that your work has reassured me that I am not the only person with this problem. Using your theory, I can give my situation a clear definition—NOW WHAT DO I DO? I reread your article almost daily, to clarify what is going on in my head, and just that relieves my anxiety. However, I don't feel that giving this thing a name will resolve it. I am an underpaid and overspent welfare caseworker who cannot afford the services of a professional. Free clinical assistance is out because I make too *much* money. I anxiously look forward to reading more about your work, but until then, I could use some advice.

If you could only drop me a line with a couple of suggestions to keep me going, I would be grateful. If you would like to call me some weekday evening collect, please do that. I WOULD JUST LIKE TO HEAR FROM YOU.

I answered:

I was somewhat reluctant to answer your letter, because you seem to be asking for help that I cannot give, and that I don't think would be good for me to give if I had it available.

I am worried that you still want to be relieved of a burden—by a lover, by me or by someone—that it is impossible to give up. I think that you must be willing to maintain your consciousness of yourself, at the same time that you make that consciousness more pleasant, by working to increase your appreciation of yourself.

In your letter, you seem to be saying that you wish men were more willing to tell you they love you, and that they be genuinely in love with you. I know that it is gratifying to be loved, and that everyone seeks this feeling. But if in doing so you deny too much of yourself, you lose what it is that might make you attractive as a person.

In the same way, I think you are too concerned with finding a therapist, relative to finding your own cure. And this, I fear, includes your communication to me. I would like to know more about your work as a caseworker. How do you proceed with welfare clients who are uncertain or concerned? How do you get them to think better about their problems and to decide what they want to do and how to do it? How do you know when you have done a good job? Is it possible to try to go through some of these steps for yourself? Perhaps in thinking about this, you will be able also to improve your techniques in your work.

In response to your request for my aid with the difficulties you are having relating to men, I would say start on a very modest scale. Develop your analysis of your problem into some specific steps you would like to take. Later, review how well you are keeping to your plan, and how successful this plan is. Talk to people you know about your efforts. If you don't have people with whom you find this possible, make such intimacy with people part of what you are attempting to achieve.

As I hope my letters show, I am not primarily concerned with being a therapist. What I want to do, at least, is honestly to set forth the impressions I gather about people from what they tell me about their attempts to be more whole. I search for where their understanding or their life is already strong, and advise them to build on that strength in devising a strategy for self-development. I would like them to mix their discontent equally with their self-love, so as to provide ballast for their continued growth as individuals. And I try to dissociate myself from their progress in any too close a way, because it is unrealistic for me to enter further into their lives.

When I become involved in counseling, as I do with some people I already know, I believe my approach combines the recommendations of Carl Rogers with those of Albert Ellis. That is, I try simply to help people sharpen their ideas about their goals—the kind of people they want to be, the values and aims they find it most important to realize, and the types of relationships they really want to have. I work with them to draw up a scheme for achieving these goals. We thus arrive at, hopefully, some methods for doing those things which they feel would be most constructive for them. Then, except for an occasional push when I see them losing sight of their goals, I leave them alone to pursue their chosen course of action. If a reassessment is necessary, then I accept their expressions of doubt and desire for new directions. But I insist that that be only the preliminary stage in our work together, and that they show their good faith by acting.

Actually, I am uncomfortable with the word—and concept— "therapy." I prefer to deal with people who present themselves in a fully self-respecting light, but who, at the same time, want to improve themselves, and perhaps me, through our association. As a result, I am not interested in remedying our defects so much as in realizing our ideals. These two aims are at times almost interchangeable, but I find it much more reassuring and energizing to think in terms of pursuing goals than to assume that I have already lost my way. Therefore, I would like to present a model for the way a person approaches relationships. It is partly real and partly imaginary, but I find it nonetheless compelling.

If you can come to love with a sense of self-possession and security, you are able to relate to people in a life-seeking way. You can be generous but demanding, can seek things you want from others without being overly calculating or unwilling to give of yourself. While you are open to see how things develop, and slow to make final acceptances or rejections, you do not give up your critical awareness. Simply, you are ready and eager to know people who will help you expand, and you feel able to attract such people.

In normal social intercourse you are relaxed, because you know your own value, and because you are not desperate to find someone on whom to peg your life. Since you are applying standards of your own, you are active but calm, seeking out those who seem attractive and making an effort to get to know them. When someone to whom you can relate does not seem available or willing to respond, you are only slightly disturbed, because your personal resources are still with you and your options have really not been reduced at all. Your only regret is that you have missed a possible friendship or a new knowledge of someone valuable. If something wrong definitely seems to have happened in the situation, you try in retrospect to fathom it and to learn from the mishap.

When, on the other hand, you find grounds for a relationship, you pursue it with a zest which doesn't take away from your respect for the other person. Your enthusiasm is not a diffuse and unstable infatuation, because it is based on an appreciation of the unique individual. You do not decide immediately that the person is what you needed all along, but you come to know him or her slowly, recognizing that there is still much to explore as the relationship becomes a loving one. When it reaches that depth of caring, you can handle it with the same dignity you showed at its genesis. Your confidence that your lover means well toward you enables you to feel that your lover values your happiness and growth, as you do his, independently of the gratification it gives him. You do not see other involvements on your lover's part as opposing or threatening the relationship. Thus you are prepared to accept the kind of growth that may lead one of you temporarily or permanently away from the relationship. For if as lovers you grow apart, you will probably still be friends, and the nonaddicted lover always has the final consolation that his own possibilities can never be exhausted.

After I write such an optimistic, visionary description of nonaddictive behavior, I am forced back to the gritty details of how two people can try to conceive a reasonable relationship which is warm and caring, and yet not overdependent and stifling. While I think it is helpful to have an image before our eyes of ideal conduct, I also think that most people need more specific, modest aids to their relating. I know that I do. However aware I am of the pitfalls in relationships, and of the drawbacks of my own style, I find it very hard to escape them. When these same situations arise, I tend to react to them in my habitual manner, without showing all of the benefits of my thinking.

I have experienced the typical problems in relating to others that I have been describing. I now have a relationship with a woman who has had her own share of interpersonal failures. I am trying to give something of myself to this relationship, and I am—probably as always—guardedly optimistic. The woman I am involved with is a very thoughtful person. By nature, we both conceptualize and express a large part of our experience.

So when we came together, we were very self-conscious, I think. We were passionate, too, but a lot of our interaction centered around discussions of what we wanted, and what we had done in the past, and what we were doing now. Sometimes I got the impression that I wasn't very much in control of myself; that I was going to do just what I had always done, which had not always been that successful. We talked about that, about what to do to prevent it, for both of us. Because we were afraid we would blow a good thing.

One way in which I try to rein in my less healthy impulses is to make a few rules to call into play whenever I see that I'm slipping. I try to pull back slightly—without panicking—and remember how I decided I had better behave in situations like the one I am in. These rules are like a framework, without which I would see no structure, or feel no rhythm, to my relationships. Together, my woman friend and I thought about rules for relationships between lovers. We came up with these:

> Don't get together all the time. Restrain yourself from expressing a total need for your partner's company. See what comes up when you're apart, even making the separations last a day or two, or more, as in taking a trip alone or with other people.
>
> Reserve some experiences for private contemplation. Decide on one involvement or activity that you won't keep your lover informed about. Not something you want to hide; just something you won't feel pressure to reveal instantaneously, as though you must keep your lover in constant touch with it.
>
> See other people when you are in your lover's company, especially in the fast, furious weeks at the onset of love. Try talking about these group interactions afterwards, and about what they have told you about you and your lover as well as the people you were with. Inquire and reveal, but try not to criticize or scrutinize. As you come to understand each other, though, you shouldn't need to do this all the time.
>
> Include trips with your partner and other forays into the outside world as a regular part of your experience together. These joint experiences are among the most informative ways to spend your shared time, and ultimately form the most solid and enduring basis of the relationship.
>
> Be patient. Don't force your feelings, or your partner's; especially the vocalization of them. Don't ask questions where you want certain set answers; don't constrain the truth to make yourself or the other person feel better, or more loved.
>
> Don't take these rules too seriously. Make up some rules that seem sensible to the two of you. Follow them, change them, replace them; talk about why.

And, finally, take it easy. No one relationship can give you life or take it away from you. Don't worry about anything you do or don't do. If you live and grow, your commitment is to life, and love comes in that same spirit—love that is a joyous desire to share all that is best in yourself and others.

Appendix

A. Responses to Morphine and a Placebo

In the Lasagna experiment, patients were given injections of an allegedly pain-killing drug which was sometimes morphine and sometimes a placebo. The drugs were administered under double-blind conditions; that is, neither the patients nor the technicians who administered the drugs knew which was which. Depending on the sequence of administration of the two drugs, which was varied in several ways, between 30 and 40 percent of the patients found the placebo as adequate as the morphine. Those who believed in the efficacy of the placebo also were somewhat more likely to obtain relief from the morphine itself. The average percentage of times relief was obtained from morphine by those who never responded to the placebo was 61 percent, while for those who did accept the placebo at least once, it was 78 percent.

B. *Shared Action of Chemically Distinct Substances*

In grouping barbiturates, alcohol, and opiates into one category, we depart, of course, from a strictly pharmacological approach to drugs. Since these three kinds of drugs have different chemical structures, a pharmacological model cannot explain the fundamental similarities in people's reactions to them. Consequently, many biologically oriented researchers have attempted to discount such similarities. Foremost among these scientists is Abraham Wikler (see Appendix F), whose position may have ideological overtones. It is consistent, for instance, with the importance he gives physiological habituation in his reinforcement model of addiction, and with the conservative public position he has maintained on such issues as marijuana. However, nowhere have pharmacologists been able to demonstrate a link between the particular chemical structures of the major depressants and the unique addictive properties that Wikler believes each of them has. In any case, there are other biochemical researchers who claim, as do Virginia Davis and Michael Walsh, that "Because of the resemblance of symptoms occurring on withdrawal of either alcohol or the opiates, it seems possible that the addictions may be similar and that the real distinctions between the two drugs could be only the length of time and dosage required for development of dependence."

Generalizing from Davis and Walsh's argument, differences in the effects of many drugs are perhaps more quantitative than qualitative. Marijuana, for instance, would have small potential for addiction simply because it is too mild a sedative to engage fully a person's consciousness in the manner of heroin or alcohol. Even these quantitative distinctions may not always be intrinsic to the drugs in question, but may be strongly influenced by the dosage strengths and methods of administration that are characteristically employed with these drugs in a given culture. The Bushmen and Hottentots may have reacted violently to smoking tobacco because they swallowed the smoke rather than exhaling it. Coffee and tea may be prepared in milder concentrations in present-day America than in nineteenth-century England. Smoking a cigarette may provide a small and gradual infusion of nicotine, compared to the amount of heroin one gets from injecting a strong dose directly into the bloodstream. These circumstantial differences are not inconsiderable, and should not be mistaken for categorical differences between substances which in important respects operate similarly.

C. Effects of Expectations and Setting on Reactions to a Drug

Subjects in the Schachter and Singer study received an injection of the stimulant epinephrine (adrenalin), which was presented to them as an "experimental vitamin." Half of the subjects were told what to expect from the injection (i.e., generalized arousal); the other half were kept in the dark about these "side effects" of the supposed vitamin. Then each subject was left in a room with another person—a stooge paid by the experimenter to act in a specified way. Half the subjects in each of the original two groups were exposed, individually, to a stooge who acted as though he were euphoric, joking and throwing paper around, and half were put in with a stooge who took offense at the experiment and stalked out in anger. The result was that uninformed subjects—those who had not been told what their physiological reaction to the injection was going to be—picked up the mood set by the stooge, while informed subjects did not. That is, if the subject experienced an effect from the drug, but didn't know why he was feeling that way, he became very suggestible. Seeing the stooge react to the experiment in a certain way served to explain for the subject why he himself was physiologically aroused—i.e., that he was angry, or that he was euphoric. On the other hand, if the subject could link his physiological state with the injection, then he had no need to look around him for an emotional explanation for his arousal. Another group of subjects, who were grossly misinformed about what the injection would do to them, were even more suggestible than were uninformed subjects.

To investigate what happens generally when people mislabel the drug they take, or anticipate effects that actually are characteristic of a different kind of drug, Cedric Wilson and Pamela Huby gave subjects three classes of drugs: stimulants, depressants, and tranquilizers. "When the subjects guessed correctly which drug they had received," reported Wilson and Huby, "they responded to it vigorously. When they guessed incorrectly, the effects of the drug were partially or completely inhibited."

D. Comparison of Health Hazards of Commonly Used Drugs with Those of Heroin

The major health hazards of tobacco are in the areas of lung cancer, emphysema, chronic bronchitis, and heart disease. Coffee, according to Marjorie Baldwin's article "Caffeine on Trial," is being implicated in heart disease, diabetes, hypoglycemia, and stomach acidity. In addition, recent research has concentrated on the increased incidence of birth defects and increased risks in pregnancy with both of these drugs, as well as with aspirin. The U.S. Public Health Service has reported that smoking on the part of mothers is an important contributor to the high rate of fetal mortality in this country. Lissy Jarvik and her colleagues, investigating chromosomal damage from LSD (see Appendix E), find that long-time aspirin users and "coffee or Coca-Cola addicts" run similar risks of genetic damage and congenital abnormality in their offspring, and women who take aspirin daily are now being observed to show a higher than normal rate of irregularities in pregnancy and childbirth.

While American society has been slow in recognizing the deleterious consequences of these familiar drugs, it has from the outset exaggerated those of heroin. Along with the myths of addiction after one shot (for which only a psychological explanation is possible) and unlimited tolerance, heroin is thought to lead to physical degeneration and death. But the experience of lifetime users in favorable social climates has shown that heroin is as viable a habit to maintain as any other, and medical research has not isolated any ill effects on health from heroin use alone. The main cause of illness and death among street addicts is contamination from unhealthy conditions of administration, such as dirty hypodermic needles. The addict's lifestyle also contributes in many ways to his high mortality rate. Charles Winick has concluded, "Opiates usually are harmless, but they are taken under unsatisfactory conditions. Malnutrition caused by loss of appetite probably is the most serious complication of opiate addiction."

The physical danger that heroin is most widely believed to present for its users is that of death by overdose. Constituting perhaps the most persistent misapprehension about the drug, "heroin overdoses" have vastly increased in recent years while the average heroin content in doses available on the street has been shrinking. Citing an investigation by Dr. Milton Helpern, New York City's Chief Medical Examiner, Edward Brecher shows that so-called deaths by OD could not possibly result from that cause. The best current guess is that deaths attributed to overdosing are actually due to the use of heroin in combination with another depressant, such as alcohol or a barbiturate.

The information presented here is not intended as an argument favoring the use of heroin. In fact, it is true that heroin offers the most sure and complete chance for eradicating one's consciousness, which is the basic element in an addiction. The premise of this book is that addiction as a way of life is psychologically unhealthy both in its causes and consequences, and the values which the book is meant to encourage run directly counter to those of a drugged or otherwise artificially supported existence. The exculpatory data on heroin, together with the evidence of ill effects from cigarettes and coffee, are offered in support of the proposition that a culture's—our culture's—estimate of the physical as well as psychological hazards of different drugs is an expression of its overall attitude toward those drugs. What must be dealt with is our society's need to condemn heroin from every possible angle, regardless of the facts, even while that society is so strongly susceptible to heroin and other forms of addiction.

E. LSD Research

Sidney Cohen's study was based on a survey of 44 LSD researchers who, among them, had collected data on 5000 individuals who had been given LSD or mescaline on a total of 25,000 occasions. These subjects, broken down into "normal" experimental volunteers and patients undergoing psychotherapy, showed the following rates of complications associated with hallucinogenic trips: attempted suicides—0 per 1000 for normal subjects, 1.2 per 1000 for psychiatric patients; psychotic reactions lasting longer than 48 hours (roughly the duration of a trip)—less than 1 per 1000 for normal subjects, less than 2 per 1000 for psychiatric patients.

The refutation of the Maimon Cohen study on chromosomal breakage caused by LSD focused on the fact that the study employed human leukocytes (white blood cells) cultured artificially in a test tube (*in vitro*), rather than in the living organism (*in vivo*). Under these conditions, where the cells cannot easily rid themselves of toxins, many chemicals cause increased chromosomal breakage. These include aspirin, benzene, caffeine, antibiotics, and even more innocuous substances, such as water that has not been twice distilled. Subsequent *in vivo* studies of users of pure and illicit LSD, along with further *in vitro* studies with proper controls, showed that there is no special danger with LSD. Reporting that caffeine doubles breakage rates just as LSD does, Jarvik and her colleagues note that any substance introduced into the body in sufficient quantity during gestation can cause congenital abnormality.

F. Conditioning Models of Addiction

A major line of thought in addiction research—the conditioned learning approach of Abraham Wikler and the animal experimenters at the University of Michigan (see Appendix B)—is explicitly concerned with the psychological rewards and punishments associated with drug use. The chief limitation of this theorizing and research, however, is that it takes withdrawal distress for granted and assumes that the relief of withdrawal pain is invariably the addict's primary reinforcement for taking an opiate past the period of initial involvement with the drug. Other rewards (such as those provided by environmental stimuli) are considered, but only as secondary reinforcements that are linked to the relief of withdrawal.

The mechanistic character of conditioning theories is associated with their origins in the observation of laboratory animals. Human consciousness entails a greater complexity of response to drugs, and withdrawal, than animals are capable of. Only animals respond to drugs in a predictable way, and only animals (especially encaged animals) respond uniformly to the onset of withdrawal by renewing their dosage of a drug. For a conditioning theory to explain the behavior of human addicts, as well as nonaddicted drug users, it must take into account the various social and personal reinforcements—ego-gratification, social approval, security, self-consistency, sensory stimulation, etc.—that motivate human beings in their drug-taking as in other activities.

Recognizing the limitations of animal-based hypotheses, Alfred Lindesmith has proposed a variation of conditioning theory which adds to it an important cognitive dimension. In *Addiction and Opiates,* Lindesmith argues that addiction occurs only when the addict understands that physiological habituation to morphine or heroin has taken place, and that only another dose of the drug will protect him from withdrawal. Despite Lindesmith's insistence that addiction is a conscious, human phenomenon, his theory is just as narrowly based on physical dependence and withdrawal as all-purpose reinforcers as are other conditioning models. It posits only one kind of cognition (i.e., the awareness of an association between withdrawal and taking an opiate) as influencing the psychological process of conditioning, rather than allowing for the range of cognitions of which human beings are capable. Lindesmith notes marginally that hospital patients who know that they have received morphine, and who are knowingly withdrawn from the drug, still do not usually become addicted. This is because they think of themselves as patients, not addicts. Lindesmith fails to draw what seems a reasonable inference from this observation: that self-image is always a factor to be considered in the addiction process.

G. Physiological and Psychological Mechanisms of Addiction

The publication in *Science* of a study by Louise Lowney and her colleagues on the binding of opiate molecules in the brains of mice, which is part of an ongoing line of research in that area, has convinced many people that a breakthrough has been achieved in understanding addiction physiologically. But for every study of this sort that reaches the public eye, there is also one like *Psychology Today*'s report on Richard Drawbaugh and Harbans Lal's work with morphine-addicted rats who had been conditioned to accept the ringing of a bell (together with a placebo injection) in place of morphine. Lal and Drawbaugh found that the morphine antagonist naloxone, which is presumed to counteract the effects of morphine chemically, inhibited the effects of the conditioned stimulus (the bell) as well as those of morphine itself. Clearly, the antagonist was working at something besides a chemical level.

Chemical reactions in the brain can, of course, be observed whenever a psychoactive drug is introduced. The existence of such reactions, and the fact that all psychological processes ultimately take the form of neural and chemical processes, should not be used to beg the questions raised by the impressive array of research, observations, and subjective reports that testify to the variability of *human* reactions to drugs.

Bibliography

Adams, Robert Lynn, and Fox, Robert Jon. "Mainlining Jesus: The New Trip." *Society* (February 1972): 50–56.

Atkinson, John W. *An Introduction to Motivation.* Princeton: Van Nostrand, 1964.

Bakwin, Harry. "Pseudodoxia Pediatrica." *New England Journal of Medicine* 232 (1945): 691–697.

Baldwin, Marjorie V. "Caffeine on Trial." *Life and Health* (October 1973): 10–13.

Ball, John C.; Graff, Harold; and Sheehan, John J., Jr. "The Heroin Addicts' View of Methadone Maintenance." *British Journal of Addiction to Alcohol and Other Drugs* 69 (1974): 89–95.

Bancroft, Raymond L. "America's Mayors and Councilmen: Their Problems and Frustrations." *Nation's Cities* (April 1974): 14–24.

Bandura, Albert. "Behavioral Psychotherapy." *Scientific American* (March 1967): 78–86.

Beck, Alan M. "The Dog: America's Sacred Cow?" *Nation's Cities* (February 1974): 29–35.

Becker, Howard S. *Outsiders.* London: Free Press of Glencoe, 1963.

Bettelheim, Bruno. *The Children of the Dream.* London: Macmillan, 1969.

Blum, Richard H., & Associates. *Drugs I: Society and Drugs.* San Francisco: Jossey-Bass, 1969.

Brecher, Edward M. *Licit and Illicit Drugs.* Mount Vernon, N.Y.: Consumers Union, 1972.

Brodsky, Archie. "D. H. Lawrence's Theory of Character as an Informing Principle of *Women in Love.*" Unpublished honors essay. Philadelphia: University of Pennsylvania, 1967.

Bronfenbrenner, Urie. *Two Worlds of Childhood: U.S. and U.S.S.R.* New York: Russell Sage Foundation, 1970.

————. "The Origins of Alienation." *Scientific American* (August 1974): 53–61.

Bruch, Hilde. *Eating Disorders: Obesity, Anorexia Nervosa, and the Person Within.* New York: Basic Books, 1973.

Burack, Richard. *The New Handbook of Prescription Drugs.* New York: Ballantine Books, 1970.

Cameron, Dale C. "Facts About Drugs." *World Health* (April 1971): 4–11.

Canadian Government Commission of Inquiry. *The Non-medical Use of Drugs.* Middlesex, Eng.: Penguin, 1971.

Cantwell, Dennis P. "Psychiatric Illness in the Families of Hyperactive Children." *Archives of General Psychiatry* 27 (1972): 414–417.

Carter, Hugh, and Glick, Paul C. *Marriage and Divorce: A Social and Economic Study.* Cambridge, Mass.: Harvard University Press, 1970.

Chein, Isidor. "Psychological Functions of Drug Use." In *Scientific Basis of Drug Dependence,* edited by Hannah Steinberg, pp. 13–30. London: J. & A. Churchill Ltd., 1969.

————; Gerard, Donald L.; Lee, Robert S.; and Rosenfeld, Eva. *The Road to H.* New York: Basic Books, 1964.

Chesler, Phyllis. *Women and Madness.* New York: Doubleday, 1972.

Clausen, John A. "Drug Addiction." In *Contemporary Social Problems,* edited by Robert K. Merton and Robert A. Nisbet, pp. 181–221. New York: Harcourt, Brace & World, 1961.

Cohen, Jozef. *Secondary Motivation.* Vol. I. Chicago: Rand McNally, 1970.

Cohen, Maimon M.; Marinello, Michelle J.; and Back, Nathan. "Chromosomal Damage in Human Leukocytes Induced by Lysergic Acid Diethylamide." *Science* 155 (1967): 1417–1419.

Cohen, Sidney. "Lysergic Acid Diethylamide: Side Effects and Complications." *Journal of Nervous and Mental Disease* 130 (1960): 30–40.

Cooper, Kenneth H. *Aerobics.* New York: M. Evans, 1968.

Davis, Virginia E., and Walsh, Michael J. "Alcohol, Amines, and Alkaloids: A Possible Biochemical Basis for Alcohol Addiction." *Science* 167 (1970): 1005–1007.

Dishotsky, Norman I.; Loughman, William D.; Mogar, Robert E.; and Lipscomb, Wendell R. "LSD and Genetic Damage." *Science* 172 (1971): 431–440.

Drawbaugh, Richard, and Lal, Harbans. "Reversal by Narcotic Antagonist of a Narcotic Action Elicited by a Conditional Stimulus." *Nature* 247 (1974): 65–67.

Dunnell, Karen, and Cartwright, Ann. *Medicine Takers, Prescribers and Hoarders.* London: Routledge and Kegan Paul, 1972.

Ellis, Albert. *Reason and Emotion in Psychotherapy.* New York: Lyle Stuart, 1962.

Eysenck, H. J. "The Effects of Psychotherapy: An Evaluation." *Journal of Consulting Psychology* 16 (1952): 319–324.

Fidell, Linda S. "Put Her Down on Drugs: Prescribed Drug Usage in Women." Paper presented at the Western Psychological Association Meeting, Anaheim, Calif., April 12, 1973.

Flink, James J. *America Adopts the Automobile: 1895–1910.* Cambridge, Mass.: MIT Press, 1970.

Frank, Jerome D. *Persuasion and Healing.* Baltimore: Johns Hopkins Press, 1961.

Freidson, Eliot. *Profession of Medicine.* New York: Dodd, Mead, 1970.

Freud, Sigmund. "Being in Love and Hypnosis" (1921). In *Group Psychology and the Analysis of the Ego,* pp. 54–61. New York: Bantam Books, 1965.

Fromm, Erich. *The Art of Loving.* New York: Harper & Row, 1956.

———. "Marx's Contribution to the Knowledge of Man." In *The Crisis of Psychoanalysis,* pp. 61–75. Greenwich, Conn.: Fawcett, 1970.

Ginott, Haim G. *Between Parent and Child.* New York: Macmillan, 1965.

———. *Between Parent and Teenager.* New York: Macmillan, 1969.

Goffman, Erving. *Asylums.* Garden City, N.Y.: Anchor Books, 1961.

Goode, Erich. *Drugs in American Society.* New York: Knopf, 1972.

Graham, Sheilah, and Frank, Gerold. *Beloved Infidel.* New York: Bantam Books, 1959.

Greer, Germaine. *The Female Eunuch.* New York: McGraw-Hill, 1971.

Hatterer, Lawrence J., with Ramsey, Judith. "Are You an Addictive Personality?" *Family Circle* (June 1974): 138–139.

Heider, Fritz. *The Psychology of Interpersonal Relations.* New York: Wiley, 1958.

Henry, Jules. *Culture Against Man.* New York: Random House, 1963.

Holt, John. *How Children Fail.* New York: Pitman, 1964.

Illich, Ivan. *Deschooling Society.* New York: Harper & Row, 1971.

Isbell, Harris. "Clinical Research on Addiction in the United States." In *Narcotic Drug Addiction Problems,* edited by Robert B. Livingston, pp.

114–130. Bethesda, Md.: Public Health Service, National Institute of Mental Health, 1958.

Jaffe, Jerome H., and Harris, T. George. "As Far as Heroin Is Concerned, the Worst Is Over." *Psychology Today* (August 1973): 68–79, 85.

Jarvik, Lissy F.; Kato, Takashi; Saunders, Barbara; and Moralishvili, Emelia. "LSD and Human Chromosomes." In *Psychopharmacology: A Review of Progress 1957–1967*, edited by Daniel H. Efron, pp. 1247–1252. Washington, D.C.: Public Health Service Document No. 1836; U.S. Department of Health, Education, and Welfare, 1968.

Jessor, Richard; Young, H. Boutourline; Young, Elizabeth B.; and Tesi, Gino. "Perceived Opportunity, Alienation, and Drinking Behavior Among Italian and American Youth." *Journal of Personality and Social Psychology* 15 (1970): 215–222.

Kolb, Lawrence. "Factors That Have Influenced the Management and Treatment of Drug Addicts." In *Narcotic Drug Addiction Problems,* edited by Robert B. Livingston, pp. 23–33. Bethesda, Md.: Public Health Service, National Institute of Mental Health, 1958.

————. *Drug Addiction: A Medical Problem.* Springfield, Ill.: Charles C Thomas, 1962.

Kubie, Lawrence S. *Neurotic Distortion of the Creative Process.* Lawrence, Kan.: University of Kansas Press, 1958.

Laing, R. D. *The Divided Self.* Middlesex, Eng.: Penguin, 1965.

Lasagna, Louis; Mosteller, Frederick; von Felsinger, John M.; and Beecher, Henry K. "A Study of the Placebo Response." *American Journal of Medicine* 16 (1954): 770–779.

Lawrence, D. H. *Women in Love* (1920). Middlesex, Eng.: Penguin, 1960.

Lennard, Henry L.; Epstein, Leon J.; Bernstein, Arnold; and Ransom, Donald C. *Mystification and Drug Misuse.* San Francisco: Jossey-Bass, 1971.

————; Epstein, Leon J.; and Rosenthal, Mitchell S. "The Methadone Illusion." *Science* 176 (1972): 881–884.

Lepper, Mark R.; Greene, David; and Nisbett, Richard E. "Undermining Children's Intrinsic Interest with Extrinsic Reward: A Test of the 'Overjustification' Hypothesis." *Journal of Personality and Social Psychology* 28 (1973): 129–137.

Lindesmith, Alfred R. *Addiction and Opiates.* Chicago: Aldine, 1968.

Livingston, Jay. "A Culture of Losers." *Psychology Today* (March 1974): 51–55.

Lolli, Giorgio; Serianni, Emidio; Golder, Grace M.; and Luzzatto-Fegiz, Pierpaolo. *Alcohol in Italian Culture.* Glencoe, Ill.: Free Press, 1958.

Lowney, Louise I.; Schulz, Karin; Lowery, Patricia J.; and Goldstein, Avram. "Partial Purification of an Opiate Receptor from Mouse Brain." *Science* 183 (1974): 749–753.

Lukoff, Irving F.; Quatrone, Debra; and Sardell, Alice. "Some Aspects of the Epidemiology of Heroin Use in a Ghetto Community." Unpublished manuscript, Columbia University School of Social Work, New York, 1972.

McCarthy, Colman. "Ousting the Stranger from the House." *Newsweek* (March 25, 1974): 17.

McClelland, David C. *The Achieving Society*. Princeton: Van Nostrand, 1961.

———; Atkinson, John W.; Clark, Russell A.; and Lowell, Edgar L. *The Achievement Motive*. New York: Appleton-Century-Crofts, 1953.

———; Davis, William N.; Kalin, Rudolf; and Wanner, Eric. *The Drinking Man*. New York: Free Press, 1972.

Mailer, Norman, "The White Negro" (1957). In *Advertisements for Myself*, pp. 311–331. New York: Putnam, 1966.

Marais, Eugene. *The Soul of the Ape*. New York: Atheneum, 1969.

Martinson, Floyd M. "Ego Deficiency as a Factor in Marriage." *American Sociological Review* 20 (1955): 161–164.

Masterton, Bruce. "Molecules, Neurons, Brains, and Thoughts." *Contemporary Psychology* 17 (1972): 1–2.

Miller, Daniel R., and Swanson, Guy E. *The Changing American Parent*. New York: Wiley, 1958.

Mizener, Arthur. *The Far Side of Paradise*. Boston: Houghton-Mifflin, 1949.

Morgan, Edmund S. *Visible Saints: The History of a Puritan Idea*. New York: New York University Press, 1963.

Nesbitt, Paul David. "Chronic Smoking and Emotionality." *Journal of Applied Social Psychology* 2 (1972): 187–196.

Oates, Wayne. *Confessions of a Workaholic*. New York: World, 1971.

O'Donnell, John A. *Narcotic Addicts in Kentucky*. Chevy Chase, Md.: National Institute of Mental Health, 1969.

Peele, Stanton, and Brodsky, Archie. "Addicted to Food." *Life and Health,* in press.

Rainwater, Lee. "A Study of Personality Differences Between Middle and Lower Class Adolescents." *Genetic Psychology Monographs* 54 (1956): 3–86.

———. *Family Design: Marital Sexuality, Family Size, and Contraception*. Chicago: Aldine, 1965.

Riesman, David. *The Lonely Crowd*. New Haven, Conn.: Yale University Press, 1950.

Rogers, Carl R. *Client-Centered Therapy*. Boston: Houghton-Mifflin, 1951.

Rosenhan, David L. "On Being Sane in Insane Places." *Science* 179 (1973): 250–258.

Sagov, Stanley E., with Brodsky, Archie. *The Art of Being a Patient: How to Help Your Doctor Help You*. New York: David McKay, forthcoming.

Sanford, Nevitt, ed. "Personality Development During the College Years." *Journal of Social Issues* 12 (1956): entire issue.

Schachter, Stanley. "Obesity and Eating." *Science* 161 (1968): 751–756.

————, and Singer, Jerome E. "Cognitive, Social, and Physiological Determinants of Emotional State." *Psychological Review* 69 (1962): 379–399.

Schur, Edwin M. *Narcotic Addiction in Britain and America.* Bloomington: Indiana University Press, 1962.

Seligman, Martin E. P. "Fall into Helplessness." *Psychology Today* (June 1973): 43–48.

Snyder, Solomon H. *Madness and the Brain.* New York: McGraw-Hill, 1974.

Solomon, Richard L., and Corbit, John D. "An Opponent-Process Theory of Motivation. I: Temporal Dynamics of Affect." *Psychological Review* 81 (1974): 119–145.

————. "An Opponent-Process Theory of Motivation. II: Cigarette Addiction." *Journal of Abnormal Psychology* 81 (1973): 158–171.

Sonnedecker, Glenn. "Emergence and Concept of the Addiction Problem." In *Narcotic Drug Addiction Problems,* edited by Robert B. Livingston, pp. 14–22. Bethesda, Md.: Public Health Service, National Institute of Mental Health, 1958.

Sorensen, Robert C. *The Sorensen Report: Adolescent Sexuality in Contemporary America.* New York: World, 1973.

Spock, Benjamin. *Baby and Child Care.* Rev. ed. New York: Pocket Books, 1968.

Srole, Leo; Langner, Thomas S.; Michael, Stanley T.; Opler, Marvin K.; and Rennie, Thomas A. C. *Mental Health in the Metropolis: The Midtown Manhattan Study.* New York: McGraw-Hill, 1962.

Steinberg, Hannah, ed. *Scientific Basis of Drug Dependence.* London: J. & A. Churchill Ltd., 1969.

Stunkard, Albert. "New Therapies for the Eating Disorders: Behavior Modification of Obesity and Anorexia Nervosa." *Archives of General Psychiatry* 26 (1972): 391–398.

Szasz, Thomas S. *The Myth of Mental Illness.* New York: Hoeber-Harper, 1961.

————. "The Ethics of Addiction." *Harper's* (April 1972): 74–79.

Turner, Frederick Jackson. "The Significance of the Frontier in American History." In *Annual Report for 1893.* Washington, D.C.: American Historical Association, 1894.

White, Robert W. *Ego and Reality in Psychoanalytic Theory.* New York: International Universities Press, 1963.

————. *Lives in Progress: A Study of the Natural Growth of Personality.* 2d ed. New York: Holt, Rinehart & Winston, 1966.

Wikler, Abraham. "Some Implications of Conditioning Theory for Problems of Drug Abuse." In *Drug Abuse: Data and Debate,* edited by Paul H. Blachly, pp. 104–113. Springfield, Ill.: Charles C Thomas, 1970.

———, and Rasor, Robert W. "Psychiatric Aspects of Drug Addiction." *American Journal of Medicine* 14 (1953): 566–570.

Wilbur, Richard S. "A Followup of Vietnam Drug Users." Press conference, U.S. Department of Defense, April 23, 1973.

Williams, Lawrence P. *How to Avoid Unnecessary Surgery.* Los Angeles: Nash, 1971.

Wilson, Cedric W. M., and Huby, Pamela M. "An Assessment of the Responses to Drugs Acting on the Central Nervous System." *Clinical Pharmacology and Therapeutics* 2 (1961): 587–598.

Winick, Charles. "Physician Narcotic Addicts." *Social Problems* 9 (1961): 174–186.

———. "Maturing Out of Narcotic Addiction." *Bulletin on Narcotics* 14 (1962): 1–7.

Zinberg, Norman E. "G.I.'s and O.J.'s in Vietnam." *The New York Times Magazine* (December 5, 1971): 37, 112–124.

———, and Jacobson, Richard. *The Social Controls of Nonmedical Drug Use.* Washington, D.C.: Interim Report to the Drug Abuse Council, Inc., 1974.

———, and Lewis, David C. "Narcotic Usage I: A Spectrum of a Difficult Medical Problem." *New England Journal of Medicine* 270 (1964): 989–993.

———, and Robertson, John A. *Drugs and the Public.* New York: Simon & Schuster, 1972.

Zola, Irving Kenneth. "Medicine as an Institution of Social Control." *The Sociological Review* 20 (1972): 487–504.

Index

abstinence, 217, 253

achievement motivation, 64, 127, 228

Adams, Robert Lynn, 168

addiction. *See also* group addictions; habit; maturing out; one-sided addictions; simultaneous or successive addictions

  to alcohol and barbiturates, 36–37, 39–41, 50–53, 67, 162, 213–14, 262

  in America, 16–17, 30, 41–48, 162

  to consumer goods, 163–64

  cycle of, 27–28, 62, 69

  to food, 67, 153, 165, 213–15, 232

  to formal education, 149–50

  to gambling, 165

  interpersonal, 17, 27–28, 70–75, 81–82, 84–87, 139, 171, 194, 247–48, 252–56

  lower-class and middle-class forms, 45, 73–75, 194

  to nicotine and caffeine, 37–40, 50, 52–53, 67, 162, 213–15

  to opiates, 27–28, 32–33, 39, 41–42, 50–53, 67, 213–15, 262

  as outgrowth of normal experience, 15–16, 52, 91–92, 203–4

  to pets, 165–67

  to psychotherapy, 156–58

  reformulation of concept, 16, 48–54

  to religion, 71–72, 168–69

  as social norm, 18, 139, 169, 199, 213

  social-psychological definition, 60–61

  as subjective experience, 18, 29,

addiction (*continued*)
50–54, 60–63
to television, 164–65
transferred from one object to
another, 36–37, 63, 71–72, 213
treatment of, 213–15, 225–36,
247–57
to work, 16, 65, 165
addicts
drug and interpersonal compared,
27–28, 73–75
ideology of, 68–70, 204–5, 241
personality traits of, 56–60
private world of, 28, 68–70, 84, 87
psychology of, 27–28, 32, 50–54,
56–63
public image of, 30, 44–45
adrenalin, reactions to, 38, 263
advertising, 161–64
alcohol, 34, 36–37, 39–41, 45–46,
50–51, 67, 162, 262
Alcoholics Anonymous, 213–14
alcoholism, 37, 40–41, 45–46, 73–74,
213–14
Alice (vignette), 124–26
Allbutt, Clifford, 34, 40
Allen and Gail (vignette), 92–103,
115–19
Alsop, Joseph, 37–38
America
communes in, 207–8
conflict between individualism and
institutionalization, 42–44
ease in handling stimulants, 40, 162
mid-twentieth-century social conditions, 14, 119–24, 126–36, 143–
69, 208
problems with alcohol, 40, 45–46,
162
response to marijuana and LSD,
46–48
response to opiates, 41, 43–45, 162
susceptibility to addiction, 16–17,
30, 41–48, 143, 162
American Indians, response to alcohol, 41
American Medical Association, 44,
161–62
amphetamines, 52, 67, 149, 177
animals addicted to drugs, 62–63,
266–68
Anne (vignette), 173–80, 204–5
Art of Loving, The (Erich Fromm),
79–83
aspirin, 37, 47, 264, 266
Atkinson, John W., 64, 127, 228
autonomous personality, 221

Bakwin, Harry, 152
balance theory, 190
Baldwin, Marjorie V., 264
Ball, John C., 36
Bandura, Albert, 155
barbiturates, 36–37, 45, 50–51,
161–62, 262
basketball, 222
Bea and Mel (vignette), 112–13
Beauvoir, Simone de, 218
Beck, Alan M., 166
Becker, Howard S., 38–39, 68
behavior therapy, 214–15, 225–27,
232, 244, 248
Beloved Infidel (Sheilah Graham and
Gerold Frank), 77–80
Bettelheim, Bruno, 207
Blum, Richard H., 39–42, 60
brain, physiology of the, 158–60
Brecher, Edward M., 37, 50, 265
Bronfenbrenner, Urie, 207–9
Bruce and Vicky (vignette), 24–28
Bruch, Hilde, 214

Burack, Richard, 161

caffeine, 37, 40, 47, 52, 264, 266
Cameron, Dale C., 49
Cantwell, Dennis P., 159
Carl and Shelley (vignette), 103–8
Carter, Hugh, 136
Cartwright, Ann, 160
Chein, Isidor, 15, 35–36, 57–58,
    61–62, 74, 123
Chesler, Phyllis, 157
childrearing
    collective upbringing, 207
    constructive patterns, 208–11
    current trends, 138–39
    patterns contributing to addiction,
        122–34, 208, 210
China
    tobacco ban, 39
    use of opium, 39, 41
cigarettes, 37–38, 50, 52, 67, 213–15,
    262
Civil War, use of morphine in, 41
Clausen, John A., 44
cocaine, 52, 67
coffee, 37, 39–40, 47, 262, 264
Cohen, Jozef, 64
Cohen, Maimon M., 47, 266
Cohen, Sidney, 46, 265
cola, 37, 47, 264
communes, 139, 207–8
    religious, 71–72, 168–69
competence as antidote to addiction,
    145, 228–29
conditioning theories of addiction,
    266–67
Confessions of a Workaholic (Wayne
    Oates), 16
Console, A. Dale, 161
controlled drug users, 34–35, 58–59

Cooper, Kenneth H., 229
Corbit, John D., 53
criteria for addiction and nonaddic-
    tion, 63–67, 223–25
    in love relationships, 83, 243–47
cross-dependence, 36–37
cultural variations in drug use, 38–41

dating patterns, 134–38
Davis, Virginia E., 262
Daytop Village, 39, 214
Demerol, 35, 45
depressants, 37, 51–53, 161–62, 262
depression, 158–59
Depression of 1929–1940, 121–22,
    128–29
"deprogramming," 168
Dishotsky, Norman I., 47
divorce rate, 136
Dixon, W. E., 34, 40
Don Juan role, 185, 194
Doyle, Sir Arthur Conan, 35
Drawbaugh, Richard, 268
Drugs and the Public (Norman E. Zin-
    berg and John A. Robertson), 33,
    39
Drugs in American Society (Erich
    Goode), 33
Dunnell, Karen, 160

education
    current trends, 150–51
    patterns contributing to addiction,
        146–50
égoisme à deux, 26, 84, 92
Ellis, Albert, 256
expertise, 122, 145, 148, 151, 160

Eysenck, H. J., 155

family
  constructive evolution, 207–9,
    251–52
  extended, 120–22
  nuclear, 119–24, 134
  as object of addiction, 119, 133–34
  as source of addiction, 17, 119–24,
    126–34, 208
fear of failure, 64, 127, 148
Federal Bureau of Narcotics, 30, 36,
    44
Fidell, Linda S., 161
Fitzgerald, F. Scott, 76–80
Fitzgerald, Zelda, 76
Flink, James J., 122
food as an addiction, 67, 153, 165,
    213–15, 232
Fox, Robert Jon, 168
Frank, Jerome D., 152
Frazier, Walt, 222
Freidson, Eliot, 152
Freud, Sigmund, 72–73
Fromm, Erich, 79–83

Gail and Allen (vignette), 92–103,
    115–19
gambling, 165
Germany
  craving for tobacco, 37
  tobacco ban, 39
Ginott, Haim G., 128, 130, 138
Glick, Paul C., 136
Goffman, Erving, 154
Goode, Erich, 33, 49–50
Graham, Sheilah, 76–80

Great Britain, 34–35, 40, 45, 74
Greece, response to alcohol, 41
Greer, Germaine, 83, 85
group addictions, 28, 38–39, 68–70,
    139, 142, 168
Guy (vignette), 185–94

habit, 15, 224
hallucinogens, 46–48, 51
Halsted, William, 35
Harrison Act, 44
Hatterer, Lawrence J., 165
Hearst, Patricia, 141–42, 209
Heider, Fritz, 190
Henry, Jules, 127
heroin. *See also* opiates
  harmful effects, extent of, 264
  overdose myth, 265
  profile of addict, 30–32
  rehabilitation programs, 213–15
  subcultures of users, 68–70
  use in U.S. ghettos, 35–36, 57–58,
    74
  use in Vietnam, 34, 39, 59–60
  use in youth culture, 58–59, 74
  welcomed as nonaddicting pain-
    killer, 45
High School, 127
Holt, John, 148
hospital patients receiving morphine,
    34, 36, 56–57, 59–60, 267
Huby, Pamela M., 263
hyperkinetic children, 159–60
hypnotism, 72–73

Illich, Ivan, 146, 148, 150
India, use of opium, 41
infants addicted to drugs, 62–63

institutions
  as objects of addiction, 146
  predominance of, in modern soci-
    ety, 17, 122, 144, 146, 152–53
  respect for authority of, 131, 144,
    146, 148, 160
  response to opiates, 43–45
  as sources of addiction, 17, 122–23,
    145–46
Isbell, Harris, 37, 41
Israel, collective upbringing, 207
Italy, use of alcohol, 40

Jacobson, Richard, 58–59, 67
Jaffe, Jerome H., 34
Jarvik, Lissy F., 264, 266
jazz, 222
Jessor, Richard, 40
Jesus freaks, 71–72, 168–69
Joan (vignette), 109–12
joy as antidote to addiction, 145, 224

Kolb, Lawrence, 37, 44, 56
Kubie, Lawrence S., 63–64

Laing, R. D., 75, 149
Lal, Harbans, 268
Lasagna, Louis, 36, 56–57, 261
Lawrence, D. H., 26, 75, 84, 199–203
learned helplessness, 159
Lennard, Henry L., 33, 160–61, 164,
  213
Lepper, Mark R., 147
Lewis, David C., 33
Lindesmith, Alfred R., 41, 59, 267
Lolli, Giorgio, 40
Louria, Donald, 35
love
  as an addiction, 13, 21–23, 53,
    70–73, 78, 80, 242
  positive concept of, 80–83, 87–90,
    242–43, 257–59
Lovers and Other Strangers, 126
Lowney, Louise I., 267
LSD, 39, 46–48, 51, 67, 265–66
Lukoff, Irving F., 35

McCarthy, Colman, 164
McClelland, David C., 43, 46, 127,
  228
Mailer, Norman, 69
Malcolm X, 46
Man with the Golden Arm, The (Nelson
  Algren), 30
Marais, Eugene, 39
Marie (vignette), 180–84
marijuana, 38–39, 46, 49, 51–52,
  67–69, 149, 251, 262
marriage, 133–38
Martinson, Floyd M., 136
Marx, Karl, 66, 252
Masterton, Bruce, 159
maturing out of addiction, 36, 57,
  219–20
media as source of addiction, 162–64
medicine
  belief in omniscience of, 151–53
  drug prescription, 160–62
  as established institution, 161–62
  as source of addiction, 151–54
Mel and Bea (vignette), 112–13
men's addictions, 184–85
mental hospitals, 154–55
methadone, 45, 213
Midtown Manhattan Study, 155
Miller, Daniel R., 127
Mitch (vignette), 236–40
Mizener, Arthur, 76
Morgan, Edmund S., 43

morphine. *See also* opiates
  administered to animals, 62–63,
    268
  administered to hospital patients,
    34, 36, 56–57, 59–60, 261, 267
  used by doctors, 35
Mystification and Drug Misuse (Henry
  L. Lennard *et al.*), 33, 160

naloxone, 268
narcotics. *See* opiates
Nat (vignette), 132–33
Nesbitt, Paul David, 52
Neugarten, Bernice, 136
neuropsychology, 158–60
Newsweek, 158–59
nicotine, 37, 50, 52, 162. *See also*
  tobacco
nonaddiction
  as in controlled drug use,
    58–59
  criteria for, 63–67, 223–25
  in love relationships, 83, 87–90,
    257–59
  a model of, 219–23

Oates, Wayne, 16
O'Donnell, John A., 37
one-sided addictions, 108–9
ontological anxiety, 75, 149
open households, 208
opiates. *See also* heroin; morphine
  in America, 41, 43–45, 162
  controlled use, 34–35
  effects of, 51, 61–62, 264–65
  history of, 39, 41
  interchangeability with other de-
    pressants, 37, 262
  relationship to addiction, 32–33,
    51, 61–62

opponent-process motivation, 53–54

pain-killer, nonaddictive, 45, 52
Paton, W. D. M., 48, 50
Patrick, Ted, 168
Persia, tobacco ban, 39
pets, 165–67
peyote, 51
physical dependence, 32, 49
physician narcotic users, 35, 58
placebo effect, 36, 50, 56–57, 151, 261
Plague, The (Albert Camus), 235
Portnoy's Complaint (Philip Roth), 212
prescription drugs, 160–62
psychic dependence, 49
psychoactive drugs, 30, 40, 48, 160,
    162, 268
  attempts to classify, 21, 49
psychosurgery, 160
psychotherapy
  belief in effectiveness of, 154–55
  institutionalization of, 154–55
  as object of addiction, 156–58
  relevance for addiction treatment,
    226, 233, 253, 256
  as source of addiction, 155–56
  as substitute for human communi-
    cation, 155
Puritanism, 42–43

Quaalude (methaqualone), 162

Rainwater, Lee, 74
religion as an addiction, 71–72,
    168–69
Ric (vignette), 31–32
Riesman, David, 43, 221
Ritalin, 159

ritualistic drug use, 35–36, 50, 65
Road to H, The (Isidor Chein *et al.*),
  35–36, 57–58, 61–62, 86
Robertson, John A., 33, 39
Rogers, Carl R., 256
Rosenhan, David L., 154
running, 229–30
Russia
  collective upbringing, 207
  tobacco ban, 39

Sagov, Stanley E., 153–54
Sanford, Nevitt, 136
Sartre, Jean-Paul, 218
Schachter, Stanley, 38, 153, 263
schizoid alienation, 75
school
  as object of addiction, 149–50
  reforms in, 150–51
  respect for authority of, 127–31,
    146, 148
  as source of addiction, 146–50
Schur, Edwin M., 74
Scientific Basis of Drug Dependence
  (Hannah Steinberg, ed.), 48–49
Seligman, Martin E. P., 159
set and setting, 38, 263
sex roles and addiction, 171–73, 180,
  184–85, 194, 209
sexual revolution, 136–38
Shelley and Carl (vignette), 103–8
simultaneous or successive addictions, 84, 169, 171, 194
Singer, Jerome E., 38, 263
Snyder, Solomon H., 159
social change, 206
social class and addiction, 45, 73–75,
  194
social dependency constellation, 74
Solomon, Richard L., 53

Sonnedecker, Glenn, 39, 41
Sorensen, Robert C., 136
soul, 222–23
South Africa, use of tobacco and
  marijuana, 39
Spock, Benjamin, 122
Srole, Leo, 155
stimulants, 37–38, 40, 52–53, 162
Stunkard, Albert, 214
Supreme Court, 44
Swanson, Guy E., 127
Sybil (vignette), 194–97
Szasz, Thomas S., 155

tea, 37, 40, 262
technology
  awe of, 122–23, 144–45
  predominance of, in modern soci-
    ety, 122, 144
  as source of addiction, 145
television, 164–65
tobacco, 39–40, 262, 264. *See also*
  nicotine
tolerance, 67
  in drug addiction, 33–35, 38
  in interpersonal addiction, 86–87
tonsillectomy, 152
tranquilizers, 37, 45, 161
Trial, The (Franz Kafka), 144
tribes (of LSD users), 39
Turkey, tobacco ban, 39
Turner, Frederick Jackson, 43

U.S. Public Health Service, 56, 264

Vicky and Bruce (vignette), 24–28
Vietnam veterans, 34, 59–60

Walsh, Michael J., 262
Weed, Steven, 142, 209
Western culture, 40, 143, 207–8
White, Robert W., 228
Wikler, Abraham, 262, 266
Wilbur, Richard S., 34
Williams, Lawrence P., 152
Wilson, Cedric W. M., 263
Winick, Charles, 15
    on effects of opiates, 264
    on maturing out, 36, 57
    on physician narcotic users, 35, 58
withdrawal, 62
    craving, 37, 59, 67, 86–87
    from drug addiction, 28, 33–39, 48,
        51, 53, 266–67
    from interpersonal addiction, 28,
        53, 72, 79–80, 87
    symptoms of, 33, 37, 39, 72
women
    addictions of, 172–73, 180

drugs prescribed for, 161
in psychotherapy, 157–58
social roles of, 172–73, 180, 209
Women in Love (D. H. Lawrence), 75,
    199–203
women's movement, 172–73
Wonder, Stevie, 249
"workaholic" syndrome, 16, 65, 165
World Health Organization, 49
World War II, 37, 122

Zinberg, Norman E., 15, 50
    on controlled drug use, 58–59, 67
    on Daytop Village, 39
    on G.I.'s in Vietnam, 39
    on hospital patients, 34
    on types of narcotic use, 33
Zola, Irving Kenneth, 152–53